Medieval Africa, 1250–1800

This is a radically revised and updated edition of *The African Middle Ages 1400–1800* (first published in 1981), a companion volume to the authors' well-known *Africa since 1800* (now in its fourth edition). Although this volume follows the overall plan of the original, the story now begins 150 years earlier, and takes into account the wealth of supportive literature in African historical studies over the last twenty years. The earlier starting date has enabled the authors to look at the entire continent from a more distinctly African viewpoint. By about 1250 AD African societies were greatly expanding their political and economic scope. Islam was spreading south across the Sahara from Mediterranean Africa, and down the Indian Ocean coast. *Medieval Africa* continues into the period of European contacts from the fourteenth century onwards, with much, but not exclusive, emphasis on the growth of the trans-Saharan, Atlantic and Indian Ocean slave trade. The book stresses the strengths, while not overlooking the weaknesses, of African societies as the eighteenth century drew to a close. This volume will be an essential introduction to African history for students, as well as for the general reader. It is illustrated with a wealth of maps.

ROLAND OLIVER is Professor Emeritus of African History at the University of London, and member of the British Academy. He has published widely on African history, including *A Short History of Africa* (1962, translated into 14 languages, 6 revised editions), *The African Experience* (1990, revised 1999) and *In the Realms of Gold* (1997).

ANTHONY ATMORE has taught African history in both the UK and Africa. He is the co-author of the companion to this volume, *Africa since 1800* (with Roland Oliver, 4 editions since 1967).

Medieval Africa, 1250–1800

ROLAND OLIVER
ANTHONY ATMORE

CAMBRIDGE
UNIVERSITY PRESS

PUBLISHED BY THE PRESS SYNDICATE OF THE UNIVERSITY OF CAMBRIDGE
The Pitt Building, Trumpington Street, Cambridge, United Kingdom

CAMBRIDGE UNIVERSITY PRESS
The Edinburgh Building, Cambridge CB2 2RU, UK
40 West 20th Street, New York, NY 10011–4211, USA
10 Stamford Road, Oakleigh, VIC 3166, Australia
Ruiz de Alarcón 13, 28014 Madrid, Spain
Dock House, The Waterfront, Cape Town 8001, South Africa

http://www.cambridge.org

Revised and updated version of *The African Middle Ages, 1400–1800*, first published
in 1981 and © Cambridge University Press

Printed in the United Kingdom at the University Press, Cambridge

Typeface Monotype Plantin 9.75/12pt   *System* QuarkXPress™ [SE]

A catalogue record for this book is available from the British Library

Library of Congress Cataloguing in Publication data

Oliver, Roland Anthony.
  Medieval Africa, 1250–1800 / Roland Oliver [and] Anthony Atmore.
    p. cm.
  Rev. and updated version of: The African middle ages, 1400–1800. 1981.
  Includes bibliographical references and index.
  ISBN 0 521 79024 7 – ISBN 0 521 79372 6 (pbk)
    1. Africa–History–To 1884. I. Atmore, Anthony. II. Oliver, Roland
  Anthony. African middle ages, 1400–1800. III. Title.
  dt25.039 2001
  960'.2–dc21   00-067608

ISBN 0 521 79024 7 hardback
ISBN 0 521 79372 6 paperback

Contents

Maps

Preface

This book has emerged in response to an invitation by Cambridge University Press to prepare a Revised Edition of *The African Middle Ages 1400–1800* published by them in 1981. We felt that after so long an interval the degree of revision needed to be radical and that this might be best achieved by setting an earlier starting date for the work as a whole. On the one hand this would enable us to look at the entire continent from a more distinctively African viewpoint, free from the bias inevitably imparted by the reliance from the outset on European written sources. On the other hand it would ensure that each of our regional chapters, the strongest no less than the weakest, would have to be redesigned to accommodate the new angle of approach. For the rest, we have divided our treatment of Mediterranean Africa into three chapters rather than two, and we have added a completely new chapter on the least known region of the continent, which is that lying at its geographical centre to the north of the Congo basin. Thus, while we have reused many passages from the earlier work, so much of the writing is new that we feel it right to give it a different title.

Like its predecessor, *Medieval Africa, 1250–1800* should be seen as a companion volume to our earlier book, *Africa since 1800*, now in its Fourth Revised Edition and still in wide demand. We hope that, in its new form, it may serve to encourage more teachers and students to explore the pre-modern history of Africa, which has so much of real interest to teach us about how small societies faced the challenges of very diverse, and often hostile, environments and yet managed to interact sufficiently to create significant areas of common speech and culture, to share ideas and technological innovations, and to meet the outside world with confidence at most times earlier than the mid-nineteenth century.

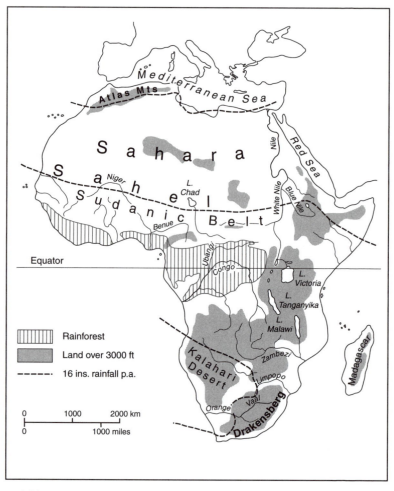

1 Africa: geography, rainfall and vegetation

1   Introduction: the medieval scene

If it is universally acknowledged that geography and climate shape and mould the course of history, it is a truism peculiarly self-evident in Africa, where humankind has had to contend with environmental conditions often harsh and always challenging. The continent's broad vegetation zones are best portrayed on a map, which will show at a glance the contrast between the areas lying roughly to the north and south of the equator. In the northern sector, the lines demarcating these zones march horizontally across the continent with almost the precision of the lines of latitude, and the determining factor is that of rainfall. The Mediterranean zone, with its coastal plains watered by regular winter rains, and at its western end the high pastures of the Atlas ranges, is bordered by the arid and stony Sahara, measuring more than 1700 miles from north to south, and stretching for more than 4000 miles from the Atlantic coast to the Red Sea. On its southern 'shore' (in Arabic, *sahel*) the desert merges into the open savanna of the Sahel, free from the tsetse-fly and offering pasture for most domestic animals, notably, cattle, sheep and goats, donkeys and the small horses native to the region. Southwards, the Sahel merges into the bush and light woodland of the Sudanic belt, offering rainfall enough for cereal agriculture, but where infestation by tsetse-fly poses a mortal danger to the larger domestic animals, especially to cattle and all the regular beasts of burden and traction. The hard, sun-baked soil must be tilled with hoes and not with ploughs. The bush of the Sudanic belt ends abruptly with the margin of the equatorial forest, where vegetables and root crops, nut and fruit trees can be grown in clearings. There is no doubt that during the second millennium a general drying of the climate has caused the zonal boundaries to shift southwards, perhaps by as much as 600 miles, but the sequence of the vegetation zones has been largely maintained.

South of the equator, the vegetation map shows a very different picture. Here, the vegetation zones criss-cross, with forest or woodland running from the Cameroon highlands in the north-west to coastal Mozambique in the south-east, and dry savanna from Somalia in the north-east to Namibia in the south-west. Here, the determining factor is not so much rainfall as height above sea level.

Very much of Africa south of the equator is covered by mountain and tableland at heights varying from 3500 to 6000 feet, with peaks rising to 15,000 feet or even more. This mountain country begins in the Ethiopian highlands and runs with scarcely a break from there to the South African highveld. Most of it is in vegetational terms savanna, corresponding to the Sahelian and Sudanic belts of Africa north of the equator. Much of it until recently abounded in wild game and was heavily infested by tsetse-fly. But over the course of 3000 years of bush-clearing by humans, fly-free grasslands were gradually established on a scale which enabled cattle pastoralism to become the main occupation of significant groups of people living all the way down the highland spine of the subcontinent at heights between 3500 and 6000 feet. This central tableland is cut through by two great volcanic rifts, one running down the centre of the Ethiopian and Kenyan highlands, and the other cleaving the watershed which divides the Congo drainage system from that of the Nile. The escarpments of these deep valleys offer specially rich opportunities for combining agriculture and pastoralism, and the floors of both hold chains of lakes, round the shores of which some of the earliest fishing industries of the world developed. At higher levels, mountain valleys and ridges offer fertile volcanic soils to those prepared to undertake the heavy work of forest clearance. Areas below 3000 feet occur mainly in the coastal plains and in the great basins of the Congo and the lower Zambezi river systems, where most of the land remains under primeval forest and where human populations have traditionally lived by a combination of fishing and riverside agriculture.

Thus far, it might seem that humans living in the southern half of the continent have enjoyed a better range of natural environments than the northerners. But, for the whole period covered by this book, we have to consider not only the natural conditions of each zone, but the possibilities for creative interaction between one zone and another. Viewed from this angle, the situation of northern Africa looks in nearly every way preferable to that of the south. This vital distinction has been seen by some scholars as one between those parts of Africa that were open to influences from the outside world and those which lacked this advantage and so were left to develop in isolation. While there is some truth in this view, its weakness lies in the unspoken premise that everything of value to Africa was introduced from the outside, with the initiative coming always from the outsiders. More pertinent is the fact that throughout northern Africa there have long been in existence more effective means of transport than the human head or shoulder. The southern coast of

West Africa, for example, is honey-combed with lagoons and barrier islands, where people lived by fishing and salt-boiling, but depended for their vegetable food on the surplus produce of the forest dwellers on their landward side, which reached them down the rivers in fleets of huge dug-out canoes. Several major river systems, including those of the Senegal, the Gambia, the Casamance, the Comoe, the Volta, the Niger and the Cross, offered waterways cutting right through the forest zone to the agricultural country of the Sudanic belt. The great Niger waterway made a double traverse of the entire savanna belt, from the Guinea forest north-eastwards to the desert edge and thence south-eastwards to its delta in the forest. Thus, the boat traffic of the Niger and its many tributaries could carry the surplus grain of the Sudan to feed the textile weavers and leather-workers of the Sahel cities and return southwards with the all-important salt of the central Sahara which was brought on camel-back to the river-ports around the river's northern bend. The Niger waterway had its eastern counterpart in the Logone-Chari river system draining northwards from the Cameroon highlands to Lake Chad, where it connected with the camel trade of the central Sudan and the salt deposits of Bilma in the central Sahara, midway between Bornu and Tripoli.

Eastwards again, the valley of the great River Nile crossed all five vegetation zones in its step-by-step descent from the Ethiopian mountains and the great lakes of eastern equatorial Africa to the south-eastern corner of the Mediterranean. On the Nile flood depended the unique fertility of riverine Egypt and the ease of navigation within the boundaries of that country, although from the cataract region southwards the camel and donkey trails offered a shorter and swifter mode of transport than the river boat. In Ethiopia and the Horn it was once again these two beasts of burden which carried the salt of the Afar desert to the dense agricultural population of the highlands and brought down the grain surplus of the Christian kingdom to feed the Muslim pilgrims visiting the holy cities of Islam.

Seen in the light of these interzonal exchanges within the northern half of Africa as a whole, the connections with the outside world across the Mediterranean and the Red Sea do not seem quite so all-important. The gold of the Sudan and the ivory of the forest contributed a small, luxury element to this general pattern of interregional trade, the role of which has been much exaggerated by historians, because these items travelled much further afield than the rest. But right through our period, and on a steadily increasing scale, it was   3 the exchange of produce between the different climatic zones that really signified. For northern and western Africa itself, the salt deposits of the central Sahara were more important than all the gold of Guinea and the camel-breeders of the desert more indispensable than the merchants of the Maghrib.

The existence of the interzonal trade of course made it easier for individuals to travel, not merely as merchants and caravan drivers, but as captives, as pilgrims, as students, and as skilled artificers of every kind. Many of these travellers remained permanently at their various destinations. During the early centuries of Islam the armies of North African states, as also the harems of their more prosperous urbanised citizens, were largely recruited from the captives brought across the Sahara, whose descendants merged with the local populations at a whole variety of social and occupational levels. No less certainly, the populations of the Sahelian and Sudanic belts were deeply penetrated by the centuries-long westward migration of pastoral Arabs, most of whose descendants turned themselves into semisedentary cattle farmers on the Sahelian pattern, all the way from Upper Egypt and the Nilotic Sudan to the shores of the Atlantic Ocean. The Saharan camel pastoralists who mined the salt and carried it across the desert in both directions were among the first black Africans to convert to Islam, and to the south of the desert the first to follow their example were the Sudanese Dyula traders who met them at the terminals of the desert trails with their river boats and their caravans of donkeys and human porters, and conducted the trade from there southwards to the margins of the forest belt. Thus, as a concomitant of its interzonal trade, the Sudanic belt of West Africa joined the wider household of Islam. No more than in other medieval societies did any but a handful of clerics actually read the sacred texts, written in classical Arabic, but many could listen to those who did, and many more could learn something at second or third hand and so pick up a rudimentary knowledge of a world wider than that of their home towns. They knew that Muslims dressed in decent cotton clothing, washed before eating and abstained from alcoholic beverages. And that, in itself, meant much. It signalled that Africa north of the equator was on the move.

In Africa south of the equator the environmental conditions were far less favourable to the interchange of produce over any distance. Here, the continuing prevalence of the tsetse-fly over large parts of the highland savanna meant that beasts of burden were unknown except in the far south. And waterways, although they existed in the forested centres of the great river basins, were seldom viable for the interchange of produce between different climatic zones. Their highland tributaries tended to be too shallow and fast-flowing for canoe traffic, and their lower reaches were nearly always broken by cataracts where they made their final descent to sea level. There remained the central basins, where people who lived mainly by fishing also used their boats for river trading, and carried metal goods and other artefacts from one community to the next. But it seems to have been only towards the end of our period that systems for relays and portages were organised capable of handling any quantity of long-distance trade.

For the rest, which included all of inland East and South-East Africa, trade was limited to what could be carried by human porters, and therefore to produce of light weight and high value, such as gold and copper, ivory and rare skins, glass beads and cotton textiles and, later, tobacco and spirits, guns and gunpowder. A porter's load might weigh 60 or 70 pounds. The journey to the coast and back might take anything up to five or six months. Food would have to be purchased along the way, and tolls paid for safe transit. Given all the difficulties, it is hardly surprising that the earliest oral record of imported textiles reaching the kingdom of Buganda, on the western shores of Lake Victoria, dates from the second half of the eighteenth century.

In fact, in the southern half of Africa, the only climatic zone which saw the development of a really active exchange of bulk produce was the coastal plain which faced the Indian Ocean. It used to be assumed that this was entirely due to the commercial enterprise of the Asian settlers who came to live there, but it is becoming increasingly clear that the dominant factor was the comparative ease of navigation in the western Indian Ocean, which enabled even the outrigger canoes of the Indonesian islanders to make the voyage there, providing only that they observed the regular alternation of the monsoon winds. The sea-going craft of the Persian Gulf and southern Arabia were no doubt more strongly built, but archaeological research is showing that the earliest Muslims to build their little mud-and-wattle mosques on the East African coast during the eighth and ninth centuries were few and poor, and that it was only with the awakening of the African coastal peoples, and also those of Madagascar, to the opportunities offered by the export of foodstuffs and the gathering of hardwood timber for the Arabian market that the coastal cities grew prosperous enough to build mosques, tombs and palaces in coral rag. Significantly, only the slightest signs have as yet emerged of any commercial interchange between the populations

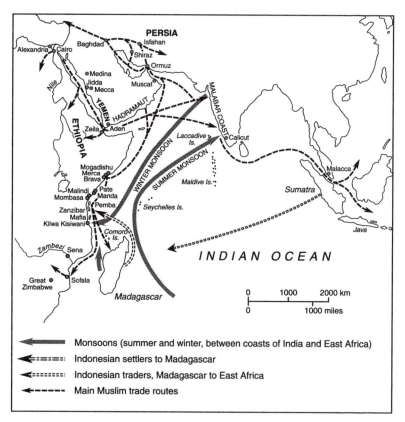

2 Indian Ocean trading activities, 1250–1400

of the coastal plain and the interior tablelands behind – except in the hinterland of southern Mozambique, between the Zambezi and the Limpopo, where gold, copper and ivory were close enough and valuable enough to stand the cost of human porterage. All down the Indian Ocean coast, the outreach of Islam remained confined to the harbour towns of the coastal plain, which recruited their citizens from the fisherman-farmers of the surrounding countryside, who, on coming to town, became Muslims and learned to speak the Bantu lingua franca called Kiswahili. But it was only in the nineteenth century that coast-based caravans began trading into the interior in a regular way. Until then, it was left to the peoples of the interior to get their trade goods to the coast. The gold and ivory trade of Zimbabwe may well have influenced the concentration of political and economic power in that region, but there is no shred of evidence to suggest that individuals from there travelled northwards up the sea routes of the Indian Ocean to learn from the knowledge and experience of a wider world.

The contrast between the northern and southern halves of Africa appears no less strongly when we turn from the consideration of peaceful commerce and travel to the nature and significance of warfare. Here, the most essential distinction was that between the horsed and the unhorsed, and the most crucial military frontier was that where the two modes of warfare interacted. Roughly speaking, Africa as far south as the Sahel lay within the horse belt, and as far back as the first millennium BC horses harnessed to light war-chariots had been used for slave-raiding in the Saharan highlands. In the first millennium AD the Christian Nubians, riding their small horses bareback, were respected for their skill as cavalry archers in the manner of the steppe peoples of Central Asia. The Arabs brought the bridle and stirrup in their conquest of North Africa. Chain-mail and horse-armour followed as luxury imports from southern Europe and put a premium on the big Barbary horses of North Africa, which were exported southwards across the desert in increasing numbers by the beginning of our period. Thenceforward, politics in the city states of the Sahel were dominated by the aristocracies of armoured knights, whose dry-season raiding brought in both the slaves needed for the agricultural work and other industries of the towns and those exported northwards across the desert for more horses and their equipment. Gradually, during our period it was discovered that horses, if stabled in town and attended by four to six slaves each to cut and carry in fodder from the surrounding countryside, could survive through the wet season even within the fly-ridden Sudanic belt, and so the cavalry frontier moved south to the fringes of the forest. Even within the forest, as in Benin city for example, these animals enjoyed so much prestige that they were kept by rulers purely as symbols of political power.

Very different was the warfare of the southern half of Africa, where, prior to the late eighteenth century, the only standing armies consisted of the personal bodyguards of kings and other great men, and where military action could normally take place only as a temporary response to the summons of the big war drum. In some cases specified areas of land could be allotted, together with rights over the services of those who lived on them, to military leaders who could muster a following to join in a campaign or in dealing with an attack from the outside. In pastoral kingdoms a frontier district might be entrusted to the herdsmen of a section of the royal cattle. But, most typically perhaps, military prowess was associated, at least in legend, with the smithing skills of a band of hunters, living apart from the ordinary people of a farming community, in the uncleared wood-lands where they could be close to their prey and at the same time preserve the technical secrets of their trade as armourers and makers of agricultural tools. In a later chapter we shall see how easily an ivory-hunting expedition could turn itself into an army of conquest (below, pp. 182–3). Very occasionally, a whole community, smitten by some natural disaster, or finding itself overcrowded in its home territory, would temporarily abandon its own efforts at food produc-tion, put itself on to a war footing and live by terror and predation on the harvests and domestic stock of their neighbours – 'cultivating with the spear', as the leader of one such episode called it. In general, pastoralists were more warlike than cultivators, if only because they had to defend their herds against wild animals and human predators by day and night. They did their everyday work spear in hand. But it was also the case that in good times herds increased faster than the human population, so that herders were always competing with each other for the best pasturelands and trying to infiltrate the spaces between, and within, agricultural settlements.

Our starting-date in the middle of the thirteenth century, then, was not one which had continent-wide significance in any particular field. The Muslim heartlands of Africa, however, did experience a series of decisive changes around this time. In Egypt, Mamluk rule, which was to last into the nineteenth century, was established in 1250, and in 1260 the Mamluk sultans consolidated their rule and their reputation in the Muslim world by defeating and turning back the advance of the Mongols towards the eastern Mediterranean. One of the earliest initiatives of the Mamluks in Africa was to drive the Arab nomads of upper Egypt southwards into Nubia, and so set in motion the Islamisation of the Christian kingdoms of the middle Nile. Likewise, beyond Egypt's western frontier, the middle years of the thirteenth century were those in which the Hafsid governors of Tunis were establishing their independence from the fading empire of the Almohads in Morocco and southern Spain, and were creating the new sultanate of Ifriqiya, stretching from Tripoli to eastern Algeria, which in the sixteenth century would fall, like Egypt, under the dominion of the Ottomans. To the south of Ifriqiya, the kings of Kanem, ruling around the basin of Lake Chad, had been Muslim since the eleventh century and by the thirteenth century several of them had made the pilgrimage to Mecca and had even built a hostel in Cairo for their subjects studying at the university mosque of al-Azhar. By about 1300 the rulers and courtiers of the rising empire of Mali on the upper Niger were Muslims and already participating in the pilgrimage to the holy cities of their faith. There, as also in Kanem, a literate class was emerging, and the *shari'a* law was beginning to be applied in the highest courts.

The attraction of key groups towards Islam is, however, only one perspective on the history of Africa, even of northern Africa, at this period. Looked at from within the continent, and searching for the connections of any one neighbourhood, encampment, village, town, chiefdom, kingdom or empire, it is obvious that Africa was still moving mostly to its own rhythms, following its own procedures and seeking its own paths, channels and routes. Socially and economically, the tendency during the period covered by this book was for societies to expand, sometimes by natural increase, but often by conquest, by the absorption of war captives and of people in various other forms of dependency, who can be described in some cases as subjects, and in others as slaves. If the economic gain was favourable enough, such dependent people might be traded abroad – in the case of the Muslim world, across the Sahara or over the Red Sea and Indian Ocean. But in many other cases war captives might be deported from a frontier district and resettled in a mining area to clear the forests and dig the shafts, or else to help with the production of food around a growing capital town. In political terms, this tendency to enlargement covered a broad continuum, from village to neighbourhood, from chiefdom to kingdom, from kingdom to empire. Always, however, political enlargement had to reckon with the limitations imposed by distance and the available means of travel and transport. This meant that conquered territories could seldom be directly administered. Most were simply placed under tribute, which generally meant that the task of slave-raiding or ivory-hunting was delegated to subordinate rulers, leaving the paramount to enforce prompt payment by occasional punitive expeditions to the periphery of the kingdom or empire. It was, generally speaking, a typically medieval scene, which remained in place in most of Africa until the nineteenth century.

The historical processes represented by the encroachment of the wider world on the one hand, and by the political and economic enlargements and accommodations of the different regions of Africa on the other, are mirrored in the changes in the nature of the evidence available to historians of the continent. The first volume in this series, *Africa in the Iron Age*, by Roland Oliver and Brian Fagan, dealt with the period from about 500 BC to the early centuries of the second millennium AD. This is a period for which, although there are some important literary sources, the evidence comes mainly from archaeology. What we here call Medieval Africa from about 1250 to 1800 is, in contrast, one for which, although archaeology continues to contribute, the dominant sources are literary and traditional. For that part of the continent open to the wider world, we now have chronicles, by which we mean historical information collected and written down more or less within the lifetime of living witnesses of the events, by learned men concerned to establish facts accurately and to arrange them in chronological order. For our period there is continuous evidence of this kind for Egypt and the countries of the Maghrib, and for Ethiopia, the western and central Sudan, the Nilotic Sudan and a considerable portion of the East African coast.

At one end of the spectrum, chronicle material shades off into recorded tradition, by which we mean information about the past remembered by non-literate witnesses of events, and passed on by word of mouth from one generation to another until eventually it was told to a literate person who recorded it in writing. Most of the evidence about most of Africa between 1250 and 1800 is of this kind, and obviously it is less reliable than evidence directly recorded from eye-witnesses. People tend to forget the things which are not in some way relevant to their daily lives, and non-literate people lack the means to place past events within an accurate chronological framework. Also, for so long as it remains in an oral state, tradition is liable to be distorted in order to serve the ideological and propaganda needs of succeeding generations. Much therefore depends on how soon and how carefully oral tradition came to be recorded.

In most of Africa this process had to wait until some members of the societies concerned began to adopt literacy in the late nineteenth or early twentieth century. However, in that part of Africa which was in some kind of touch with the outreach of Islam, some traditional history was recorded much earlier. Ibn Khaldun, the great historian and philosopher, who was born in Tunis in 1332 and died in Cairo in 1406, incorporated much traditional material from the Sahara and the western Sudan, as well as from the Maghrib itself, in his 'History of the Berbers'. The mid-seventeenth-century chronicles of Songhay and Timbuktu by al-Saʿdi and Ibn al-Mukhtar incorporate traditions of the earlier empires of Ghana and Mali. The fragmentary chronicles of Hausaland, Aïr and Bornu, though known only in nineteenth-century versions, clearly contain material that had existed in written form long before. The same is certainly the case with the Swahili chronicles of several of the harbour towns on the East African coast, but especially the nineteenth-century version of the Kilwa chronicle, an earlier version of which had been seen and used by the Portuguese historian João de Barros in the mid-sixteenth century.

Lastly, there is the most valuable kind of historical evidence, which is the record written by the eye-witness personally. This may take the form of the narrative of a journey, or the report of a mission, or the accounts of a trading venture, or the correspondence generated by any ongoing enterprise by literate people, whether commercial, religious, diplomatic, military or colonial. Here, although the world of Islam has the first word, it is the European world, Christian at least in name, that comes by the end of our period to occupy the dominant role. Until the fifteenth century there was no European foothold on African soil, and no European had made any significant journey into the African interior. Yet, from the mid-fourteenth century, we have Ibn Battuta's lively accounts of his journeys across North Africa from Morocco to Egypt and from the Persian Gulf down the East African coast to Mogadishu, Mombasa and Kilwa, and from Morocco across the Sahara to the western and central Sudan. Again, from the early sixteenth century we have the no less vivid reminiscences of the Granadan Moor, al-Hassan ibn Muhammad al-Wazzani, later converted to Christianity as Leo Africanus, who travelled extensively in Morocco and Songhay, and perhaps as far afield as Hausaland, Bornu and Kanem.

Between Ibn Battuta and Leo Africanus, however, came the dramatic entry of Portugal on to the African scene. Following the conquest of Ceuta in Morocco in 1415, the Portuguese began their systematic exploration of the oceanic coastlines of Africa, reaching Cape Verde in 1446, the Bight of Benin in 1475, the Congo estuary in 1483, and the Cape of Good Hope, Sofala, Kilwa, Mombasa and Malindi all in 1497-8. Spurred on by the spread of the printing-press and the expansion of secular education, the Christians of western Europe made a much wider use of literacy than their Muslim contemporaries. From the fifteenth century onwards, royal and ecclesiastical archives began to bulge with instructions, reports, accounts and itineraries, and from the sixteenth century on there issued from the printing-presses a swelling stream of voyages, handbooks, histories and geographies, all of which constitute precious sources for the 11 history of the coastal regions. Alongside these printed records came a flood of more mundane correspondence and account books of the various European merchant houses. Nevertheless, it is only here and there that these European records shed their light at any distance into the interior. Taking the continent as a whole, between 1250 and 1800 AD, it is to the traditional sources of African history, with all their difficulties of interpretation, that the historian must mainly turn.

The first edition of this book, published in 1981, had AD 1400 as its starting-point. The putting back of this date by 150 years has forced us, as nothing else could have done, to begin our consideration of each and every region of the continent from the inside, by seeking first the evidence, however scanty, about the condition of the African peoples as it was before the earliest contemporary reports of them by outsiders. It has enabled us to see more clearly how many of the more fundamental staples of human history had already been long established in Africa before the always selective and often superficial impressions recorded by travellers from Asia or Europe. We have been reminded that agriculture and stock-raising were being practised with the help of iron tools and weapons from one end of the continent to the other. We have been impressed by the evidence from the study of language relationships that, even at the beginning of our period, most Africans were speaking the same languages that their successors were speaking in the nineteenth and twentieth centuries. In other words, populations had in general remained stable enough to absorb the migrations caused by conquest or natural disaster. No less impressive is the fact that, despite the huge number of the African languages, usually reckoned at between 2000 and 3000, all can be grouped within one of only four language-families, the emergence of which would seem to go back at least to the origins of food production. There is the Afroasiatic family, which spreads across both sides of the Red Sea and includes Ancient Egyptian, Berber, Hausa, Omotic, Amharic, Arabic and Hebrew. There is the Nilo-Saharan family, based in the central Sahara and Sudan and including the Nilotic languages spoken in parts of northern East Africa. There is the great Niger-Congo family, which spreads across the southern half of West Africa and includes as a sub-family all the Bantu languages spoken in Africa south of the equator. And there is the Khoisan family, today clearly associated with the hunters and herders of southern Africa, which at one time extended far up into eastern Africa from there. All this argues that, beneath the great diversity of languages and cultures visible in modern times, there lies, if not an absolute and original unity, then at least a respectable simplicity of ancestral forms. On the whole, it would seem that Africans were divided from each other culturally by the multitude of different environments of their continent rather than by any fundamental antagonisms that could be attributed to race.

2 Egypt: al-Misr

For more than 4000 years before the start of our period, from the first emergence of the Pharaonic kingdom, Egypt had carried the most densely packed and the most easily accessible agricultural population of any part of Africa or, possibly, of the world. This population was concentrated entirely in the Delta and beside the flood plain of the Nile, where the fertility of the soil was maintained by the silt carried down by the river and deposited over the farmlands by the annual flood. The water which carried the precious silt carried also the boats of the corn merchant and the tax gatherer. Every cultivated holding was within sight of the river or the canal bank. Every peasant smallholder could be forced to disgorge his taxes in kind, money and labour. Thus, although the peasants might live very near the subsistence level, suffering severely in the seasons following a poor flood, their combined taxes could support a rich and powerful superstructure of centralised government and military might. It seemed to make little difference to the system whether or not the ruling élite was a foreign one, and in fact since early in the first millennium BC it had always been so. Persians were followed by Greeks, Greeks by Romans, Romans by Byzantines, Byzantines by Arabs, and Arabs by Turks.

But there was more to Egypt than downtrodden peasants and exotic rulers. By 1250 Islam had been established in Egypt and the Maghrib for nearly six centuries. Starting as the religion and culture of the Arab conquering armies, it had been strengthened by the wholesale westward movement of Arab nomads (in Arabic, *kabila*), the camel and cattle pastoralists with their flocks of sheep and goats, away from the desiccating pasturelands of Arabia and into the marginal country adjoining the closely settled flood plain of the Nile. There, through interaction and intermarriage, Islam had been adopted by a steadily growing proportion of the indigenous populations. By the thirteenth century Muslims had come to outnumber Christians, and Arabic, which had long supplanted Coptic as the literary language, was displacing spoken Coptic, even in the countryside. The peasant farmers of Egypt, the *fellahin*, were by now a mixed population of indigenous Copts and large numbers of formerly nomadic Arabs who had managed to transform themselves into sedentary cultivators.

At the village level, Islam was a homely faith, kept lively by holy men, the *shaykhs*, many of them claiming descent from the Prophet as the authentication of their ministry. But Egypt in 1250 was also a land of great cities, peopled by traders, clerks, craftsmen, boatmen, carters and water carriers as well as by officials, clerics and lawyers. Town dwellers were more susceptible than countrymen to the Islamic disciplines of prayer and fasting, in which laxity would quickly attract censure and sanctions. The Mamluk capital at Cairo was, of course, one of the very great cities of the Mediterranean world. Founded in 969 by the Fatimid conquerors from Ifriqiya, it stood just to the north of the first Arab capital at Fustat. It was first and foremost a palace city, where the Fatimid sultans and their Ayyubid successors lived in splendour, served by 30,000 slaves and attended by poets and scholars who made it the global centre of Arabic letters and learning. Cairo was likewise the seat of the religious establishment, of sophisticated, learned, juridical and philosophical Islam. Its al-Azhar mosque was the premier university of the Islamic world. It was also, and especially under the Mamluks, a military city, dominated by the citadel, now the headquarters of the army of mainly Turkish soldiers that protected Egypt from external foes and kept itself in a state of prosperity and power.

MAMLUK EGYPT: THE EMPIRE OF THE TURKS

Turkish-speaking slaves had been recruited into the armies of the 'Abbasid Caliphs of Baghdad as early as the ninth century. The Turkish slave general Ibn Tulun, who was sent by the Caliph to rule the Egyptian province in 868, became Egypt's first semi-independent Muslim ruler. When the Fatimids conquered Egypt in 969, they recruited Turkish slaves as cavalrymen to supplement the black slave infantry whom they had brought with them from Ifriqiya. Their Ayyubid successors, who ruled Egypt from 1171 until 1260, purchased yet more slave cavalrymen as an answer to the threat posed by the Christian Crusaders from western Europe. These were the famous *mamluks*, which was the Arabic term generally used for the white slaves, Turks and later Circassians, who were captured or purchased as young boys on the Kipchak steppe adjacent to the Caspian and Aral seas, and shipped, mainly by European merchants, via the Bosphorus to Egypt. There the slave boys were sold into the households of the great military commanders, at first the Ayyubid and then the Mamluk *amirs*, to be brought up as members of a *corps d'élite*. Once trained, they were manumitted and given an income corresponding to their rank, which consisted of the tax from a specified area of land, called an *iqta*. For the higher ranks these revenues were large enough for the great amirs to purchase and train fresh mamluks for their regiments. An iqta, however, was essentially a grant in usufruct, which ended with the life of the owner. Moreover, although mamluks could marry, their children could never become mamluks. Thus, the foreign élite had constantly to be replenished by fresh recruits from the northern borderlands of Islam, educated in the discipline of a military household, and dependent for their manumission and their subsequent promotion upon their professional patrons and superiors. The number of royal mamluks, consisting of those troopers who had been fully trained in the Cairo barrack schools and on the hippodrome, rarely exceeded 10,000, ruling over an Egyptian population of between 4 and 8 million.

In 1250, following two decisive victories over the crusading army of King Louis IX of France, at Mantra and al-Fariskur in the Nile Delta, a group of mamluk officers staged a *coup d'état* against Turan Shah, the last of the Ayyubid sultans. The transition was eased by the marriage of the concubine of an earlier Ayyubid sultan to one of the great amirs, Aybeg, who thus became the first Mamluk sultan. Henceforth, for the next 267 years, the sultanate was always held by a mamluk, and the Mamluk kingdom was known to contemporaries as *Dawlat al-Atrak*, 'the empire of the Turks'. At the death of a sultan, a designated son or nephew carried on the office for a few days or weeks, while the leading amirs fought among themselves for the succession. When a new sultan was elected, the natural heir was expected to withdraw into an honourable retirement. Once in office, the new sultan became by far the largest iqta-holder, receiving one quarter of all the revenues levied in this way. The first line of Mamluk sultans, who ruled from 1250 until 1382, was drawn from the Turkish regiment that was given the nickname Bahri, probably because their barracks were on an island in the River Nile (*Bahr al-Nil*). The Bahris never became a hereditary dynasty, despite the fact that a number of sultans were in fact succeeded by their children or relatives. They were followed from 1382 to the end of Mamluk rule in 1517 by the Burji line, named from a Circassian regimental garrison in the towers (*burj*) of the Cairo citadel, but their ascendancy, while marking a change in the balance of power between Turkish and Circassian elements in the military élite, had little effect on the Mamluk system of domination.

The Mamluks seized power in Egypt at a time that was critical for the whole of the Islamic world. For the fading threat of the

Crusaders there was now substituted the far more terrifying menace of the Mongol armies advancing from Central Asia, and rolling up year by year the map of the old 'Abbasid empire. Baghdad fell in 1258 to the Mongol general Hulugu, grandson of the great Genghis Khan. In 1259 Hulagu's armies marched into Syria, where they sacked Damascus and Aleppo and reached the shores of the Mediterranean. The Mamluks rose to the historic occasion. The newly elected sultan, Qutuz, and his principal amir, Baybars, led the Mamluk army out of Egypt into Palestine. On 3 September 1260, near 'Ain Jalut in Galilee, the Mamluks inflicted a heavy defeat on the Mongols and their Armenian Christian allies. 'Ain Jalut was a decisive battle, although its military significance has often been exaggerated. In reality the Mongol expansion into Persia and the Fertile Crescent had overreached itself, and the nomad armies were exhausted. Hulagu himself had returned to his base in Persia, following the death of the Great Khan in far away China. The Mamluk army vastly outnumbered the Mongol detachment that remained in the west. Nevertheless, the Mamluk sultanate basked in the glory of having been the first Muslim power to defeat the awesome invaders. The chief beneficiary of 'Ain Jalut was Baybars, who soon after the battle treacherously murdered Qutuz and had himself proclaimed sultan. An able general, administrator and statesman, Baybars was the real founder of the Mamluk kingdom.

Baybars (1260–77), Qala'un (1279–90), al-Nasir Muhammad (1293–1340, with two intervals) – these were the great sultans of the Bahri line, who reorganised and defended the western half of the Islamic world during the vital half-century of the Mongol threat. Their first contribution was military. They modernised their armies, even engaging Mongol bands to impart the latest techniques in cavalry warfare. But their tactics in the field were basically those perfected over the centuries by mounted archers on the steppes of Central Asia. The battles fought by the Mamluks were outside Egypt, mainly in Palestine and Syria, where they finally dislodged the Crusaders, annexed the remaining Ayyubid principalities, defeated another Mongol army in Anatolia, and established Syria, with its capital at Damascus, as the northern province of their empire. Thereafter, the imperial communications through Palestine were so good that Baybars boasted that he could play polo in Cairo and Damascus in the same week, while an even more rapid carrier-pigeon post was maintained between the two cities. The Mongols continued to threaten Syria for several decades, until a Mamluk army won a decisive victory over them near Damascus in 1303.

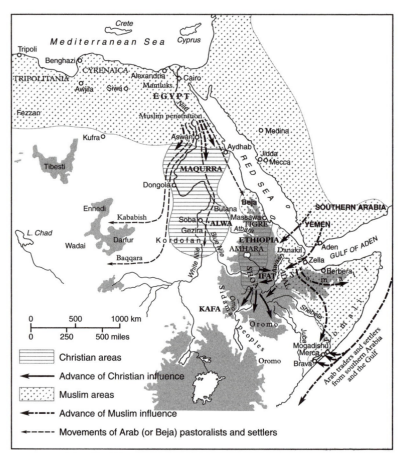

3 Muslim and Christian North-East Africa, 1250–1400 (see also Map 10, p. 101)

Once the Mongol tide had been stemmed, refugees from Iraq and Persia poured into the more peaceful Mamluk domains. One of the earliest was an 'Abbasid prince from Baghdad, who was installed as caliph in Cairo in 1261. Although politically powerless, the reinstatement of the caliphate in Egypt hugely enhanced the prestige of the Mamluk sultanate, especially in the Arabic-speaking world. One corollary advantage was the allegiance of the rulers of Mecca and Medina. Another was the increased importance of Cairo as a focal point on the pilgrimage routes to the Holy Cities. Other refugees included teachers, preachers and scholars from Baghdad and other eastern cities, who helped to make Cairo the undoubted centre of orthodox Sunni Islam and also of Arabic scholarship. Moreover, Mamluk Egypt gained greatly by the Mongol disruption of the more northerly trade routes connecting Europe and Asia. The Mamluk sultans sent embassies to the Indian Ocean lands to advertise the merits of the Red Sea route, and even while they were chasing the Crusaders from their last outposts in the eastern Mediterranean, they were carefully encouraging the settlement of European merchants, Venetians, Genoese and others, in specially protected quarters (*funduqs*) in Alexandria. The great merchant and banking families of Egypt, known collectively as *karimi*, who had begun their operations under the Ayyubids, were far more than mere middlemen who bought at the Red Sea ports and sold at those of the Mediterranean. They operated fleets on the Red Sea and the Indian Ocean. They had agencies in Ethiopia and Nubia, in Arabia and the Persian Gulf, in India and Sri Lanka, in Indonesia and southern China. At home in Egypt, they vied with the sultans and amirs as patrons of religion and the arts. But, like all other non-Mamluks, they were excluded from the ruling élite.

Finally, during the early Mamluk period direct trading links were opened with the countries of the western and central Sudan. In particular, Egypt developed a series of caravan routes passing via the oasis of Awjila in the western desert, to the Fezzan, and thence to Kanem and Bornu on the one hand and to the cities of the Niger bend on the other. Awjila became the leading market for slaves from the central Sudan, thus avoiding the problems of transit through Christian Nubia. But the chief interest for Egypt in these trading connections was in gold, especially after the exhaustion of the country's only gold mines in upper Egypt. From the fourteenth century on, Mamluk coins were minted in gold brought all the way from Bambuk and Bouré around the sources of the Niger and the Senegal. It was paid for mostly in Egyptian textiles which were greatly sought after in the western Sudan. Alongside the trade from across the desert came the pilgrims. The pilgrimage of Mansa Musa, the ruler of Mali, to Mecca in 1325 is justly famous. The Mansa spent three months in Cairo and, except for having to abase himself before Sultan Qala'un, was as impressed by his experiences there as his hosts were by him. He is said to have distributed gold on such a lavish scale as to cause a monetary inflation in the town. At all events, Mansa Musa's visit was remembered for centuries by Egyptians.

Meanwhile, on their southern border the measures taken by the Mamluks against the Arab nomads of upper Egypt were so drastic that they led by the fourteenth century to the migration of large 19 numbers of the nomads into Nubia and so to the disintegration of the Christian kingdom of Maqurra. The Mamluks did not have the same reasons as their predecessors to keep on good terms with their Christian neighbours. They could get their military recruits from Eurasia and their domestic slaves from the great market at Awjila. If their nomads gave trouble, they could afford to drive them out and put the burden on others. During the reign of Sultan Baybars the Mamluks endeavoured to by-pass Maqurra by occupying the Red Sea port of Suakin and developing more direct trade links with 'Alwa and Ethiopia. In 1272 King David of Maqurra raided Egyptian territory and captured the port of 'Aydhab, probably as a response to this Mamluk initiative. Four years later Baybars sent an army into Maqurra, and after plundering as far south as Dongola, installed David's cousin as a vassal ruler (below, pp. 98–9). Likewise, the Mamluks had no truck with unruly nomads, who were driven southwards into Nubia, where they formed the nucleus of a Muslim population in this hitherto Christian land..

During the first century of Mamluk rule Egypt prospered exceedingly. But then, in 1347, the country was struck by the Black Death, the first of a series of disasters that inaugurated a period of crisis that lasted until 1412. The two plagues, the bubonic and the highly infectious pneumonic, originated on the steppes of Central Asia and spread east and west along the trade routes, carried by migrating nomads. The pandemic, which later in Europe became known as the Black Death, was trasmitted by rats. It reached Alexandria by ship in 1347, via the Crimea and the Bosphorus, and, in the words of the Egyptian chronicler al-Maqrizi, 'burst upon Egypt at the end of the growing season, when the fields were at their greenest', and spread rapidly across the Delta and up the Nile valley, breaking out in Cairo in 1348.[1] Unlike the experience of Europe, pneumonic plague became endemic, so that during the following century and a half Egypt suffered no less than twenty-eight outbreaks. Michael Dols, the historian of the pandemic in the Middle East, estimated that between one quarter and one third of a population of 4 to 8 million died in the course of these epidemics. 'The initial depopulation caused by the Black Death, despite all of its dramatic qualities, was far less important for the history of the later Mamluk empire than the cumulative loss, as exemplified by the deterioration of the Mamluk army.'[2] The Mamluks themselves suffered catastrophically,

[1] Cited by André Raymond, *Le Caire* (Paris, 1993), p. 143.
[2] M. W. Dols, *The Black Death in the Middle East* (Princeton, 1977), p. 223.

their military strength declined and they were unable to mount any major offensive for several decades thereafter. According to al-Maqrizi, who tended to equate the consequences of the plague with the oppression practised by the regime, mortality during the epidemic of 1437–8 was 'terrible among the mamluks inhabiting the barracks: there died in this epidemic about one thousand. And there died of the castrated servants 160 eunuchs; of the slave-girls of the sultan's household, more than 160, beside 17 concubines and 17 male and female children.'[3]

In 1382 Sultan Barquq inaugurated the Burji line of Circassian rulers. The change indicated the increasing costs and difficulties of obtaining Turkish boy slaves on the Kipchak steppe, partly as a result of the plague. Egypt had hardly begun to recover from the dislocation of the epidemics when a further wave of mixed Mongol and Turkish invaders led by the great conqueror Timur (Tamarlane) broke upon the northern frontiers of the Mamluk empire. In 1400 Syria was invaded and completely devastated. Damascus and other cities were put to the sack, and their inhabitants deported to the east. Egypt was saved by Timur's decision to turn his attention to the Ottoman Turks rather than to the Mamluks, and finally by his abrupt departure for a campaign in China, where he died in 1405. But the tale of Egyptian crises continued. A low Nile flood in 1403 was followed by famine. And the later reign of Sultan Faraj has been described as 'a long and painful history of appalling atrocities', marked by 'bloody and burlesque episodes' of civil war among the Mamluk factions.[4] The finale came in 1412, when Faraj was assassinated in Damascus by his valets. Thereafter, order was restored and economic conditions gradually improved.

The Mamluk recovery in the fifteenth century was a patchy affair, more apparent in Egypt than in Syria, and within Egypt more visible in Cairo and the great cities of the north than in the countryside. The Burji sultans were great builders and restorers of mosques, schools, hostels, baths and other public works, and the long reign of Qayt Bey (1468–96) saw some of the finest flowerings of Mamluk art and architecture. Roads, bridges, markets and caravanserais were well maintained right up until the end of Mamluk rule, and so were the splendours of the royal pavilion (*maqad*), the hippodrome and the *maydan*, the botanical garden within the Cairo citadel, where incense burned and wine flowed, while musicians played and poets

[3] al-Maqrizi, *As Suluk*, p. 834, cited in Dols, *The Black Death*, p. 158.
[4] Gaston Wiet, *L'Egypte arabe* (Paris, 1937), p. 538.

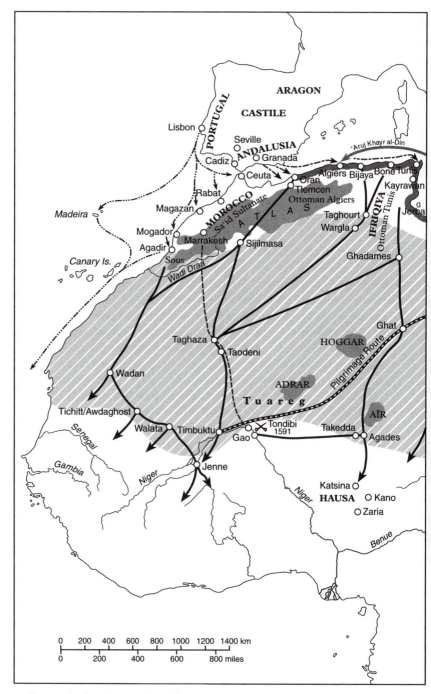

22   4 Egypt, the Maghrib and the Saharan trade routes, 1400–1800

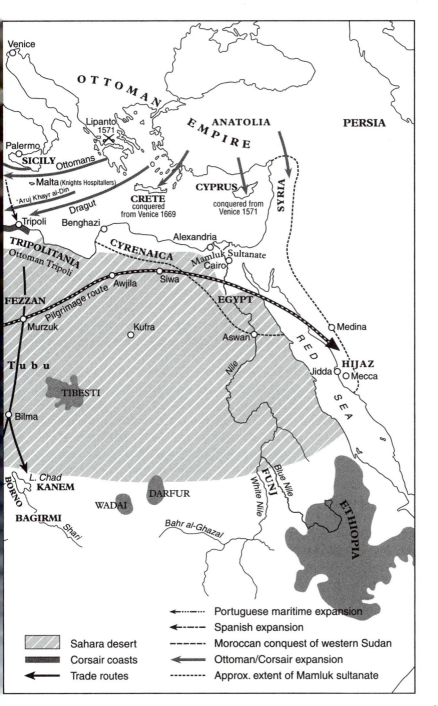

Venice

O T T O M A N

Lipanto
1571

Palermo

SICILY Ottomans

Malta (Knights Hospitallers)

'Aruj Khayr al-Din

Dragut

Tripoli   Benghazi

TRIPOLITANIA
Ottoman Tripoli

CYRENAICA

ANATOLIA

E M P I R E

PERSIA

CRETE
conquered
from Venice 1669

CYPRUS

conquered from
Venice 1571

SYRIA

Alexandria

Mamluk Sultanate
Cairo

FEZZAN

Pilgrimage route   Awjila   Siwa

Murzuk

Kufra

EGYPT

Aswan

T u b u

TIBESTI

Bilma

Nile

Medina

RED

HIJAZ
Jidda Mecca

SEA

BORNO

L. Chad
KANEM

WADAI

DARFUR

BAGIRMI   Shari

Bahr al-Ghazal

White Nile

Blue Nile

FUNJ

ETHIOPIA

←······ Portuguese maritime expansion

←---- Spanish expansion

------ Moroccan conquest of western Sudan

← Ottoman/Corsair expansion

········· Approx. extent of Mamluk sultanate

Sahara desert

Corsair coasts

← Trade routes

23

recited to a court society clad in silk and sprinkled with rosewater, the beards of its male luminaries perfumed with the musk of civet. Like many invaders of the sown lands from the steppe or desert, the Mamluks delighted in conspicuous consumption. This was the Cairo visited by the great men of the western Sudan on their way to the pilgrimage and from which they took home with them ideas and symbols of grandeur like the state umbrellas used on ceremonial occasions. This, even more importantly, was the Cairo where West African scholars went to study the authentic doctrines of Sunni Islam in a bookish atmosphere very different from the popular enthusiasms of the Maghrib or the Nilotic Sudan, in the Cairo of the al-Azhar mosque and the renowned *madrasa* high schools. To the traveller and historian Leo Africanus, who arrived in the capital the day after the entry of the Ottoman army, Cairo was still 'one of the greatest and most wonderful cities in the world'.[5] Though ruled by Turks and Circassians, Mamluk Egypt preserved the old Arabic civilisation of Islam, which was being replaced to the east and the north by new Islamic cultures of recent converts, whose main languages were Turkish and Persian, and whose influence upon Africa was to be much slighter.

Strangely enough for a set of military rulers, the chief failure of the Mamluks was in the field of military technology. The military expenditure of the Burji sultans put a severe strain on an already overstretched economy and a stagnating population. The great campaigns of 1485–91 against the Ottoman Turks, which ended in a stalemate, cost an astronomical million dinars. The construction of a fleet of warships in the Red Sea to counter the threat from the Portuguese cost another fortune. Overtaxation, state monopolies and depreciation of the currency were short-term remedies which produced long-term damage. The initiative of the karimi merchants in the eastern trade was already declining when the Portuguese at the end of the fifteenth century sailed into the Indian Ocean and began to divert the maritime trade of the East around the Cape of Good Hope. But, far more serious was the fact that by the later fifteenth century the military machine of the Mamluks was becoming outdated, and mainly because of the etiquette of proud cavalrymen, whose instinct led them to reject the use of firearms. The cavalrymen of their main rivals, the Ottoman Turks, fully shared this prejudice, but the Ottoman military also had the regiments of janissaries, recruited like the mamluks as boy slaves, but from the mountains of

[5] Léon l'Africain, *Description de l'Afrique* (Paris, 1956), p. 503.

the Balkans and not from the steppes of Central Asia, who became highly skilled in the use of guns and firearms. The janissaries were the Ottomans' secret weapon.

On 18 May 1516 the aged Mamluk sultan Qansawh al-Ghawri rode out of Cairo in the midst of a fabulous procession of his troops and followers, carrying with him the treasure of Egypt in gold dinars, on the first stage of his expedition to Syria, to defend his northern lands from the threat of Ottoman aggression. Before the summer was out, he was to die among his defeated soldiers on the battlefield of Marj Dabiq, near Aleppo, a defeat greatly assisted by the defection of Khayr Bey, Mamluk governor of Aleppo, to the Ottomans. Against the advice of some of his officers, the Ottoman sultan Selim continued his advance through Palestine and across the Sinai desert into Egypt. On 23 January 1517 his troops stormed the fortified camp of al-Raydaniyya, outside Cairo. The next day detachments of the Ottoman army entered the city, and the sultan's name was proclaimed from the city's mosques. Selim remained in Egypt until September, the first and last Ottoman sultan to visit the new province.

THE OTTOMAN PROVINCE

The Ottoman sultanate had emerged in the fourteenth century as one of many Turkish principalities engaged in spirited holy war (Arabic *jihad*, Turkish *ghaza*) against the retreating frontier of the Byzantine empire in Anatolia. Within a century it had grown into a world power, first by conquering the Byzantine provinces in southeastern Europe and then, in 1453, by capturing Constantinople itself. This great city, known to the Turks as Istanbul, became the capital of an empire of quite exceptional flare and individuality, which for more than two centuries seriously threatened the very future of Western Christendom. On their Asian flank, the Sunni Ottomans were themselves threatened by the rise of a new dynasty in Persia, the warlike Shi'ite Safavids, while to the south there was Mamluk Syria. There was a real danger that populist Shi'ite Islam would spread westwards into Anatolia. For their part, the Mamluks could not rely on the loyalty of any of the Turkish- or Kurdish-speaking vassal states north of the Syrian plain. In 1514 the Ottoman army defeated Shah Isma'il at Tabriz. Two seasons later, in 1516, it prepared to march eastwards for a further attack on Persia. The Mamluks took fright, and Sultan Qansawh led the Mamluk army into northern Syria. At all costs, the Ottoman sultan Selim had to prevent the rumoured alliance between Mamluks and Safavids. He therefore diverted his forces against the Mamluks, and a few months later rode into Cairo.

Egypt was conquered, and was reduced to the position of a province (Arabic *wilaya*, Turkish *eyalet*) of the Ottoman empire, and merely one of thirty-two. Syria and Palestine were detached and broken up into a number of separate provinces. This proved a blessing in disguise for Egypt, as its economy was no longer drained of financial and other resources for the futile task of defending a remote northern frontier. Turkish became the imperial language, partly replacing Arabic among the ruling groups of Egypt. Yet, except for the shift in status, the Ottoman conquest brought little change to the vast majority of the urban and rural population, who remained subjects under the Ottomans as they had been under the Mamluks. Indeed, when he left Egypt, Sultan Selim appointed as his viceroy the rebel Mamluk, Khayr Bey, and left the Mamluk apparatus with its recruitment of boy slaves largely intact.

However, the accession of Selim's son Suleyman (known to Westerners as 'the Magnificent') in 1520, led to a series of revolts against Ottoman overrule, and order was not restored until 1525, with the arrival in Egypt of the redoubtable Ibrahim Pasha, the grand vizier of the empire. Ibrahim issued an edict which, legally at least, was to regulate the civil and military administration of the province until the end of Ottoman rule in 1798. This introduced some specifically Ottoman elements into the structure of government. Henceforward, the governor was to be a *wali*, and his council a *diwan*, while the judicial system was to be reorganised under *qadis*. The military system was to be strengthened by the addition of an imperial garrison, consisting of two infantry regiments, the janissaries and the *'azeban*, with their headquarters in the citadel at Cairo, and five other detachments, three of cavalry and two of infantry. But the base of the ruling triangle remained the Mamluk amirs, who retained control over the rural districts and the minor towns, although they were required to reside in Cairo. The main result of Ottoman rule was to multiply the areas of conflict for power between these ruling groups.

For much of the sixteenth century the Ottoman governors held the upper hand, reflecting the prestige of the great sultans, Suleyman the Magnificent and Selim II. During this period Egypt contributed greatly to the economic well-being of the empire, proving by far the most profitable of the Ottoman provinces. The wealth of the country was in its population, its agriculture and its commerce, all of which were recovering their momentum at the time of the conquest, following the dreadful crisis of the fourteenth century. With the conquest, most of the agricultural land reverted to the sovereign. The Mamluks thus lost their iqta holdings, but when in due course the land was parcelled out again for tax purposes, the Mamluks again became the main holders of the tax farms (*iltizam*). The imperial tribute, assessed at about one quarter of the total state taxes, was fixed and comparatively light. Despite the activities of the Portuguese in the Indian Ocean, Egypt's share of the Eastern trade remained very considerable throughout the sixteenth and most of the seventeenth century. The Ottomans inherited and developed the Mamluk interests in Arabia and on the African shores of the Red Sea. In 1538 the Ottoman governor of Egypt, Sulayman Pasha, led an unsuccessful expedition to oust the Portuguese from the Indian port of Diu, but on his return voyage took control of Aden. A few years later, Ozdemir Pasha, a Circassian Mamluk commander in the service of the sultan, led an expedition through upper Egypt into northern Nubia (known to the Turks as Berberistan), where he captured and garrisoned Aswan, Say and Ibrim, all important river-ports in the Nile valley. Ozdemir then led his forces across the eastern desert to the Red Sea ports of Suakin, Massawa and Zeila. The Ottomans set up a new province there, which they called Habesh (Abyssinia), with its capital at Massawa, in a largely successful attempt to exclude the Portuguese from the Red Sea and Christian Ethiopia. Suez, with easy access to both Cairo and the Mediterranean coast, became the great Egyptian port on the Red Sea.

The authority of the Ottoman governors was seriously undermined in 1596, when the imperial garrison turned insubordinate as empire-wide inflation devalued their pay. Tumult on the streets of Cairo led to the suspension and recall of the governor. In 1609 an even more serious revolt was put down only with the aid of the Mamluk beys. By the 1630s the beys were imposing their will on the Ottoman authorities. From 1631 till 1656 politics in Egypt were dominated by Ridwan Bey, the leader of a Mamluk faction. But after about 1660 the Mamluk ascendancy waned, and the officers of the Ottoman regiments (*ojakat*), especially the janissaries, came to the fore, with an ambitious janissary subaltern, Kuchuk Muhammad, playing a popular role in the convoluted politics of Cairo. Kuchuk was assassinated while riding through the city in 1694. His place was taken by another janissary, Afranj Ahmad (Ahmad the European), who met a similar fate in 1711. Nevertheless, despite all this instability among the governing caste, it could be that the thirty years before and after 1700 constituted the golden age of Ottoman Egypt. The   27 janissary ascendancy was marked by a mutually beneficial alliance between them and the wealthy artisans of Cairo, in which the soldiers protected the artisans and exploited them by becoming their business partners, while assuring their security and mitigating the exactions levied upon them by the authorities. For their part, the janissaries and the other soldiers were becoming increasingly Egyptianised, marrying into the local Cairene families. In the words of al-Sayyid Marsot, 'the ascendancy of the *ojakat* ensured the well-being of the Egyptian artisans, and the ordered and reasonable exploitation of the urban tax farms, the *iqtaat*'.[6]

MODERNISING TENDENCIES IN EIGHTEENTH-CENTURY EGYPT

When, in the 1760s, the janissaries gave way once again to the Mamluk beys, it was in a changed economic environment for Egypt and the Ottoman empire generally. Basically, this was because the terms of trade had altered in favour of European commercial interests, especially those of the French textile manufacturers and traders, who were outperforming local cloth production in Egypt. Up to this time the Mamluks had in general lived off their rural tax farms, many of which had become hereditary. But in the straitened economic circumstances the beys seized the urban tax farms from the janissaries and jacked up the taxes. They raised mercenary armies to enforce their demands, and even purchased naval vessels to expand their control over the trade formerly in the hands of the great merchant families, the *tujjar*. Those beys who managed to fight their way to the top attempted to modernise and centralise the administration of Egypt, and this brought them into contention with their Ottoman suzerains.

The foremost of the brash 'new men' of Egyptian politics was Ali Bey al-Kabir, who was nicknamed *Bulut kapan*, 'the cloudcatcher'. He came to prominence in 1760, when he schemed for the office of *shaykh al-balad*, senior bey. 'I will take command by my sword alone, and not through the support of anyone else', the chronicler al-Jabarti reports him as boasting.[7] Ali Bey set aside the old Ottoman regiments, hired a mercenary army equipped with vastly expensive firearms and cannon, established law and order, and ruthlessly

[6] A. L. al-Sayyid Marsot, 'Egypt under the Mamluks', in *Egypt in the Reign of Muhammad 'Ali* (Cambridge, 1984), p. 5.
[7] al-Jabarti, *Aja'ib al-athar*, in C. Mansour (trans.), *Merveilles biographiques et historiques* (Cairo, 1888–96), vol. I, p. 258.

eliminated rivals and seized their wealth. Once in power, he set about impressing the Cairenes in the traditional manner, by vast displays of conspicuous consumption. Contemporaries thought that Ali Bey would declare himself the independent ruler of Egypt, but he remained outwardly loyal to the Ottoman state, at least until 1770, when he conspired with the Russians in an attempt to recover Syria for Egypt in the Turco-Russian war. In the event, he lost control of Egypt, was taken captive and died in 1773. For much of the last quarter of the eighteenth century power was shared by two Mamluk grandees, Ibrahim Bey and Murad Bey, who exploited the country in their own interests and in plain defiance of the Ottoman sultans. In 1786 they even ceased to pay the tribute, which caused the sultan to send an expedition, commanded by his admiral Hasan Pasha, to re-establish Ottoman authority over the province. The admiral attempted to impose a number of reforms, but without durable results, for in 1791 the duumvirs Ibrahim and Murad regained power, and it was they who were defeated by the French army of General Bonaparte at the battle of the Pyramids in July of 1798.

In conclusion, it may be said that in many ways Egypt had greatly benefited from having been a large and important province of the Ottoman empire. Cairo, in particular, had won a central place in the internal commerce of the empire, which was facilitated by the absence of frontiers and the free circulation of goods and people. One indication of its growing prosperity can be seen in the multiplication of its caravanserais from the fifty-eight mentioned by Maqrizi in the fifteenth century to 360 by the end of Ottoman times. By the close of the eighteenth century, the city had a population of 263,000, still hierarchically ranked, but with a significant growth in the numbers and prosperity of its middle class. At the top of the social ladder there was still the Turko-Circassian élite, headed by the Ottoman governor and his court, the janissary and other regiments of the military, and the households of the Mamluk beys. The fact that some of these were now living on their country estates was one sign of the social change that was taking place. Next in the hierarchy came the members of the learned professions: the *'ulama*, the teachers in the law schools (*maddhab*) and the high schools (*madrasa*), the *imams* and other personnel of the mosques, and the clerics of the *zawiya*, which were the Muslim equivalents of the Christian monasteries. At the heart of the learned class was the university mosque of al-Azhar, around which congregated the schools (*riwaq*) of the foreign religious communities, such as the students from the Maghrib and those from Adal.

Next below the learned professions came a class composed of merchants and traders, ranging in the scope of their dealings from a certain Ahmad al-Saʿadi, a seller of peas, who in 1703 had an income of 145 paras, to one Qasim al-Sharaybi, a coffee merchant who, when he died in 1735, left 12,642,372 paras, together with a fleet of ships and extensive landed property. Dominating the economically active population were the high bourgeoisie, the great merchants and financiers, the tujjar, who controlled the long-distance trade both within the empire and further afield to India and the Sudanic regions of Africa. By the last quarter of the eighteenth century tujjar were taking over Mamluk properties and exploiting their tax farms. They had numerous links with the governing caste, and lived in veritable palaces rivalling those of the élite. Below the tujjar were the host of smaller merchants and shopkeepers and the skilled artisans, who performed a bewildering variety of trades. Closely connected with the high bourgeoisie were the minority groups and foreign communities, comprising Copts, Jews, European Christians, Turks, Maghribis, Syrians, Greeks and Armenians. In the 1760s Ali Bey had begun the process of dispossessing the native Egyptian tujjar in favour of Syrian Christians of the Melkite rite, so as to secure better control of the financial and commercial resources of the country. These Monophysite Christians, who had fled to escape persecution by the Greek Orthodox Church in the 1730s, settled in the ports of Damietta and Rosetta and engaged in trade with the countries of the eastern Mediterranean. By the 1780s some of the Syrian Christian merchants had forged links with entrepreneurs in the Italian ports and in Marseilles, and had intermarried with their trading partners, thus paving the way for the penetration of the Egyptian economy by French commercial and industrial interests.

At the bottom of the social ladder struggled the populace (*al-ʿamma*) – the donkey-men, porters, water carriers, hawkers, cleaners and day labourers. As artisan production declined during the difficult closing decades of the century, so the number of day labourers increased, to the extent that the great historian of Cairo, André Raymond, has no hesitation in using the term 'proletariat' to describe this large group of urban people, forced to support themselves miserably by 'vague activities'. For many, 'their only belongings consisted of a piece of matting, on which they slept with their wives and children'.[8] The participation of this Cairene proletariat in

[8] M. Charbol, *Description de l'Egypte* (Paris, 1822), cited in Raymond, *Le Caire*, p. 211.

street uprisings marked a new phase in Egyptian politics. Equally significant were the members of the 'ulama who joined, and in some cases even led, these popular uprisings. There were social stirrings even in the countryside. Small numbers of fellahin were becoming comparatively affluent, and new and powerful rural figures were emerging among the shaykhs who served as the local representatives of the absentee tax farmers. These village shaykhs were to play a large part in the history of nineteenth-century Egypt. Lastly were those who lacked even a toe-hold on the social ladder – the slaves, mostly from black Africa, who were the domestics and concubines in the Mamluk palaces and in the villas of the wealthy merchants.

After occupying Cairo in 1798, Napoleon Bonaparte drove most of the surviving Mamluks into upper Egypt. In 1802 the Ottomans placed an embargo on the export of further white slave boys for recruitment into the Mamluk households. In 1811, after nearly a decade of fighting his way to the top of the heap of conflicting interests left by the departure of the French, Muhammad Ali, an Albanian major in the Ottoman forces which, jointly with the British, had driven the French out of Egypt, destroyed those Mamluks still remaining in Cairo in a ruthless act of slaughter. Thus ended for Egypt eight centuries of domination by this peculiar institution. Muhammad Ali then set about modernising Egypt along the lines attempted fifty years earlier by Ali Bey, the 'cloudcatcher', with much more success but with many unforeseen consequences.

3 Ifriqiya and the Regencies

To the Arabs the Mediterranean lands west of Egypt were known collectively as the *Maghrib* (the West). The nearer part of it, comprising Tripolitania, Tunisia and eastern Algeria, was also known by the name of the former Roman province of Africa, arabised as *Ifriqiya*. The western Maghrib, comprising western Algeria, Morocco and Mauritania, was *al-Maghrib al-Aqsa* – the Far West. By the thirteenth century, Islam had been established in the Maghrib for more than five hundred years – so much so that the former Latin Christianity of the coast and its immediate hinterland had long ceased to exist. The Berber language had largely disappeared from the towns and coastal plains of the Mediterranean shore, and the use of Arabic was spreading rapidly even among the rural populations of the interior, thanks to the westward migration of Arab pastoralists in search of new grazing grounds for their sheep and camels. These last, often given the generic name of Banu Hilal, had begun their expansion from the Egyptian province of Cyrenaica during the eleventh and twelfth centuries by moving across the steppe country of Tripolitania and southern Tunisia, towards the Atlas foothills and the desert fringes to the south of them. By the fourteenth century their vanguard had reached the Atlantic seaboard of Morocco and Mauritania.

The Banu Hilal have traditionally been presented as a destructive element in Maghribi society. In reality, however, they performed a very positive function within it by acting as the frontier defence force, the policemen and the tax gatherers of the coast-based rulers, who rewarded them for their services with grants of land. By the sixteenth century the cultivators and herdsmen of the hinterland of the eastern and central Maghrib had become thoroughly arabised, the poorer people speaking the rough tongue of the Banu Hilal, while the petty warlords and the dynasties of 'holy men', who between them dominated the countryside, appropriated fictitious genealogies to claim Arab descent. Thus, Berber and Arab nomads combined to create a syncretistic kind of Islam, of which the characteristic leaders were the holy men, known as *marabouts*, rather than the teachers, preachers and jurists who animated the religious life of the towns. In this way, Islam achieved in the Maghrib what neither Roman rule nor Latin Christianity had succeeded in doing, by uniting the Berbers within a single ideology.

Following the defeat of its armies in Spain in 1212 (below, p. 51), the brilliant Almohad empire in North Africa soon disintegrated. By the end of the 1230s independent Berber dynasties had taken control of Morocco in the west, Ifriqiya in the east and the central Maghrib in between. These dynasties fought among themselves in the attempt to restore the unity achieved by the Almohads and also did what they could to control the turbulent warlords of the hinterland. But despite the rough and ready nature of political power, there remained in the Maghrib enough basic security and good order to permit a good deal of regular, long-distance movement by civilians in the service of trade, religion and education. Trade routes ran mainly north and south, linking the Maghrib with southern Europe on the one hand and with the western and central Sudan on the other. Land transport on both sides of the Mediterranean was by pack animals and not by wheeled vehicles. In the Maghrib donkeys, mules and horses were used for short hauls, but the main long-distance baggage animal was the camel. Though usually associated with the desert, it was a familiar sight in every port and market town from the Mediterranean coast to the Senegal and the Niger.

Hand in hand with these movements of trade went those occasioned by religion and education. The world of Islam revered knowledge, and stressed the virtues of pilgrimage. Knowledge acquired abroad was preferred to the home product, and the aspiring scholar would migrate from one famous law school to another, keeping open regular links between Fez, Meknes, Tlemcen, Tunis, Kayrawan, Cairo and places further to the east. Pilgrimage attracted even larger numbers. Young men and old, rich and poor, some riding but many on foot, swelled the camel and donkey trains moving to and fro across the Maghrib towards the holy cities of Mecca and Medina beyond the Red Sea. Merchants, clerics and pilgrims alike were helped on their journeys by the fortified monasteries (zawiyas) of marabouts or Sufi devotees, which provided protection and succour in a dangerous countryside.

Much of the merchant shipping of the Maghrib was in European hands, and communities of European and Jewish traders lived in factory enclaves in all the large ports – Tripoli, Tunis and Bijaya (Bougie), all in Ifriqiya; and Oran, the port of Tlemcen. Andalusian Muslims and Christian mercenaries or renegades played leading roles in the North African sultanates, especially as pirates. Privateering or 'corsairing' (from the Italian *corsare*, to chase) went back to the earliest years of contact between the northern and southern shores of the western Mediterranean and its islands, and was practised by both Muslims and Christians. Only from the late fifteenth century, however, did privateering become the predominant form of Muslim shipping, well organised and often animated by the active intention to convert the Christian captives so taken, who became an important element in all Maghribi armies and navies.

Between the lands of the Moroccan sultanate and the port of Bijaya lay the territory of the 'Abd al-Wadid or Zayyanid dynasty, with its graceful capital city of Tlemcen, situated in the hills behind its port at Oran. Tlemcen was the only city in the central Maghrib to have a strong connection with the African interior, for it bestrode a caravan route leading southwards between the Saharan Atlas and the Great Atlas to Sijilmasa, the oasis terminal of the western desert crossings. It thus competed with Ifriqiya and Morocco for the gold and slaves of Mali and Songhay, and was the main intermediary for these commodities with Andalusia and the expanding Christian kingdom of Aragon.

THE HAFSIDS AND THEIR NEIGHBOURS

The great power of the eastern Maghrib from the early thirteenth century onwards was the Hafsid kingdom of Ifriqiya, with its capital at Tunis, its agricultural base in the fertile Tunisian plain, and its long coastline stretching all the way from the Egyptian frontier east of Tripoli to that of Tlemcen a little to the west of Bijaya. The Hafsids were in origin shaykhs of the Almohad empire at the period of its widest expansion, who had been placed in Tunis as military governors of the eastern province. But with the fragmentation of that empire following its disastrous defeats in Spain, a succession of long-lived Hafsid shaykhs, starting with Abu Zakariyya (1228–49) and al-Mustansir (1249–77), gradually turned their command into an independent kingdom.

The economic strength of Ifriqiya lay in its rich agricultural lands, laid out in a patchwork of vegetable gardens, wheat fields and olive groves, covering the whole northern half of the Tunisian plain. From Carthaginian and Roman times onwards these had enabled it to absorb and acculturate wave upon wave of immigrants, and to feed a great metropolitan city. The earlier Muslim rulers of Ifriqiya had placed their capitals to the south of the Tunisian plain, near the main land routes to the Far West, but, with the growth of the maritime trade of the Mediterranean, Tunis was in every way to be preferred. With easy access to a superb natural harbour nearby at Halq al-Wadi (Goletta), Tunis was the natural hub for the maritime trade between the eastern and western Mediterranean, already much boosted by the traffic between Muslim Spain and the heartlands of Islam, as well as by the crusading activities of the Christians of western Europe. Crusading led to the growth of merchant shipping, and when the military tide turned with the loss of the Christian principalities in the Levant, both traders and Crusaders looked for new points of contact in Egypt and North Africa. In 1248 King Louis IX of France led a disastrous crusade against Egypt, and in 1270 he returned to lay siege to Tunis, where he died of a fever. Leadership of the expedition reverted to his brother Charles, Count of Anjou and King of Sicily, who evacuated it on the promise of a large tribute by al-Mustansir. Nevertheless, Tunis was among the earliest of the North African towns to welcome the Christian merchants of southern Europe – from Barcelona and Marseilles, Pisa, Genoa and Venice – and to provide them with protected enclaves where they could do their business in safety. Moreover, under Hafsid rule, Ifriqiya grew into a maritime power in its own right, importing timber for shipbuilding from as far afield as Norway, and manning its shipyards and its galleys with Christian captives taken in privateering raids around the coasts of Malta, Sicily and southern Italy. Its population, swollen by a steady accretion of black slaves from the Sudan, as well as by Moorish Muslim refugees following the conquest of Sicily by the Normans in 1091, had grown by the mid-fourteenth century to around 100,000. It was thus among the great cities of the world at that time.

Though Tunis was comparatively distant from the desert, its control of the central Mediterranean enabled it to command a goodly share of the profits from the Saharan trade. One major caravan route led south from Tunis to Ghadames, and thence to Timbuktu. On the southern shore of the Gulf of Sirte, the smaller port of Tripoli stood almost in the desert, at the head of the great central route to the Fezzan and Kawar, Bornu and Hausaland. The Hafsids of Ifriqiya, no less than their contemporaries in Morocco, minted the gold of Mali and Songhay. In addition, they received the slaves and ivory of the central Sudan. In this direction, they were in touch with the rulers of Kanem and Bornu, with whose emissaries they discussed arrangements for the safety of the trade routes. The royal family of Kanem had converted to Islam as early as the eleventh century, no doubt under the influence of traders from Ifriqiya. In the words of 35

Ibn Khaldun, the fourteenth-century historian and philosopher, who was himself a native of Tunis: 'The merchants who dare to enter the Sudan country are the most prosperous and wealthy of all people. The distance and the difficulty of the road they travel is great. Therefore, the goods of the Sudan country are found only in small quantity among us, and they are particularly expensive. The same applies to our goods among them. Merchandise becomes more valuable when merchants transport it from one country to another. They get rich quickly.'[1]

Moulded by the pleasant environment of the Tunisian plain, the rulers of Ifriqiya were cultivated and civilised men, who kept a sumptuous court and were punctilious in their public appearances, when they processed on horseback through the city, accompanied by their principal shaykhs and men at arms, to the beating of drums and tambourines, and the twirling aloft of their huge and richly embroidered state umbrellas. Literacy in Arabic was promoted, along with religious education, in every large mosque, while three major university mosques at Kayrawan, Tunis and Bijaya provided the training for an intellectual élite of preachers, judges and administrators. Of these, the great mosque at Kayrawan had been held in repute throughout the Islamic world since the ninth century, as the centre of the Maliki 'school' of orthodox, Sunni, doctrine and jurisprudence. Of Kayrawan, the eleventh-century poet, Ibn Rashiq had written:

How many were in her of nobles and gentles, white of face and proud of right hand, joining in worship and obedience to God in thought and deed, a school of all excellencies, pouring out its treasure to lord and people; men of God, who brought together the sciences of religion, and burnished all the usages of Tradition and the problems of the Koran; doctors who, if you asked them, rolled away the clouds with their knowledge of the Law, their pure language and explanations.[2]

The puritanical Almohads had forbidden the teaching of the Malikite school in all the great mosques of their empire, and it was some time before the Hafsid rulers of Ifriqiya returned to the older religious practices and restored not only Malikite teaching at Kayrawan but also the doctrinal unity so vital to the spread of Islam in the western and central Sudan. Then, once again, students from all over the western Islamic lands gathered under the university's

---

[1] Ibn Khaldun, *Muqaddimah* (London, 1967), p. 310.

[2] Cited in Michael Brett and Werner Forman, *The Moors* (London, 1980), p. 60.

ample colonnades to sit at the feet of learned professors of scripture and tradition, and the Maliki version of the shari'a law derived from them. Alongside the formal and legalistic religious precepts of the Malikite school, however, there flourished the more popular Sufi practices of Muslims in the towns and countryside of Ifriqiya, so much so that a school of Sufi learning was established at Kayrawan. Many African students came to Ifriqiya in the course of making the pilgrimage to Mecca from places far to the west and south. Often they stayed for years on the way, and returned to become religious leaders in their own countries.

The prosperity and civilisation of the urban élite of Ifriqiya during the first century of Hafsid rule suffered a severe setback when the Black Death was brought from Sicily to Tunis in 1348. Ibn Khaldun, who lost both parents to the plague, described its effect in telling language. 'Civilisation', he wrote, 'decreased with the decrease of mankind. Cities and buildings were laid waste, roads and way-signs were obliterated, settlements and mansions became empty, dynasties and tribes grew weak.'[3] Successive outbreaks of the plague hit the rural cultivators of the Tunisian plain even more sharply than the inhabitants of the coastal towns. Agricultural output fell. The revenues of the state were diminished. Weakened central government had a shorter outreach, and could no longer protect its rural subjects from the predatory inroads of the wild pastoralists of the southern frontier, who seized the opportunity to raid and steal. Faced with this situation, the sultans of Ifriqiya could only resort to the classic remedy of making alliances with warrior chiefs of the Banu Hilal and other Arab tribes, who provided military contingents in exchange for the right to gather taxes from specific areas of the countryside. The first such iqta, the Egyptian type of military fief or tax farm, had been granted by Sultan Abu Zakariyya to an Arab warrior chief as early as 1248, but after the Black Death the expedient proliferated. The fifteenth century saw a partial recovery, particularly in the coastal cities, where an emerging middle class showed vigour in developing the maritime trade with southern Europe. But the overall picture is one of a population that was no longer increasing in line with its European contemporaries and rivals. It would appear that by the end of the fifteenth century the Maghrib as a whole was supporting only about half as dense a population as the comparable lands to the north of the Mediterranean sea.

[3] Ibn Khaldun, *Muqaddimah*, p. 30.

THE STRUGGLE FOR POWER IN THE MEDITERRANEAN: SPAIN AND THE OTTOMAN EMPIRE

In the eastern Mediterranean the dominant development of the fifteenth and early sixteenth centuries was the rise and deployment of Ottoman power. We have already seen (p. 25) how, beginning in Anatolia, it had spread into the Balkan provinces of the Byzantine empire, encircling and finally capturing Constantinople in 1453. From there on, its progress into Greece and the Aegean islands, and up the Dalmatian coast of the Adriatic, brought it at once into conflict with Venice, which could only be successfully pursued by turning itself into a naval as well as a military power. Sultan Bayezid II (1481–1512) accordingly set in motion an ambitious programme of naval construction, which established Ottoman supremacy in the eastern Mediterranean and lasted through most of the sixteenth century. The conquest of Egypt and Syria by his successor, Selim, was the most spectacular result of this policy, but by no means the only one. The Knights of St John had already been driven from Rhodes, and an Ottoman enclave established on the mainland of Italy at Otranto. Add to these naval exploits the land victories of Suleyman the Magnificent in Serbia and Hungary and his threat to the eastern half of the Habsburg empire by laying siege in 1529 to Vienna, and there could be no doubt that Ottoman advances in the eastern Mediterranean would lead on to others in the west. The security of the Iberian peninsula, along with that of southern Italy, Sicily and the other Mediterranean islands, was at stake.

In so serious a conflict the whole of the African coastline of the Mediterranean had necessarily to be involved, and it was inevitable that Hafsid Ifriqiya, with its strategic position at the narrows of the sea, would suffer interference from both sides. Indeed, Spain, following its conquest of Granada in 1492, had already moved to forestall a Muslim counterattack by occupying and placing garrisons (*presidios*) in several of the main harbours of North Africa, including Bijaya and Tripoli, at either end of the Ifriqiyan coastline. These operations were carried out between 1496 and 1511. Meanwhile, as early as 1504 a band of Turkish corsairs, acting initially under licence from the Hafsid ruler Muhammad ibn al-Hasan (1493–1526), established a base in the great harbour of Tunis at Goletta, from which they conducted highly successful privateering operations against Christian shipping passing through the narrows, and raided for booty and captives in the fishing villages of Sicily and southern Italy. The leaders were three brothers, Turkish Muslims from the recently conquered

Aegean island of Lesbos, of whom the two elder ones were called ʿAruj and Khayr al-Din. They shared their booty with the ruler, and as the number of their ships and crews increased, he authorised them to open a second base on the offshore island of Jerba in the southwestern corner of the Gulf of Sirte and within easy reach of the Spanish presidio near Tripoli. Next, in 1512, still working closely with the Hafsid ruler, ʿAruj led the first of several unsuccessful expeditions to Bijaya, where the Spaniards had driven out the Hafsid governor and planted a garrison of their own. After failing at Bijaya, the brothers responded in 1516 to an appeal from the inhabitants of Algiers, then only an insignificant fishing port in the neighbouring state of Tlemcen, for help in ridding themselves of the Spanish garrison recently planted on an offshore island called the Peñon, which faced their harbour. Here, it could be said that the brothers, in accepting, crossed the always narrow boundary between piracy and imperialism. From their toe-hold in Algiers they inevitably became involved in the politics of Tlemcen, in which they held no licence from the local Zayyanid ruler to intervene. In 1518 ʿAruj was driven out and killed by a combined force of Spaniards and Zayyanids. Thereafter, Khayr al-Din, nicknamed Barbarossa, 'the redbeard', by his Spanish foes, declared a jihad against the Spaniards. He appealed to the Ottoman sultan for military help, placing himself under his protection and receiving in return the Ottoman title of *pasha* and the military rank of *beylerbey* (commander-in-chief) in respect of the force of Turkish janissaries, armed with muskets and cannon, which were sent to his aid.

Although initially forced to retreat from Algiers, Khayr al-Din gradually built up a successful bridgehead a little further to the east, at Jijilli. From there, he returned to capture Algiers in 1525, occupying first the town and then the Spanish fortress on the Peñon. By building a causeway between the Peñon and the mainland he created a nearly impregnable harbour, which was to become the main Ottoman naval base in the western Mediterranean and the headquarters of an extensive and profitable corsairing enterprise. Territorially, his dominions now comprised the coastline of eastern Algeria and the island base of Jerba in the Gulf of Sirte. In between lay the crumbling state of the Hafsids. However, his contribution to the whole momentum of Ottoman maritime expansion in the Mediterranean was so highly appreciated by the Porte (the English name for the Ottoman government) that in 1533 he was summoned to Istanbul and appointed by Sultan Suleyman as high admiral of all the Ottoman fleets. Acting from this position, which he held for the next thirteen years, he was able to send a fleet of eighty-four ships to capture Tunis briefly for the Ottomans. But the Turkish garrison there was soon ejected by the Spaniards, who restored the Hafsid sultanate, which endured, but with steadily diminishing significance, for another forty years. Meantime, the main theatre of Ottoman expansion had moved west to Algiers, where Khayr al-Din's fleet successfully resisted a mighty assault by the Spaniards in 1541, which was said to have consisted of 500 ships, carrying an invasion force of 24,000 men. The expedition was commanded by the Emperor Charles V in person, who lost one-third of his ships and himself narrowly escaped capture.

The successful defence of Algiers in 1541 marked the high point of Ottoman naval power in the Mediterranean. It marked also the beginnings of Ottoman imperial rule in North Africa. It meant that beylerbeys were henceforth regularly appointed from Istanbul to command the Algiers government in succession to the more personal and territorially indeterminate command given to Khayr al-Din. It meant the steady development of Algiers into a capital city which rapidly eclipsed that of the Zayyanid sultans of Tlemcen, who now became politically dependent on the Ottoman beylerbeys. Not least, it set the pattern of Ottoman overrule in the rest of their North African dependencies.

Following Khayr al-Din's death in 1546, he was succeeded as high admiral by Sinan Pasha, who in 1551 laid siege to the fortress of Tripoli and drove out the Knights of St John, who had replaced the Spanish garrison. A famous corsair captain named Dragut was appointed governor of the town, and soon developed it into the capital of an Ottoman province comparable to that of Algiers. The political authority of the Hafsids of Tunis over Tripoli was simply ignored. Under Dragut's rule corsairs from Tripoli relentlessly raided the coasts of Sicily and southern Italy. The Spaniards, as the rulers of Sicily and Naples, attempted a counterattack on Tripoli, but were ignominiously defeated. The Ottomans in their turn suffered a parallel reverse in 1565 in their attempt to capture Malta, when an Ottoman expeditionary force of 20,000, led by Dragut and the Ottoman admiral, ʿUluj ʿAli, was successfully resisted by a handful of Knights. In 1571 the Ottoman navy suffered a far more serious disaster when 230 of its ships, assembled for the invasion of Cyprus, were surprised in their winter quarters in the Gulf of Lepanto by the combined navies of Spain and Venice, and all but thirty were lost. Nevertheless, in 1573 and 1574 ʿUluj ʿAli, with the help of Sinan Pasha, was able to achieve the definitive capture of Tunis and so put an end to Hafsid rule. At last, in 1581, Spain and the Ottomans signed a truce which effectively ended their Mediterranean contest.

THE OTTOMAN PROVINCES: ALGIERS, TUNIS AND TRIPOLI

From the final capture of Tunis in 1574, all of the eastern and central Maghrib was formally comprised within the three Ottoman provinces, known to Europeans as the Regencies. In practice, only the coastal districts were held, and each province had still to face the problems of internal conquest and consolidation inescapable from the establishment of any colonial regime. At the head of each province was a beylerbey or pasha, nominated by the sultan in Istanbul. Initially, these appointments were long-term, and in the case of Algiers 'Uluj 'Ali combined the post with that of high admiral of the Ottoman fleet. But after his death in 1587 the term of the office was set at three years, which correspondingly reduced the authority of the incumbent. Each beylerbey needed to balance two rival sources of power. First, in each province there was the seafaring élite, comprising the corporation of ship-owners (*taifa*) and the corsairing captains (*ra'is*), from whom the original impulse for Ottoman protection had come, and upon whose continuing activity the material prosperity of the provinces depended. With the exhaustion of both Spanish and Ottoman navies after their great struggle, the Mediterranean was wide open to privateering and profits were higher than ever before. Some of the corsairing captains were Turks, but most of the officers and non-slave seamen were drawn from the miscellaneous elements of the North African coast – Berbers, Arabs, Moors, Greeks, Jews and Christian renegades from Corsica, Sardinia, Malta, Sicily and Calabria.

The second power base in the Regencies were the *ojak* – the janissary musketeers, nearly all of them Turks, recruited from Anatolia under licence from the Ottoman sultan. These, though free men, followed the same system as the mamluks of Egypt. Only first-generation recruits might be members of the military caste. Their descendants by local wives (*kulughlis*) formed a privileged social élite, but were barred from military rank. When it came to the conquest and administration of the interior, the power of the ojak grew more rapidly than that of the taifa. Their numbers increased. They were tightly organised in 'rooms' and 'barracks', and the military commanders formed a *diwan* (council), which soon took over the real government of the Regencies, leaving the Ottoman governors as mere figureheads. So dominant was the military element in the life of the Regencies that the provinces were commonly referred to in Turkish as the 'garrisons of the west'.

During the Ottoman period the preponderance of power and prosperity in North Africa swung decisively from the old province of Ifriqiya to the new polity of Algiers. It was here that the move towards Ottoman rule had started, here that the ojak established their first 'barracks', and here that the most powerful navy had been built up. The most striking evidence of the gains from corsairing was seen in the rapid growth of the capital city, which soon overflowed the walls built by Khayr al-Din and his immediate successors into a circle of luxurious suburbs spread over the surrounding hills. This was the prosperous world of the taifa, based upon the harbour, the docks and the *bagnios*, the winter prisons of the galley slaves, who were allowed to exercise their religion and to communicate with their relatives in southern Europe in the hope of raising the funds for a ransom. Outside Algiers, it was the ojak who ruled. In the west of the country Tlemcen was developed as an administrative centre, and garrisons were posted in the other main towns. In the countryside the traditional shaykhs and the leaders of the religious brotherhoods conserved much of their former authority, but all those within reach of expeditions from the garrison towns were subject to taxation or tribute payments, and already in the sixteenth century the power of the ojak was felt along the caravan routes leading south from Tlemcen to Taghourt in the Atlas and Wargla on the desert margin.

In its developed form, the government was organised in four provinces, each under a bey, and further into districts ruled by *qaʿids*, the central government sending out troops three times a year to assist in the collection of taxes or tribute. At headquarters, the military government of Algeria was administered in typical Ottoman bureaucratic style, with a chancellery controlled by four state secretaries, which kept efficient records of the booty brought in by the corsairs and the taxation collected in the countryside. But if the Ottomans were firmly in control of the levers of power in the coastal region, society in the hinterland remained wild and refractory, especially as the tribal warlords learned how to manufacture and effectively use muskets. Among their followers the possession of a gun became a mark of virility. 'It would be a difficult matter', wrote one eighteenth-century observer, 'for a young fellow to get a wife worth having before he is the master of a fuzil.' When the warlords fell out with the Ottomans, they did so with a vengeance. When the Banu 'Abbas, who controlled the passes between Algiers and Constantine, were at war, 'all the Turks that fell alive into their hands, the punishment inflicted on them was cutting off their genitals in the middle, and turning them loose, with their hands bound behind, so to bleed to death in the roads'.[4]

One of the functions of the chancellery in Algiers, which continued in name for 150 years, was to receive the written instructions sent from the sultan in Istanbul and to present them at a weekly meeting of the diwan held at the pasha's palace. Control of the government circulated among the great title-holders – pashas, deys and beys, representing the corsairs, janissaries and officials, the 'men of the pen'. In 1711 the office of pasha was amalgamated with that of the bey, the locally elected commander-in-chief of the ojak. As in other Maghrib countries, stability tended to go hand in hand with the longevity of the ruler. Bey Muhammad ibn 'Uthman ruled from 1766 until 1791. By this time privateering had become merely the pastime of the local fishermen. Legitimate trade flourished, especially that in grain. During the Revolutionary and Napoleonic wars the demand for North African products greatly increased. Wool, leather and grain went to France, and cattle for the British Mediterranean fleet went to Malta. Much of this trade was in the hands of Jewish merchants and bankers. Algiers became known as France's 'bastion', and it was disputes over trade that provided the pretext for the French invasion of the Regency in 1830.

Tunisia under Ottoman rule comprised only the central part of the old sultanate of Ifriqiya. As such, it was not only more compact but stabler and more coherent. Here there was a large, fully settled agricultural population, well accustomed to paying taxes. Only in the saline flats to the south of the Tunisian plain, and in the Aures mountains bordering Algeria, were there nomadic tribes requiring constant pacification by military expeditions. Above all, the whole country was far more Islamised and Arabic-speaking than Algiers. In these circumstances the few thousand Turks who formed the ojak, and also the corsair captains, became much more associated with local élites than their counterparts in Algeria. They accepted non-Turkish elements into their ranks – Greeks, people of mixed race and even renegade Christians – and within a short time the Turkish language gave place to Arabic, even among the military. Even sooner than in Algeria, the local ojak took affairs into their own hands, first

[4] Joseph Morgan, *A Complete History of Algiers* (London, 1731, reprinted New York, 1970), cited in Michael Brett and Elizabeth Fentress, *The Berbers* (Oxford, 1996), p. 160.

by collectively controlling the diwan, and then, in 1598, by allowing a single, autocratic military leader, the dey, to take over.

However, by the 1630s power had shifted significantly to another military figure, the bey or commander of the territorial forces, consisting of the tribal militias and those of the kulughli descendants of the Turkish janissaries. In 1705, in the face of an invasion from Algeria, a kulughli leader, Husayn ibn 'Ali, gained control of the Regency and set up a quasi-monarchy, founding a dynasty that was to reign over Tunisia until the middle of the twentieth century. Husayn centralised the government and greatly encouraged both trade and agricultural production, working closely with the long-established European merchants. 'The bey has such a hold over trade that he can be said to be the only trader in the state', wrote the French consul Saint-Gervais in 1730.[5] After a period of unrest in the middle of the eighteenth century, two strong rulers, 'Ali Bey (1759–82) and Hammadi Pasha (1782–1814), restored peace and prosperity. As in Algeria, so in Tunisia, agricultural products were in high demand by the European participants in the Napoleonic wars, and the country became a large exporter of foodstuffs for the first time since the fall of Rome.

The Ottoman regime in Tripoli faced much thornier problems than its counterparts in Tunisia and Algeria. In large measure these arose from the geographical environment. While Tripoli had an immense strategic importance as the terminus of the shortest trans-Saharan crossing, and as an almost inevitable staging-post on the land route from Egypt to Ifriqiya, it lacked a viable agricultural base. The coastal plain enjoying a regular winter rainfall was nowhere more than 10 miles wide. Behind it, there was only sparse grazing for a few pastoral nomads. The grain to feed the two or three coastal towns had to be carried 500 miles on camel-back from the oasis region of the Fezzan or else brought in by sea. Tripoli was a port and a caravanserai, but only with the utmost difficulty could it be made into a kingdom. Thus, while the transition from rule by the Ottoman beylerbey to that of the dey of the local ojak and the corsair captains followed much the same pattern as in the other two Regencies, violent episodes were recurrent, and it was only in the middle of the seventeenth century that Tripoli emerged as a serious power in the central Mediterranean.

As in Tunis, control shifted from the janissaries to the local notables and the kulughli, and from the dey to a bey. Two strong beys of

[5] Cited by M. H. Cherif in *General History* V, p. 253.

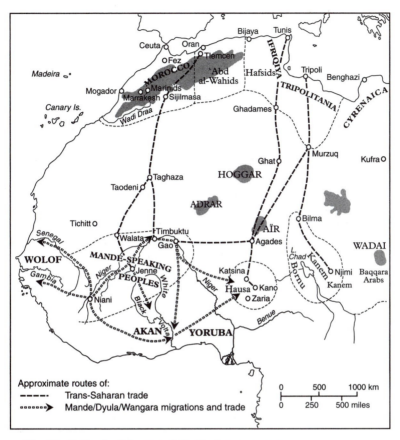

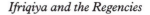

5 The Maghrib, the Sahara and the Sudan, 1250–1500

the Saqizli family, in origin Greek renegades from the island of
Chios, built up the corsairing fleet, which raided as far as Spain and
Italy, and developed a force of swift cavalry to police the caravan
routes to the Sudan. When the caravan traffic was diverted eastwards to Cyrenaica to avoid the attentions of the corsairs and the
European fleets which preyed upon them, the beys seized control of
the eastern province of Benghazi from the Ottoman authorities and
began to impose tribute on the settled Arab and Berber tribes of the
'green mountain' (*Jebel al- Akhdar*). Thus a self-sufficient economic
framework was at last erected, which reached its heyday under the
Karamanlis, a kulughli dynasty, who held power as pashas from 1711
until 1835, when Ottoman forces resumed control of the Regency.   45

SOUTH OF THE REGENCIES

The history of the Ottoman period in North Africa is too often presented as though it had no connection with the African world to the south. In fact, the struggle for command of the southern shores of the Mediterranean had a profound significance for eastern West Africa. In the first place, it was a victory for Islam, which kept open the lines of communication not only in North Africa but across the desert. Had Spain during its greatest century not been diverted from North Africa by the conquest of the New World and by dynastic ambitions in Italy and Central Europe, the history of West Africa as well as North Africa might have been very different. As it was, Muslim teachers and Arabic books continued to cross the Sahara along with Barbary horses, Turkish guns and Venetian cloth and hardware. More important, African pilgrims continued to visit the heartlands of their faith, and African slaves contributed, probably on a greater scale than in the past, to the population of the Muslim lands around the eastern Mediterranean. It has been remarked that, whereas the Atlantic slave trade removed a preponderance of young males to plantation slavery in the New World, the trans-Saharan caravans carried a majority of women and young children destined for service and concubinage in Muslim households. The penal conditions of the galleys and the mines were reserved for Christian slaves from southern Europe.

The degree of interaction between North and West Africa depended, of course, on political conditions to the south of the desert as well as to the north. As we shall see in the next chapter, the political and commercial relations of the western Sudan were concentrated during this period very largely upon Morocco and the Atlantic coast. The north-eastwards traffic was that of pilgrims, who crossed the desert from Timbuktu to Ghat and Ghadames and continued eastwards through the Fezzan and Awjila, keeping to the desert oases and avoiding the main centres of Ottoman government. The trade of the central Sudan, however, was much more closely linked with the eastern and central Maghrib. Here, throughout our period, the dominant state was Bornu, its external contacts and political dynamism based firmly on the trans-Saharan slave trade. The main instrument of slave-catching throughout the central Sudan was the horse, employed in annual dry-season expeditions against the smaller, less organised populations bordering the great Sudanic states. The Sudanic breed of horses, though long established, existed upon the very margin of horse-breeding country, and

46

needed constant enrichment from the larger Barbary stock to the north of the desert. Cavalry forces also needed horse-trappings, armour and coats of mail. And, increasingly during the Ottoman period, guns became an element in Sudanese warfare. They were certainly in use in Bornu by the sixteenth century, and at the time of their introduction they were accompanied by 'Turkish' musketmen, that is to say, soldiers of fortune from Tripoli and Tunis, trained to fire and mend them and familiar with the completely novel military tactics required for their use. All these were costly luxuries, and in a land without much gold or ivory they could be paid for only in slaves.

From Bornu the slave caravans all went northwards through Kawar, where the great salt mine of Bilma formed the hub of a wide circle of trade routes supplying all the populations of the central Sahara and Sudan. From Kawar they marched a journey of three or four weeks to the Fezzan. Along this, the most difficult section of the route, caravans depended on the co-operation as escorts and guides of the Tubu (or Teda) people, whose homeland was the mountain massif of the Tibesti, where they bred great numbers of camels for use in the long-distance trade. On arrival in the Fezzan, the caravans paused to recuperate and regroup at one or other of the oasis towns, such as Zawila, Traghen or Murzuk, where the slaves were rehabilitated, clothed and sold to the North African merchants who operated along the northern desert routes leading to Egypt, Tunisia and, above all, Tripoli, whence cargoes were despatched to Istanbul and other markets in the Ottoman empire. During most of the period the rulers of the Fezzan were a dynasty of Moroccan origin, the Awlad Muhammad, who took tolls, guarded the routes and generally acted as intermediaries between the peoples of the north and the south. From time to time military expeditions arrived from Tripoli to assert a nominal sovereignty. For the most part, these were placated with gifts and honourably entertained until they departed. Nevertheless, the existence of relatively strong powers at either end of this trans-Saharan route did contribute to its security, and in some sense Tripoli and Bornu regarded each other as neighbours and partners in policing the Saharan tribes, just as Kanem and Ifriqiya had done in an earlier period. Embassies and gifts were exchanged, and the traffic in arms and slaves was recognised as a political as well as a commercial transaction.

To the west of the grand central route through Kawar there ran another, scarcely less important, which connected the cities of Hausaland with Ghat in the northern foothills of the Hoggar massif, and thence with Murzuk on the one hand and Ghadames on the other. The camel nomads on whom this system depended were the Tuareg, who from about the eleventh century onwards had shifted their grazing lands southwards from the Hoggar to the hilly regions of Aïr and Adrar of the Ifoghas. Their earliest contribution had been in developing the routes running north-eastwards from Mali and Songhay. The connection between Aïr and Hausaland seems to have emerged only in the fifteenth century, when the Tuareg began to export the copper of Takedda and to acquire a near-monopoly in the distribution of Bilma salt. This corresponded in time with the military expansion of Kano, Katsina and Zaria, when horses and armour began to be imported in quantity from the north, and when manufactures of cotton and leather goods began to be exported across the desert in exchange. With the fall of Songhay at the end of the sixteenth century, the route between Aïr and the Niger bend fell out of use, but the Hausa trade continued to thrive. From the northern entrepôts of Ghadames and Murzuk the cotton textiles of Hausaland were distributed throughout the countries of the Maghrib, and some were even re-exported southwards again to Timbuktu. What came to be known in northern Europe as 'Morocco leather' had often an origin in Hausaland. All in all, the Tuareg trade routes seem to have had a more purely commercial flavour than those of the Tubu to the east. The Tuareg themselves acted as transport agents, carrying goods for a commission and taking responsibility for safe delivery. There was no western counterpart to the special relationship between Tripoli and Bornu, and, perhaps for this reason, firearms did not appear in Hausaland until the eighteenth century. Nevertheless Hausaland, even more than Bornu, belonged to the commercial hinterland of the Ottoman Maghrib, which in turn deserved to be known as the gateway to the central Sudan.

4   The Islamic Far West: Morocco

Morocco is shaped like a broken saucer, with its flat base facing to the Atlantic and its mountainous rim surrounding the coastal plain on every landward side. The plain of Atlantic Morocco rises gently through the undulating foothills of the mountain rim, and supports the settled cultivators and the great cities vital to the country's economy. But until quite recent times it was the wild tribesmen, the herders and high-valley farmers of the great mountains, and the camel people of the desert fringes beyond them, who again and again initiated movements of religious and political renewal which caused the Moroccans to break out of their natural fastness in wars of conquest against their neighbours. During the early centuries of Islam the main direction taken by these wars had been northwards, into the Iberian peninsula, of which the southern tip lay only 9 miles away from Morocco. The original Muslim conquest of Spain, begun in AD 711, had been undertaken as much by Moroccan Berbers as by Arabs. The eleventh-century conquest of Morocco by the Almoravids from the western Sahara had followed through into what had by then become Muslim Andalusia. So had the movement initiated by the Almohads of the High Atlas in the following century. By the middle of the thirteenth century, however, most of Muslim Spain and Portugal had been reconquered by the Christians, although it might be claimed that Spain's loss had become Morocco's gain, through the hosts of migrants fleeing from Andalusia, who came to constitute the most creative and industrious of the sultanate's urban population.

In the mid-thirteenth century the Berbers were still the majority element in the Moroccan population. Their great tribal confederations – Sanhaja, Zanata, Masmuda and others – still dominated the sultanate and provided its ruling dynasties. But the insurrections of zealot warriors were giving way in the countryside to the more peaceful charisma of holy men and saints. Likewise, the linguistic and ethnic composition of Morocco was changing. Under the Almoravids and the Almohads the language of government and of the army had been Berber, but during the second half of the twelfth century the Almohads enrolled Banu Hilal and other Arab tribesmen from Ifriqiya to fight in their armies in Spain, and later encouraged them to settle in the Atlantic plain of Morocco. Still during the thirteenth century, another Arab grouping, the Banu Maʿqil, moved in from further east to occupy the southern and eastern part of the Atlas, from where they spread out over the desert fringes south of the mountains. By the fifteenth century these pastoralists, now known as the Banu Hassan, had overrun much of the western Sahara as far as the north bank of the Senegal, where they were encountered by the earliest sea-borne expeditions of the Portuguese to the West African coast.

These Arab tribesmen were to have a profound effect on the language and culture of the sultanate in the centuries to come. Far from being the unwanted locusts depicted by Ibn Khaldun, the Banu Hilal and the Banu Maʿqil migrated primarily as warriors. They became the allies of the ruling dynasties in Tunis, Tlemcen and Fez, or, more generally, of one or other of the petty warlords who held precarious power over the small towns and countryside of the Maghrib. Before long, the Arabs had superseded the earlier Berber aristocracy and were waxing fat off the taxes and tribute they exacted from the local populations. In these circumstances Berber peasants either withdrew to previously uninhabited levels of the high mountains, or else became absorbed into the Arab tribal system. The rough vernacular of the Banu Hilal became the Arabic of the majority and fictitious genealogies from classical Arabia became the touchstone of respectability. By the sixteenth century the process of arabisation was so nearly complete that Moroccan society was divided no longer mainly by ethnicity but by wealth. The powerful became wealthy through force of arms, by extracting tribute from the less powerful. The poor became increasingly impoverished.

These problems of insecurity were mitigated in Morocco by the spiritual potency of the holy men, the marabouts, who played a role not dissimilar from that of the monks of medieval Europe. The word came from *murabit*, meaning 'a man of the *ribat*', one of the many fortresses built mostly during the time of the Almoravids for the warrior monks who defended the frontier of Islam against the infidel. In Ifriqiya, they had become in the course of time rather more the retreats of hermits, who sought sanctity through asceticism and withdrawal from the world. During the time of the Almohads both kinds of marabouts became profoundly influenced by Sufism, a new kind of mysticism developed in the eastern part of the Islamic world and introduced into the Maghrib by the Banu Hilal and other immigrant Arabs. There it fused with the maraboutism of the Berbers to inspire the dominant form of popular Islam, and gradually multiplied into a whole variety of *tariqas*, or 'ways' to the knowledge and experience of God. In the religious practice of country people, it centred upon the cult of saints. The faithful liked to live near a holy man during his lifetime, and to send their sons to serve him and so learn to follow his example. The tombs of former holy men became places of pilgrimage and spiritual revival. And the marabouts themselves often led their devotees on to make the greater pilgrimage to Mecca.

Moroccan pilgrims were well known all along the routes to the east. They travelled in great numbers, using the desert trails in preference to those which passed through the coastal towns, and paused for rest and refreshment at the zawiyas of other holy men along the way. The leading zawiyas had became places of great importance, both in the diffusion of Sufi devotion and in the resolution of disputes between the pilgrims and the local people. In the Fezzan a Moroccan dynasty, the Awlad Muhammad, ruled for more than two centuries following the retreat of the kings of Kanem from their northernmost possessions (above, p. 47). And with the Islamisation of the Nilotic Sudan, it was the Sufism of the Islamic Far West which became the practice of country people. In Morocco itself, the political and sociological significance of maraboutism was that it bridged the gap between town and country and, still more importantly, between the settled lowlanders of the *bilad al-makzan*, who paid taxes to the central treasury, and the dissident highlanders of the *bilad al-siba*, the 'land running to waste'.

THE MARINID SULTANATE

After the defeat of the Muslim army by the Christian forces at the battle of Las Navas de Tolosa in 1212, the superb military empire, created by the first Almohad caliph 'Abd al-Mumin only some sixty years previously, began to crumble. In Morocco it survived for another half-century until it was finally extinguished in its capital city of Marrakesh. As we have seen (above, p. 34), the Almohads were replaced in Ifriqiya by the Hafsid dynasty, and in the central Maghrib by the 'Abd al-Waddids or Zayyanids of Tlemcen. During this period of transition Seville, the great capital of Muslim Spain, fell to Castile in 1248. The conquest of the rich Muslim sultanates of Andalusia was largely complete. Only the mountains of Granada remained in Muslim hands. Great numbers of Spanish Muslims fled to the towns and cities of North Africa, to Tunis and Tlemcen, a few to the small port of Algiers, but the largest numbers to Fez and other towns in Morocco.

Here, in the heartlands of lowland Morocco, the Almohads came under pressure from the Banu Marin, a sub-tribe of the great confederation of Zanata Berbers, which had its home base on the desert edges of south-eastern Morocco. They were warrior pastoralists, pursuing the age-old tactics of their kind, by encroaching on the wealth of their settled neighbours as soon as there appeared to be any chink in their defences. 'Originally from the desert', wrote a nearly contemporary chronicler, 'where they belonged to the noblest among the Zanata, the Marinids knew neither silver metal nor money, neither agriculture nor trade. All their wealth consisted of camels, horses and slaves.'[1] The Marinids took advantage of the weakness of the Almohads to invade the plains of north-eastern Morocco, where they established sporadic control over the peasant cultivators, and forced towns to pay tribute to them instead of to the Almohad government. Fez succumbed to the tribesmen in 1248, and finally in 1269 the Marinid chief, Abu Yusuf Ya'qub, captured Marrakesh and proclaimed himself sultan. But his ambitions did not stop there. His long-term aim was to resurrect the Almohad empire, with its boundaries running from southern Morocco into southern Spain and from the Atlantic to Ifriqiya. For his capital he chose not Marrakesh but the ancient northern city of Fez, where he built a new administrative and military town on the outskirts of the old city, with separate Christian and Jewish quarters, a palace for himself, and a library for the benefit of the scholars who flocked to his court. Abu Yusuf, despite his warrior background, was something of a connoisseur and bibliophile, and the skills and artistry of the Andalusian refugees helped him to turn Fez into the most illustrious city of the Maghrib, rivalling in architectural glory the Muslim towns of southern Spain. Their presence strengthened the religious, intellectual and commercial life of the city, in which the manufacture of cloth and leather goods flourished, as did trade, directed in large measure to Spain and the Italian cities.

The Marinids governed Morocco with the help of their Zanata followers, but also, and increasingly, by co-opting the Arab tribesmen settled on the Atlantic plain. Indeed, the Zanata themselves soon became assimilated into the Arab tribal system. The formerly independent Arabs now functioned as *makzan*, or government tribes, exempted from the taxes they collected from the peasant subjects of the regime. When riding in state, the sultan was flanked on either side by an Arab and a Zanata chief, symbolising the relationship

[1] Ibn abi Zar, *Rawd al-Qirtas*, cited by I. Hrbek in *General History* IV, p. 85.

between the ruler and the twin pillars of his power. Within their new state the Marinids threw their weight behind the urban religious establishment. The authority of the Maliki school of law, which had been swept aside by the Almohads, was restored. The towns, with their cathedral-like mosques and resplendent madrasas, or religious colleges, of which the Marinids built no less than seven, became bastions of Islamic orthodoxy. In the countryside, on the other hand, people turned increasingly to the zawiyas of the marabouts and the shrines of the Sufi saints for religious and practical succour.

Looking beyond Morocco, the first concern of the Marinids was to secure to themselves the dominant share in the profits of the trans-Saharan trade. The old trail crossing the western Sahara had been severely disrupted by the thirteenth-century incursions of the Banu Maʿqil into the border regions of the Sus and the Darʿa in southern Morocco. The trading caravans from Mali now travelled by a more easterly route, starting from Walata at the desert's southern edge and passing the salt mines of Taghaza to Sijilmasa, the great oasis entrepôt to the south of the Atlas. From there the northern merchants found it easier to travel over the bleak plateau of the central Maghrib to Tlemcen than to cross the high passes of the Atlas to Morocco. And it was thus at the ports of Tlemcen at Oran and Hunayn, rather than those of northern Morocco, that the gold trade now passed into the hands of the European merchants from Spain and Italy. The Tlemcen trade reached its peak in the late thirteenth and early fourteenth centuries, and it so happens that a remarkable set of family records of it survives in the papers of five brothers of the Maqqari family, from which a detailed picture can be reconstructed. Two of the brothers lived in Tlemcen, one in Sijilmasa and two more in Walata. The two last had made themselves comfortable by building houses of stone and marrying local wives. 'The one in Tlemcen dispatched to his Saharan brother such merchandise [as] he requested, and the Saharan one sent him skins, ivory, [kola] nuts and gold dust. As for the one in Sijilmasa, like the needle of a balance, he informed them of downward and upward trends in prices, and wrote to them about the situation of the various traders and local events. And thus their wealth increased and their situation improved considerably.'[2]

It was only to be expected that the self-confident Marinid conquerors of Morocco would make Tlemcen their prime target for

[2] Ibn al-Khatib, *Ihata fi taʾrikh Gharnata*, cited by D. T. Niane in *General History* IV, p. 620.

further expansion. They made their first attempt before the end of the thirteenth century, by laying siege to the capital city for eight years on end, but without result. Finally in 1337 they succeeded, following another grim siege, conducted by the so-called Black Sultan of Morocco, Abu'l-Hasan. All the northern outlets of the trans-Saharan trade were thus brought under a single rule. Far to the south, the ruler of Mali, Mansa Suleyman, was quick to respond to the changed political and military circumstances in the Maghrib, sending an embassy to Abu'l-Hasan, the members of which, according to Ibn Khaldun, 'lauded the authority of the sultan, acknowledged his prerogative, conveyed the submission of their king, and his willingness to pay the sultan his dues, and to act according to his wishes and advice.'[3]

During the twenty years of his reign (1331–51) Abu'l-Hasan's armies campaigned relentlessly across the length and breadth of the Maghrib and in southern Spain. It was in 1333 that the Black Sultan first crossed the Straits of Gibraltar and captured Algeciras as a bridgehead. He returned there in 1340, when the Marinid fleet, with the assistance of Hafsid ships, defeated the Castilian navy. But later that year Christian forces inflicted a crushing defeat on the Muslim army at the battle of the Río Salada, a defeat that marked the end of active Muslim intervention in Spain. However, within a few years virtually the whole of the Maghrib was under Abu'l Hasan's control. Not content with reducing the Hafsids to a state of vassalage, he took advantage of a succession dispute and in 1347 entered Tunis and formally annexed Ifriqiya. This was the high point of the Marinid dynasty, at least in the eyes of Ibn Khaldun, then a fifteen-year-old student in the town. Years later, having been in the service of Abu 'Inan, the son of the Black Sultan, at Fez, Ibn Khaldun expressed bitter disappointment at the failure of the Marinids to achieve their lofty imperial ideals. For Abu'l-Hasan in Ifriqiya nemesis fast approached.

The Black Death arrived in Tunis (above, p. 37). The sultan foolishly stirred up an Arab revolt in Ifriqiya, and was soundly defeated. Thereupon Abu 'Inan proclaimed himself sultan, and deposed and soon defeated his father, who died a lonely fugitive in the snows of the Atlas. A few years later Abu 'Inan, who replicated his father's endeavours against Tlemcen, Tunis and the Arab tribes, was murdered by his vizier in Fez.

---

[3] Ibn Khaldun, *Ta'rikh al-duwal*, cited by N. Levtzion in *CHA* III, p. 361.

THE SHARIFIAN SULTANS AND THE PORTUGUESE

Although the Marinid dynasty survived in name for a century after the death of Abu 'Inan, it enjoyed but a shadow of its former greatness. Between 1358 and 1465 no fewer than seventeen sultans held the throne, but such central power as remained was passing into the hands of another Zanata clan, the Banu Wattas, whose members held the hereditary office of vizier from 1420 on. Such was the turbulent situation in which the Portuguese were able to establish a bridgehead at Ceuta on the southern shores of the Strait of Gibraltar.

The Christian kingdom of Portugal had come into existence in the mid-twelfth century, when the founding ruler had captured Lisbon from the Muslims, and its armies had fought alongside those of Castile at the great Christian victory of Las Navas de Tolosa in 1212. There had followed two centuries of nearly continuous warfare while the young kingdom drove out the remaining Muslims from its southern province in the Algarve and engaged in border conflicts with its Christian neighbours in Castile, with whom peace was finally concluded in 1411. In the unfamiliar state of calm, King John of Portugal, perhaps needing an outlet for the activities of his militant frontiersmen, determined to continue the struggle with the Muslims on African soil by conquering Morocco. His son, Prince Henry, later remembered as 'the Navigator', was placed in charge of the enterprise, and in 1415 Ceuta was occupied after a single bloody battle. Prince Henry is said to have learned from Muslim prisoners about the caravans laden with gold which reached Morocco across the desert from the south, and there is no doubt that initially he planned to occupy the whole country with the aim of capturing the overland trade in gold. In 1437, however, the Portuguese were heavily defeated in an attempt to capture Tangier, and thereafter Prince Henry's strategy turned increasingly to outflanking Morocco rather than conquering it. By 1444 his mariners had reached the mouth of the Senegal and were seemingly in a position to tap the gold trade at its source. In Morocco, therefore, he needed only to establish some fortified staging posts along its Atlantic coastline. Between 1458 and 1519 the Portuguese captured several Moroccan ports, including Sale, Agadir and Mazaghan, from which they occasionally raided the interior, even on one occasion plundering Marrakesh. But in general they engaged in more friendly trade, purchasing cereals, horses and woollen textiles, which they transhipped and bartered in West Africa for gold and slaves. By the end of the sixteenth century, when Morocco had acquired a powerful new dynasty of its own, the 55 country had ceased to be of major importance to Portuguese imperial or economic aspirations.

The resurgence of Morocco in the sixteenth century originated partly in opposition to the Portuguese encroachments, partly in religious zeal and partly in pure opportunism. Its leaders were marabouts, the holy men of the Islamic brotherhoods of the Saharan borderlands, and *sharifs*, the heads of local Berber and Arab noble families who claimed descent from the Prophet. However, the continuing inspiration of the movement came from the holy city of Fez. Sharifs had become prominent in the city in the fifteenth century, when the Marinid dynasty was in terminal decline. The Moroccan victory over the Portuguese outside Tangier in 1437 had coincided with a miraculous rediscovery of the grave of the founder of the city, Sultan Idris, a fifth-generation descendant of the Prophet, who had died in 828. The tomb quickly became a popular shrine, and soon the sharifian movement was flourishing all over Morocco and western Algeria, with its centre in the Saharan oases south of the High Atlas. When, in about 1510, the people of the Sus region turned to their marabouts for protection against the Portuguese, they invited Abu ʿAbdallah Muhammad, the head of one such family of sharifs in the Wadi Darʿa, to lead a jihad against them. The dynasty so founded was later known as that of the Saʿdian sharifs in order to distinguish it from that of the ʿAlawi sharifs which followed.

Abu ʿAbdallah slowly and systematically built up his power, on the one hand invoking the religious concept of the *mahdi*, and on the other hand strengthening and modernising his army by employing foreign mercenary instructors in musketry and artillery. He himself remained in the Sus, but in 1524 one of his sons was able to establish himself as sultan of Marrakesh, while in 1541 another recaptured the port of Agadir from the Portuguese, who subsequently evacuated all but one of their harbour forts. But jihad against Portugal soon took second place in the concern of the new dynasty to gain and secure their position, for the Ottoman Turks were by this time emerging as the strong power in the Maghrib, to threaten Morocco from their bases at Algiers and Tlemcen. A three-cornered struggle took place between the Saʿdian sharifs, the last of the Wattasids and the Ottomans for the control of Fez. The Ottomans took over the city for a few months in 1554, before it finally fell to Muhammad al-Mahdi. The sultan, however, felt uncomfortable and insecure in the sophisticated northern city, and made his headquarters in the ancient capital of the Almoravids at Marrakesh. Muhammad al-Mahdi adopted the caliphal title as a direct challenge to the Ottoman sultan, but paid the price for his presumption when he was assassinated a few years later by a palace guard who was in the pay of the Ottomans. There followed two decades of struggle involving the Ottomans in the area between Fez and Tlemcen, and rival claimants to the sultanate, one of whom took refuge in Portugal. The chivalrous young Portuguese king, Don Sebastian, determined on the invasion of Morocco in support of his client. In 1578 the battle of al-Qasr al-Kabir, or the Battle of the Three Kings, resulted in the annihilation of the Portuguese by a much superior Moroccan force. Three sovereigns died on the day of the battle – the sultan 'Abd al-Malik just before it began, Don Sebastian and the rival Moroccan sultan in the course of the fighting. The undeniable victor was the new sultan, 'Abd al-Malik's brother, Mawlay (My Lord) Ahmad, later nicknamed al-Mansur al-Dhahabi (the Golden Conqueror).

The victor over the Portuguese at al-Qasr al-Kabir rode high in the estimation of his subjects, and indeed of the world at large. He inherited and fine-tuned a standing army built up by his predecessor, with Andalusian and renegade Christian musketeers and artillerymen instructed by Turkish mercenaries, and set up military and administrative councils within a royal diwan, housed in a tented capital which moved around with the sultan. All this military expenditure, however, coupled with an extravagant new building programme at Marrakesh, meant that al-Mansur desperately needed to find new sources of revenue that did not suffer from the vicissitudes of primitive taxation. Like other rulers in North Africa, he sought control over the trans-Saharan trade, especially that in gold. A first, probing expedition despatched in 1584 is believed to have reached the Senegal, imposing Moroccan authority over the nomads along the westernmost desert caravan route leading to the Wolof kingdoms in Senegambia. The busier route, however, ran further to the east, passing the great salt mines at Taghaza, which were serviced by slaves of the Tuareg, who themselves paid respect to the Sudanic empire of Songhay. In 1586 Mawlay Ahmad sent musketmen to occupy Taghaza, but the miners fled with their Tuareg masters into the sandy wastes, where they soon discovered a vast and hitherto unexploited salt-pan some 120 miles to the south-east, at Taodeni. Soon afterwards Mawlay Ahmad determined to invade the heartland of Songhay itself.

To send an expedition across 1700 miles of desert, there to fight the host that held in subjection the whole of the western Sudan, was a conception of breathtaking boldness, and it is recorded that many wise heads were shaken when Mawlay Ahmad presented the plan to 57

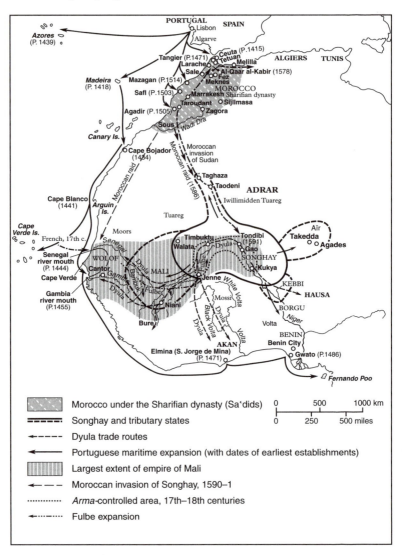

6 Morocco and the western Sudan, 1400–1800

his council. The sultan insisted, however, that such would be the superiority of firearms when matched against spears and bows that the force need be no larger than an ordinary commercial caravan. Events were to prove him right. In October 1590, 4000 picked men under the command of a Spanish renegade, Judar Pasha, with 2500 muskets, ammunition and supplies loaded on to 8000 camels, wound their way out of Marrakesh. Half perished in the desert, but the survivors reached the Niger bend in February 1591 and began to march downstream towards the Songhay capital at Gao. News of their approach had already reached Askiya Ishaq, who advanced to meet them with, at the least estimate, 10,000 cavalry and 30,000 foot soldiers. Battle was joined at the riverside village of Tondibi, and the Moroccans won a decisive victory. Ishaq made his submission to Judar and offered tribute to the sultan in gold and slaves. This, however, was refused, and another pasha was sent from Morocco to replace Judar and complete the conquest.

During the remainder of Mawlay Ahmad's reign more than 20,000 Moroccan troops crossed the desert to reinforce those already established on the Niger. The result was the creation of a military colony, with the pasha residing at Timbuktu in a citadel constructed by forced labour in the foreign merchants' quarter of the town. The Moroccans concerned themselves with tribute and taxation, squeezing the merchant community and levying tolls on the river traffic. For a few years the profits appeared to be fabulous. 'Following the conquest of the kingdoms of the Sudan, Mawlay Ahmad received so much gold dust that envious men were all troubled and observers absolutely stupified. So, from then on al-Mansur paid his officials in pure gold, and in dinars of the proper weight only. At the gate of his palace 1,700 smiths were daily engaged in striking dinars.'[4] But, unlike the Spanish conquistadors in the Americas, the Moroccans never succeeded in laying hands on the sources of the fabled wealth of the Sudan. At home in Morocco, the huge cost of the enterprise proved a heavy burden on the Golden Conqueror's subjects. His death in 1613 was followed by a long and furious wrangle over the succession, during which the whole structure of the kingdom crumbled like a house of cards. In these circumstances the Sudanese garrison, known locally as the *arma* (musketeers), could no longer be reinforced or even relieved, and, isolated on the Niger, turned itself into an increasingly indigenous ruling class (below, pp. 70–2).

MOROCCO UNDER THE ʿALAWIS

The reign of Sultan Ahmad set a pattern which was repeated during the next two centuries: that of a period of strong and brilliant rule by a long-lived monarch, which was followed in turn by serious breakdown. The Moroccan government under the Saʿdian and ʿAlawi

---

[4] al-Ifrani, *Nizhat*, cited and trans. N. Levtzion in *CHA* IV, pp. 150–1.

sultans lacked the institutional strength to survive from one high point to the next. There was nothing like the enduring quality of the city-based Ottoman structures prevailing in the Regencies, with their blend of firmness and diplomacy, of force and compromise. By the middle of the seventeenth century the Saʿdian empire had ceased to exist. The political and social vacuum was filled by a resurgence of Berber maraboutism from the Atlas mountains, so much so that between 1640 and 1660 roving bands of soldiery – all that remained of al-Mansur's proud army – occupied the cities loyal to the holy men, while yet another sharifian warlord from the Saharan foothills of the Great Atlas carved out a power base in southern Morocco. This was Mawlay Rashid from Tafilelt, who in the early 1660s declared himself sultan. In the resultant anarchy, the ʿulama clerics representing Islamic orthodoxy in Fez in 1666 called upon Mawlay Rashid and his musketeers for protection. So was instituted the ʿAlawite dynasty of sharifian sultans, who took their name from ʿAli, the son-in-law of the Prophet. The long reign of his brother Mawlay Ismaʿil (1672–1727) ensured the triumph of the sharifian principle in the politics of Morocco, a principle that was based on personalities rather than institutions. Mawlay Ismaʿil sought to rival his contemporary, Louis XIV of France, by his construction of a vast palace at Meknes and by his ostentatious style of life, while dispensing altogether with Sultan Ahmad's more Ottoman style of central administration, surviving haphazardly on forced tribute and gifts. 'The gobbling palace economy', so characterised by the historian Pat Mercer, ate up the country's revenues and was maintained by a system of awe and fear.

Mawlay Ismaʿil, like his Saʿdi predecessors, was conscious of the value of black manpower and Sudanese gold, and his long reign witnessed a considerable expansion of the trans-Saharan trade. The sultan built up his power largely through his black slaves (*ʿabid*), whose numbers were said to have reached 150,000. He conscripted into his own service slaves born in Morocco, but he imported many more from the Timbuktu pashalik and from slave-raids across the western desert. In 1678 he personally led an expedition from the Sus into the Sahara, and received the submission of the chiefs of some of the Banu Hassan clans. By the end of his reign Moroccan soldiers were fighting in the army of the amir of the Trarza Moors, who was his principal vassal on the north bank of the Senegal. His Moroccan chroniclers depicted these exploits as imperial triumphs: 'Mawlay Ismaʿil conquered the fringes of the Sudan and reached beyond [the Senegal]. His authority extended over Sudanese people. In this respect he achieved even more than Sultan [Mawlay Ahmad] or anyone before him.'[5] The black slaves were housed, men and women separately, in a specially built town near the royal palace at Meknes. They supplied his army, his garrisons around the country, his palace servants, his skilled artisans and the agricultural labour needed to feed his court and capital. But the servile character of much of the army and of the royal administration completely lacked the long-term recruitment and training system of the Ottoman apparatus. Sharifian relatives and tribal hangers-on, who were exempted from taxation, formed a huge and unproductive upper class. Morocco itself was still a country only partially under control, split between the *bilad al-makzan*, or government land, and the *bilad al-siba*, or waste land, which was parcelled out among provincial dynasties with which the sultans jockeyed for authority.

On the death of Mawlay Isma'il, the 'abid took charge of what remained of the *makzan*, initiating a state of disorder and chaos that lasted for more than thirty years. But the 'Alawi dynasty, surviving this unrest and the endless quarrels among Isma'il's sons, staggered on until the reign of the next great sultan, Sidi Muhammad (1759–90). He finally pacified the 'abid and returned to the customary system of using Arab levies to maintain government order. In 1765 Sidi Muhammad opened the new port of Mogador in southern Morocco for trade with European merchants, after a century when all contact with the infidel had been kept to a minimum. Through Mogador diplomatic relations were developed with European states. By the first decade of the nineteenth century Sultan Mawlay Suleyman had brought great tracts of the bilad al-siba to acknowledge the authority of his government and to become part of the makhzan. But within a decade most of this ground had been lost. The prestige of the sultan among his pious subjects was immense, but his power was painfully minimal. The governmental apparatus of Morocco, both centrally and locally, remained almost totally undeveloped throughout the nineteenth century. In the first as well as the last resort, the sultans relied upon military expeditions to enforce their regal power over one of the oldest independent countries in the world of Islam.

---

[5] *Ibid.*, p. 152.

5 The western Sudan and upper Guinea

Seen from a viewpoint in the western Sudan, the prime significance of our period is that it saw the slow change in its external orientation, from the north and north-east towards the west and the south. At the start it was a region centred upon the empire of Mali, high up the valley of the River Niger and close to the frontier dividing modern Mali and Guinea. The Mali empire in the middle of the thirteenth century was taking tribute from many peoples besides its own Mande-speaking ethnic core. Westwards, its area of patronage stretched for some 700 miles to the Atlantic seaboard between the Senegal and Gambia rivers, where the Wolof and the Fulbe recognised its paramountcy. Eastwards, its authority extended for a similar distance downriver to Timbuktu and Gao, the two great meeting-points of desert trails and river traffic, where the precious salt of the Sahara was exchanged for the cereal produce, the slave captives, the ivory and the gold of the western Sudan. In Mali, as in other African empires, the supreme ruler was essentially a paramount, a king of kings, the degree of whose authority varied greatly from one part of his dominions to another, according to the accessibility of each to the imperial armies and tax collectors. Within the Mande-speaking heartland the basic building-block of government was the *kafu*, a community of anything from 1000 to 15,000 people living in or near a mud-walled town and ruled by a hereditary dynast called a *fama*. The paramount ruler, though hedged around with all the splendid ceremonial of African kingship, bore the military title of *mansa*, 'conqueror', which underlined the reality that his dominion might expand or contract according to the range of his armed forces. Where the mansa's soldiers were no longer seen, there the kafus would soon resume their independence under their traditional famas. Outside the Mande-speaking nucleus, the relationship with subordinate rulers was even more essentially based upon the regular or occasional payment of tribute.

During the first two centuries of our period the armies of the mansa were at their strongest. First and foremost, they protected a line of river communications that ran from the fringes of the equatorial forest in the south to those of the desert in the north. Halfway between central Mali and Timbuktu, the Niger flowed through an

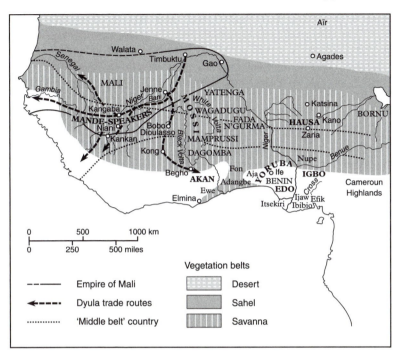

7 West Africa, 1250–1500 (see also Map 5, p. 45)

'inland delta', where a wide flood plain made possible the production of an agricultural surplus sufficient, through the use of slave
labour, to feed the cities of the arid Sahel and to provision the caravans that plied the desert trails. The 'royal slaves' of the inland delta
were among the more fortunate of those recruited by the mansa's
cavalry in their annual forays into the country lying within the great
bend of the river. They were settled in colonies, which had each to
produce a quota of grain for collection by boat at the appointed
season. It was a fate far preferable to the 1700 mile march across the
desert to a slave market in North Africa or even further afield than
that. The mansa's capital was sited close enough to control access to
the important gold-producing districts of Bambuk and Bouré, and
this was the aspect of the economy which attracted the attention of
the great merchants of the long-distance trade routes. Most of these
visitors were Muslims, and it was through their influence that the
dynasty and its high officials had long been converted to the faith.
The court circle included clerics and lawyers literate in Arabic and
well informed about the geopolitics of the outside world. Several

63

mansas of the thirteenth century had made the pilgrimage to Mecca and seen with their own eyes the mosques and palaces of Egypt and the Maghrib. In 1325 Mansa Musa, himself literate in Arabic, would lead 10,000 of his subjects on the pilgrimage, dispensing so much gold along the way as to cause a decline in its value in Cairo (above, p. 19).

The merchant class of Mali were known as Dyula, and they ranged far beyond the political boundaries of the empire. In particular, they penetrated the forested regions to the south of the upper Niger and the Gambia in search of fresh sources of gold, ivory and the nuts of the forest-growing kola tree which were the preferred stimulant of well-to-do townsfolk throughout the Sudanic belt of western Africa. The Dyula liked to travel in company, and where necessary with their own armed retainers. They tended to form settlements around the margins of the forest region, where they could store their trade-goods and where their local wives and children could be taught by Muslim clerics. Towns like Kankan in modern Guinea, Bobo Dioulasso in modern Ivory Coast and Begho in modern Ghana all originated in this way. Dyula merchants opened up the trade in gold from the Lobi fields in modern Burkina Faso and from the Akan forest in modern Ghana. Even Kano in far away northern Nigeria traced the conversion of its rulers to Islam to a party of Dyula merchants from Mali who arrived there, probably by the desert trail leading eastwards from Gao to Agades, with a consignment of fine horses and splendid horse-trappings sometime in the late fourteenth century.

THE OPENING OF THE ATLANTIC

In its long-term implications, the most significant development of the fifteenth century in West Africa was the opening of the Atlantic coastline to European shipping. Starting with the Portuguese occupation of Ceuta in 1415, this was in origin a project to gain closer access to the trade in West African gold, first of all by approaching the Moroccan termini of the trans-Saharan routes, and then by circumventing the overland traffic across the desert. As governor of Ceuta, the Portuguese prince Henry, later called 'the Navigator', gained first-hand information about the desert caravans. He devoted the rest of his life to the improvement of Portuguese shipbuilding and cartography and to promoting the exploration of the African coastline. The earliest expeditions were directed to opening the ports of southern Morocco, 600 miles closer than Ceuta to the oases where the camel caravans emerged from the desert trails. Meanwhile, along the mainland coast, the pioneers passed Cape Bojador in 1434 and Cape Blanco in 1441, south of which the little offshore island of Arguin offered a safe site for a trading settlement more than halfway down the desert coast. The place was already frequented by Moorish salt-traders, who were glad to exchange Sudanese gold and black African slaves for the commodities they were accustomed to buy more expensively in Morocco – horses, wheat, textiles, carpets and silver coin.

Beyond Arguin, the Portuguese came in 1444 to the mouth of the Senegal, which was the effective boundary between the Sahara and the Sudan. To the north of it lived the nomadic, pastoral 'Moors', to the south the sedentary Wolof, with their own ruling dynasty and their equestrian nobility already well practised in the capture and export of slaves, whom they were happy to trade to the Portuguese for Arab horses and other luxuries.

Up the broad, slow-moving waters of the Gambia, discovered in 1455, the Portuguese were able to sail their caravels for some 150 miles inland. This brought them into contact with a number of small states on the western periphery of the Mande-speaking world, and especially with the Dyula traders, who responded quickly to the new commercial opportunities presented by the ocean route. At Cantor on the upper Gambia the Portuguese were within about two weeks' march of both the Bambuk and the Bouré goldfields, which had supplied the needs of Europe and the Middle East for many centuries. Here, too, they were able to collect itineraries from merchants who had travelled as far afield as Timbuktu, and even Kukya, the traditional capital of the Songhay kingdom on the eastern arm of the Niger bend. And here they were able to learn that south-eastwards from Jenne another network of trade routes led through even richer gold-producing countries to the shores of the same great sea. This was the vital information which spurred the Portuguese to continue their explorations, despite the death of Prince Henry in 1460. In 1469 a Lisbon merchant, Fernão Gomes, was granted a temporary monopoly of the West African trade on the condition that he advanced the trading frontier by 100 leagues a year. This brought him in 1471 to the shores of the Akan country – the Gold Coast, as it would later be called – where the creekside village soon to be named Elmina, 'the mine', was henceforward to be the heart of Portugal's West African trading empire. Here, on a rocky promontory beside the village, a royal 'castle' – in reality a fortified trading depot – was built in 1482. Elmina became the centre of a local trading network, collecting the produce which came down various trade paths from the interior. At the height of its prosperity in the late fifteenth and early sixteenth centuries, an average of 800 pounds of gold a year passed through its vaults, and its warehouse was restocked at monthly intervals with copper, brass, textiles, cowry-shells – and slaves. The last, heavily in demand by the Akan for mining and porterage, were mostly brought from Benin, where a rapidly expanding military empire had many war captives to dispose of.

THE DECLINE OF MALI AND THE RISE OF SONGHAY

It has been estimated that by the end of the fifteenth century the maritime commerce of the Portuguese may have been attracting about one quarter of the total production of West African gold into its net.[1] In addition, by carrying something of the order of 2000 West African slaves a year to the Cape Verde islands, the Azores and Madeira, as well as to its own homeland, Portugal had established a far-flung sugar industry of great significance for the further development of its world-wide trading system. All this was of revolutionary importance to a small European nation, but it hardly scratched the surface of life in West Africa. There, the first century of Portuguese contact had produced some coastward reorientation in the economic life of peoples living within 100 to 200 miles of the ocean, but over most of the region the commercial arteries remained firmly linked to the Niger waterway and the desert caravans. The economic determinant of this pattern, which prevailed until the coming of the railways in the twentieth century, was undoubtedly the production and distribution of salt. There was no more economic way of getting this vital mineral into the scattered cooking-pots of the western Sudan than to mine it in mid-Sahara and carry it for a month on camel-back to the banks of the great river of West Africa at the northernmost point of its long course.

The fifteenth century did indeed see a change in the main over-arching system of political control in the western Sudan, but this was in no sense a consequence of Portuguese outreach. Already from about 1360 onwards the Keita dynasty of Mali had been subject to severe internal dissensions based on the rivalry between the descendants of Mansa Musa and those of his brother and successor Mansa Sulayman. Trouble at the centre of the system was soon reflected in disintegration at the periphery. Of the tributary states, Songhay in the east and in the west the Wolof kingdom south of the lower

[1] V. Magalhaes-Godinho, *L'Economie portugaise au XV et XVI siècles* (Paris, 1969), pp. 175–226.

Senegal were the first to break away. Next, from the region enclosed by the Niger bend, Mossi horsemen made swift, devastating raids on the rich riverside towns from Jenne to Timbuktu. The Fulbe pastoralists from the upper Senegal moved in upon the areas of cereal production around the inland delta of the Niger. Finally, the Tuareg nomads of the desert advanced southwards upon the cities of the Niger bend, occupying Timbuktu in 1433. Thus, although the great king of the interior whose existence was reported by the Dyula traders to the Portuguese on the Gambia in 1455 was still the Mansa of Mali, the range of his effective rule was already limited to the Mande-speaking heartland of the former imperial system. Within twenty years, it was to be reduced still further, to the southern half of that core region.

The state which expanded to fill the power vacuum left by the break-up of Mali was Songhay. As a kingdom embracing much of the eastern arm of the Niger bend, it already had a long history. It had been the contemporary, and in some respects the counterpart, of ancient Ghana, commanding the caravan routes leading northwards and eastwards from the Niger bend in much the same way as Ghana had controlled those leading to the north and west. With the expansion of Mali in the thirteenth century, Songhay had lost its northern province and its control of the desert routes. For much of the fourteenth century the remainder of the kingdom paid tribute to Mali. Yet the Songhay-speakers were still the predominant population of the river valley far beyond the political boundaries of the state. They were the fishermen, the boat-builders and the river traders right round the great bend of the Niger, forming the main ethnic stratum at Jenne and Timbuktu as well as at Gao and Kukya. Moreover, eastern Songhay, along with the neighbouring country of the Mossi, offered the best conditions for horse-breeding to be found anywhere to the south of the Sahara, and the mounted lancers of the Songhay aristocracy were swift and terrible, whether as slave-raiders on the eastern frontier or as the pillagers of the Sahel cities. Thus the potential existed for a Songhay revival, given only the leadership capable of directing it, and in 1464 this was found with the accession to the throne of Sonni Ali, who in a reign of twenty-eight years placed Songhay in the position formerly occupied by Mali.

Sonni Ali is remembered in the oral tradition of Songhay as a magician of unparalleled power, and in the chronicle of al-Saʿdi of Timbuktu as an impious and unscrupulous tyrant. In reality, he was first and foremost a great military commander with a well-conceived strategy of conquest, based upon the Niger waterway. Whenever   67

possible, he manoeuvred his land forces within the arc of territory
enclosed by the river, ferrying them to the north bank only to attack
specific targets. In 1469 he took Timbuktu from the Tuareg, making
his own headquarters at the river-port of Kabara, but sacking the
rich city and driving out the Tuareg and Sanhaja clerics who had
been the civil functionaries and the teachers and preachers at the
famous Sankore mosque. A poignant passage of al-Saʿdi's chronicle
describes their departure northwards to the desert city of Walata.

On the day they left Timbuktu you could see grown men with beards
anxious to mount a camel, but trembling in fear before it. When they
mounted the camel, they were thrown off when the beast rose, for our
righteous forefathers used to keep their children indoors until they grew
up. Hence they had no understanding of practical matters, since they did
not play in their youth, and play makes a child smart and gives him insight
into many things![2]

Having established this vital junction between the land and water
routes, Sonni Ali pursued his conquests upstream, reaching Jenne,
which he besieged with the aid of 400 river boats in 1473. This gave
him command of the gold and kola trade routes leading southwards
to the Volta basin. It remained to secure the important grain-pro-
ducing region around the inland delta from raids by Mossi from the
south and Fulbe from the west. It was only towards the end of his
reign that Sonni Ali's forces were in direct contact with those of the
already much reduced kingdom of Mali in the region to the west of
the upper Niger. Here, broadly speaking, he was successful in the
savanna, but not so in the forest, where his cavalry, impeded by the
dense vegetation, was at the mercy of the Malian archers.

In methods of government, it seems that the new Songhay leadership mainly took over the old Malian system, and this tendency
became clearer when, soon after the death of Sonni Ali, power was
seized by one of his generals, the Askiya Muhammad Ture, whose
name would strongly suggest that he was not of Songhay but of
Soninke (i.e., northern Mande) origin, and that his *coup d'état* represented a return to Mande leadership in what was predominantly a
Mande-speaking empire. In another important respect Muhammad
Ture's accession signified a return to the traditional Malian ethic.
Before all else he was an orthodox and pious Muslim, who was able
to re-enlist the support of the literate class of the great cities of Gao,
Timbuktu and Jenne. During his reign the scholars returned to

[2] J. O. Hunwick (ed. and trans.), *Timbuktu and the Songhay Empire: al-Saʿdi's Tarikh down to 1613* (Leiden, 1999), p. 93.

Timbuktu, the princes were educated in the Sankore mosque and the princesses were married to the rich merchants who managed the trans-Saharan trade. Relations with the Tuareg and the Sanhaja were restored, and through them Songhay established virtual control over the salt mines of Taghaza and the copper mines of Takedda, which were the keys to the successful working of the long-distance trade. Again, the Muslim clerics, once restored to favour, supplied the ideological support and the legal framework necessary for the efficient government of a large territory within which many people were constantly moving around outside their traditional ethnic areas.

At a more material level, the Songhay empire depended greatly on its colonies of royal slaves and on its privileged castes of craftsmen, which had probably been built up originally from the more skilled groups of war captives, such as smiths, weavers and leather-workers. Here again, Songhay took over a system already initiated in Mali, while adding greatly to the numbers of slaves by means of the regular, annual raids carried out by the Songhay cavalry among the unprotected, stateless peoples living south of the Niger bend. Many of these captives went to the trans-Saharan markets, especially at this time those of southern Morocco, where a sugar industry was being actively developed. Others were sold to the free citizenry of Songhay. Others again became the property of the ruler and were either recruited into the army or settled in colonies on the state farms. These were spread right across the empire, to supply the government and the garrisons, but the largest concentration was still to be found in the well-watered inland delta, whose grain harvests were so vital to the towns of the Sahel, the desert caravans and even the workers in the desert salt mines.

There is an interesting account in the seventeenth-century Sudanese chronicle of Ibn al-Mukhtar of how Sonni Ali, when he died, bequeathed to his successor twelve 'tribes' of slaves, some of which he had inherited from his own ancestors in pre-imperial Songhay, and three of which he had obtained, presumably by conquest, from the emperor of Mali. These three tribes were composed of pagan Mande, or Bambara, from the regions to the south of the Mali empire, and when they belonged to Mali each man and wife had been obliged to cultivate forty measures of land for the king. But when they were taken over by Songhay, Sonni Ali divided them into groups of one hundred – fifty men and fifty women – and each group was allotted two hundred measures of land to cultivate in common. They were given a production quota, after supplying which they were allowed to keep any surplus for themselves. The children of slaves were slaves, and if a slave married a free woman, the king would pay a dowry of 40,000 cowries to the girl's family in order to establish his right of ownership over her children. The king would also take some of the children of slaves and sell them in order to buy horses for his cavalry.[3]

The Songhay empire, like that of Mali before it, thus involved a gigantic effort of state enterprise in production and trade as well as in military operations and civil government. Under Muhammad Ture (1493–1528) its territories were greatly expanded, especially towards the west, where it encompassed the whole of the northern half of the old Mali empire. To the east of nuclear Songhay, Muhammad led at least two spectacular military expeditions, the first to Borgu, in the west of modern Nigeria, and the second passing through the Hausa states of Zaria and Kano to the city of Agades in modern Niger. But these were raids, not wars of conquest. As Muhammad himself explained, they were undertaken to distract the Songhay-speaking element in his armies from meddling in the Mande-speaking western half of his empire, where his own interests were strongest, and where he preferred to rule through slave armies recruited from his own war captives. Not under Muhammad only, but also under the succession of sons and grandsons who followed him as Askiyas until 1591, the real thrust of Songhay was towards the west and the north. It was an impetus based upon Timbuktu, both as the centre of Islamic learning in the western Sudan and as the meeting-point of river and desert communications. It was an impetus, largely successful, to reconstruct as much as possible of the old Mali empire around this northerly base. While it lasted, it was certainly more significant in every way than the reconstruction of the coastal fringes of western West Africa under the impact of the European maritime advance.

TIMBUKTU AND THE ARMA

We have seen (above, pp. 57–9) how, in 1590–1, the sultan of Morocco, Mawlay Ahmad, sent an expedition across the Sahara to invade the Songhay empire and capture the sources of West African gold. The ultimate aim was, of course, illusory, because the Songhay empire did not directly control any of the gold fields. Moreover, the

---

[3] Ibn al-Mukhtar, *Tarikh al-Fettach*, ed. and trans. O. Houdas (Paris, 1913), pp. 19–20.

Moroccans, though able to destroy a Sudanese empire by the sudden, dramatic use of firearms in trained and disciplined hands, were quite unable to maintain control of a colony separated from the metropole by 1700 miles of desert. Following their military victory, the arma (musketeers), as they were locally called, systematically pillaged the accumulated wealth of the great cities of the Niger bend and sent it north to Marrakesh. The Moroccan pashas built themselves a fortified headquarters in Timbuktu, levying tolls on the river traffic and import and export duties on the foreign merchants who managed the desert trade. But the proceeds did not begin to cover the huge cost of military reinforcement and supplies. After the initiating sultan, Mawlay Ahmad, died in 1607, his successors made no great effort to prolong the occupation. When the last of the pashas appointed from Marrakesh died, it was said by poison, in 1621, no attempt was made to replace him. Thereafter, the arma were simply left to survive as best they could under pashas elected by the senior officers, who neither paid tribute to Morocco nor received any subsidies from it. Only the Friday prayer continued to be said in the name of the Moroccan sultan until the end of the Saʿdian dynasty in 1659. Successive generations of arma, taking Sudanese wives, were gradually transformed into an indigenous ruling class.

To the learned Muslim clerics who supplied the chroniclers of this period, many of whom had suffered persecution and deportation during the violent aftermath of the conquest, the government of the Morrocan pashas appeared a sad contrast to that of the Askiyas of sixteenth-century Songhay.

The Saʿdian army [wrote al-Saʿdi] found the land of the Sudan at that time to be one of the most favoured of the lands of God Most High in any direction, and the most luxurious, secure and prosperous, thanks to the *baraka* [charisma] of the most auspicious, the divinely favoured Commander of the Faithful Askiya al-Hajj Muhammad b. Abi Bakr, because of his justice, and the strictness of his all-encompassing authority, which was as effective at the borders of his kingdom as it was in his palace – from the limits of Dendi to the end of the land of al-Hamdiyya, and from the limits of Bendugu to Taghaza and Tuwat, and what lies within them. All of this changed then: security turned to fear, luxury was changed into affliction and distress, and prosperity became woe and harshness. People began to attack one another throughout the length and breadth of the kingdom, raiding and preying upon property, [free] persons and slaves. Such iniquity became general, spreading and becoming ever more serious and scandalous.[4]

4 Hunwick, *Timbuktu*, pp. 192–3.

Nevertheless, the arma succeeded in ruling the riverine core of the former Songhay for some two centuries. Following the battle of Tondibi, the conquerors built fortresses and established permanent garrisons at the main river-ports between Gao and Jenne, which enabled them to control and tax the vital bulk exchange of Saharan salt for Sudanic grain, on which all other trade depended. Dangers constantly threatened from the peripheral peoples, such as the Mossi to the south and the Fulbe to the west. A remnant of independent, pagan Songhay survived in Dendi, downstream to the east. The Iwillimidden Tuareg of Adrar of the Ifoghas soon closed off the eastern desert route from Gao to Takedda and the copper mines along the way there. But the main northern route from Timbuktu to the Taodeni salt mines remained open to the camel caravans of the Tuareg, and the arma, by careful policing of the Niger waterway, were able to take handsome profits from the salt coming south and the cereals, slaves and gold dust passing to the north. Indeed, there can be no doubt that when the ʿAlawid dynasty seized power in Morocco, it led to a considerable expansion of the trans-Saharan trade. The ʿAlawids, like their predecessors, were sharifs from the desert fringes, very conscious of the value of black manpower as well as Sudanese gold. Sultan Mawlay Ismaʿil, who consolidated their regime during a reign which lasted from 1672 until 1727, built up his power almost entirely through his black slaves, whose numbers were said to have reached 150,000. As we saw in the previous chapter, Mawlay Ismaʿil conscripted into his own service many black slaves already in Morocco, but he imported many more both from the Timbuktu pash-alik and from his own slave-raids across the western desert to the upper Senegal. In the early eighteenth century the French, who by this time had supplanted the Portuguese on the Senegal, noted the presence of Moroccan raiding parties on both banks of the river, while upstream in Galam their advanced posts heard tell of the 'Moors' of Timbuktu, living in their forts beside the Niger and trading blocks of salt for gold and slaves. When, at the very end of the eighteenth century, Mungo Park penetrated from the Gambia to the upper Niger, he found that the trade in salt and gold was still in vigour, but the slave trade was now mostly conducted with the Europeans at the Atlantic coast, where guns were the most valued articles of import.

WESTERN WEST AFRICA AND THE ATLANTIC SLAVE TRADE

We have seen that in western West Africa the opening of the Atlantic coastline by the Portuguese had by the middle of the sixteenth century achieved only limited results. The only major diversion of the trade in gold had been that from the Akan country, which reached the coast at Elmina, while the Akan themselves had continued to be importers rather than exporters of slaves. The slaves who had been shipped overseas to Portugal and the Atlantic islands had been taken from Senegambia and the rivers immediately to the south of it, or else, and predominantly, from lands to the east of the 'Gold Coast'. From about 1530 the New World had begun to be a destination for African slaves, but for almost a century after this the numbers exported there remained quite small, amounting to something between 2000 and 4000 a year. So far as western West Africa was concerned, Morocco continued to be by far the largest market. It was only with the development of plantation agriculture in Brazil and the West Indies during the 1630s that the trans-Atlantic slave trade began to be a big business worth the active competition of the new maritime powers of northern Europe. The Dutch were the first of these newcomers to enter the West African trade. They had already supplanted the Portuguese in the Indian Ocean and who in 1621 had founded a West Indian Company to plant coffee and sugar in the Caribbean. During the 1630s the Dutch occupied the Portuguese plantations in Brazil. By 1642 they had ousted the Portuguese from all their coastal bases in West Africa, including their headquarters at Elmina on the Gold Coast. During the 1650s and 1660s, French, British, Danish, Swedish and German companies were formed to develop tropical plantations and to promote the trade in African slaves, which appeared to be the only means of providing the necessary manpower. By the second half of the seventeenth century the trans-Atlantic trade had escalated to some 20,000 slaves a year. The eighteenth century saw a further increase, rising to close on 60,000 slaves a year from Africa as a whole.

To the total figure of slave exports by sea it is likely that the contribution of western West Africa was of the order of one-third. Different parts of the area were differently affected at different periods, however, and here as elsewhere there is an obvious correlation between the processes of conquest and territorial expansion among the indigenous African states, many of them situated quite far from the sea, and the supply of slaves at particular points along the coast. During the first two centuries of the trade the main sources of slaves were the Wolof states to the south of the Senegal and the Mandinka states on both sides of the Gambia, all of which were in the course of consolidation at this period. During the third century of the trade, when most slaves were exported under the 73

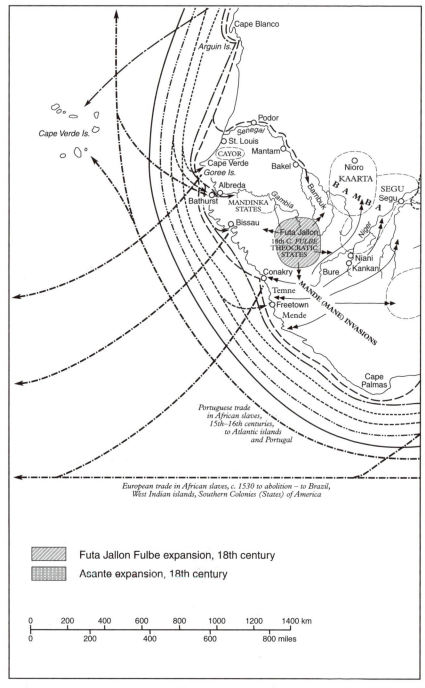

Cape Blanco

Arguin Is.

Cape Verde Is.

Podor

Senegal

St. Louis

CAYOR   Mantam

Cape Verde   Bakel

Goree Is.

Nioro

KAARTA

Albreda

Bathurst   MANDINKA   *Gambia*   *Bambuk*   B   SEGU

STATES   A   M   Segu

B

Bissau   A

Futa Jallon

18th C. *FULBE*   *Niger*

THEOCRATIC   Niani

STATES   Bure   Kankan

Conakry

Temne   MANDE (MANE) INVASIONS

Freetown

Mende

Cape
Palmas

*Portuguese trade
in African slaves,
15th–16th centuries,
to Atlantic islands
and Portugal*

*European trade in African slaves, c. 1530 to abolition – to Brazil,
West Indian islands, Southern Colonies (States) of America*

Futa Jallon Fulbe expansion, 18th century

Asante expansion, 18th century

| 0 | 200 | 400 | 600 | 800 | 1000 | 1200 | 1400 km |

| 0 | 200 | 400 | 600 | 800 miles |

8 The western Sudan, upper and lower Guinea, 1400–1800 (see also

Map 9, pp. 86–7)

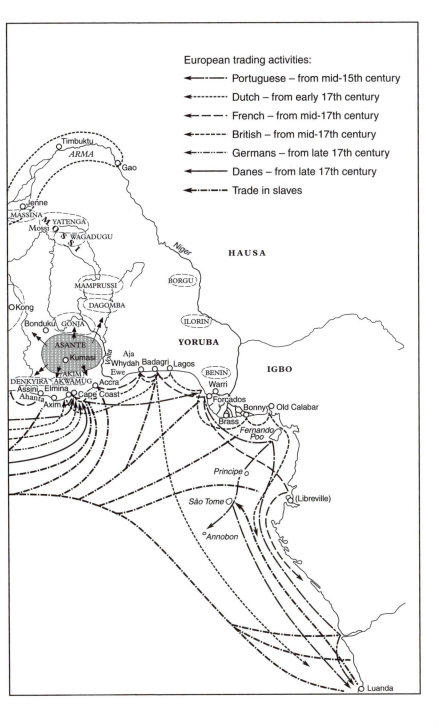

European trading activities:

◄—·—· Portuguese – from mid-15th century

◄------- Dutch – from early 17th century

◄— — — · French – from mid-17th century

◄------- British – from mid-17th century

◄—··—·· Germans – from late 17th century

◄——— Danes – from late 17th century

◄—··—·· Trade in slaves

Timbuktu
ARMA
Gao
Jenne
MASSINA
YATENGA
Mossi
WAGADUGU
Niger
HAUSA
MAMPRUSSI
BORGU
Kong
Bonduku GONJA
DAGOMBA
ILORIN
ASANTE
Kumasi
YORUBA
Aja
Volta Whydah Badagri Lagos
Ewe
BENIN
IGBO
AKIM
DENKYIRA AKWAMU
Accra
Assini Elmina
Ahanta
Axim Cape Coast
Warri
Forcados
Bonny Old Calabar
Brass
Fernando Poo
Principe
Sâo Tome
Annobon
(Libreville)
Luanda

asiento system to the silver mines in Mexico and Peru, the main area
of supply seems to have been the river estuaries of modern Guinea,
Sierra Leone and Liberia, where the hinterland was at this period
subject to a series of invasions by warlike groups of Mande origin,
who carved out a score of little states among the ill-defended 'West
Atlantic' peoples of the coastal forests. The best known among these
invaders were the Mane, who migrated from the southern margins of
the Mali empire and travelled as a plundering horde through much
of modern Ivory Coast and Liberia before settling, around 1545, in
Sierra Leone. Here they gradually broke up as their various sections
conquered and colonised different ethnic groups. The Mane migration was certainly not due in any way to the European traders at the
coast. Its warriors were armed with bows and arrows, not with guns.
Yet the existence on the Sierra Leone rivers of a ready market for
their war captives caused a mutation in the Mane mode of military
dominance which turned them into the main suppliers of the
Atlantic slave trade for the best part of a century.

During the second half of the seventeenth century, however, while
the slave trade was growing rapidly elsewhere, in Sierra Leone it
almost died out. The various Mande conquerors had become
absorbed into the local societies, and there was no more occasion for
slaving expeditions until, in the early eighteenth century, a revolution occurred among the Fulbe of Futa Jallon, a little further inland.
Here in 1726 the Muslim Fulbe declared a jihad against their pagan
Jallonke neighbours, driving them from their highland plateau and
forming a powerful and aggressive theocratic state, which for the rest
of the century conducted regular slaving wars against all the neighbouring peoples and traded their captives in huge numbers to the
Europeans at the coast. As earlier with the Mane, the origins of the
disturbance had nothing to do with the Atlantic trade, but once the
process had begun, it was no doubt carried much further than it
would otherwise have been by the fruits of the trade, in this case
mostly firearms. A similar situation developed during the same
period along the banks of the upper Niger, where Mande warlords,
armed with guns from the Gambia trading posts, built up the
Bambara kingdoms of Segu and Kaarta.

The most spectacular developments in the agglomeration of political power resulting from the intensification of European commercial activity during the seventeenth and eighteenth centuries
occurred in the hinterland of the Gold Coast. Here, the initial attraction for the Europeans was the gold of the Akan forest, mostly situated between 80 and 150 miles from the coast. Some of it was still

traded inland to Timbuktu and Hausaland. The rest found its way to the coast by a score of routes and, once the Portuguese monopoly had been broken in the 1640s, Dutch, British, Danes and Germans pressed in to build fortified trading settlements at almost every fishing village along a 200 mile stretch of palm-fringed, surf-beaten shore. The coastal peoples – Nzima, Ahanta, Fante, Gwang and Ga – soon joined in the competition, aligning themselves with one or other of the forts, and each striving to attract the upcountry caravans into their own sphere of patronage. In these circumstances larger concentrations of power could occur only in the interior. It was at the heart of the forest region that political opportunities were greatest. Here were the sources of gold. Here lay the option of trading both to the north and to the south

In the seizing of these opportunities it would seem that the Atlantic trade, as reorganised by the northern Europeans during the seventeenth century, did play a major part. Where the Portuguese had traded slaves for gold (see pp. 65–6, above), the Dutch, the British and the Danes traded guns. As a result, states of the gold-producing belt – in the west Denkyira, in the east Akyim and Akwamu – were helped on the path to rapid territorial expansion, in the course of which the Gold Coast became a large supplier of slaves for export. Akwamu, in particular, soared from very small beginnings in the eastern forest hinterland to dominate all the trade routes from Accra to the Volta. The Ga state of Accra was conquered between 1677 and 1681, and Akwamu armies rampaged across the coastlands of modern Togo and Bénin (Dahomey), capturing and enslaving tens of thousands of the Ewe and Aja peoples, and creating a series of colonial provinces among the conquered. Further west, Denkyira, though never reaching the sea, conquered and made tributary most of the Akan peoples living to the north of the Fante and Ahanta of the coastal states, thus dominating all the trade routes between Cape Coast and Axim. From each of these expanding empires a steady supply of war captives was delivered to the European forts, there to await the arrival of the next ocean-going slave ship.

At the very end of the seventeenth century, however, both Denkyira and Akwamu were superseded by Asante, in origin a group of small states formed by migrants and refugees from the earlier empires to the south. At some time around 1680 these formed themselves into a federation based upon Kumasi, in the very centre of the forest region, astride the economic watershed between trade routes running to the north and the south. Asante gathered in the political experience of almost every state founded among the Akan peoples. The founding ruler, the Asantehene Osei Tutu, had been educated at the courts of both Denkyira and Akwamu. His chief priest, his military leaders and his armoury of firearms all accompanied him from Akwamu to Kumasi. After starting as a tributary of Denkyira, Asante fought a war of independence between 1698 and 1701, which left it in control of the main gold-bearing regions. From there it went from strength to strength. By 1724 it had expanded to the savanna in the north. In 1741–2 it conquered Akyim, which had already superseded an exhausted Akwamu. Its lands thus reached the eastern seaboard. In 1744–5 its northern armies defeated and made tributary the large savanna states of Gonja and Dagomba. Here, the musketmen of the forest triumphed over the armoured cavalry of the Muslim Sudan. It was a turning-point in West African history.

During the second half of the eighteenth century Asante consolidated its vast conquests into one of the largest and most sophisticated imperial systems ever constructed without the aid of literary skills. It was based on a careful distinction between a highly centralised metropolitan region, of which the population was deliberately built up by forced deportations from the conquered lands, and an outer circle of dependent provinces held under strict military and fiscal control. A network of well-kept roads radiated from the capital, each with designated resting places for the runners and the supply caravans passing to and fro on military, commercial or diplomatic business. All high officials were required to present themselves regularly at the royal court, and something like an orderly career structure emerged in the army and the civil service. In 1819 a proud Asantehene told a European visitor that it was not his practice to make war 'to catch slaves in the bush like a thief'. This remark reflected a state of satiety in which Asante had long ceased to feel the need of further territorial expansion. There was by then no problem about the disposal of war captives, and the country's mineral wealth sufficed for its necessary purchases of foreign firearms. Asante, like other full-grown West African empires, had almost ceased to be a slave-trading power. Yet, without the Atlantic slave trade of the eighteenth century, Asante might never have emerged from the obscurity of its forest heartland.

6 The central Sudan and lower Guinea

The region of West Africa lying between the Volta river and Lake Chad, comprising in modern political terms Nigeria and the immediately adjacent countries of Bénin, Niger and Cameroon, was probably, even by the thirteenth century, one of the best-populated parts of the entire continent. It lay at the meeting-point of Africa's three main language families. It had been the scene of the earliest metalworking, in both copper and iron, anywhere to the south of the Sahara. It had therefore probably witnessed the earliest intensive agriculture made possible by forest clearance with iron tools. While it had experienced no concentration of political power on the scale of the empires of Mali and Songhay in the west, it was, even more than its western counterpart, a region in which most people lived in defended towns, from which they went out by day to till their farms in the surrounding countryside. Buildings, wherever it was climatically possible, were of puddled clay and, when these were damaged by weather or warfare, they could normally be rebuilt on the same sites, using the same materials. Urban settlements therefore enjoyed a relative permanence unusual in other regions of Africa, and these settlements, together with their surrounding farmlands, formed the basic units of government. On a wider basis, small towns might pay respect to larger ones, and newer towns might honour the older towns from which their founding ancestors were supposed to have come. The archaeological evidence, however, leaves no doubt that warfare between neighbouring towns must have been a regular occurrence, for defensive walling was already widespread by the second half of the first millenium AD. Nevertheless, warfare between neighbouring towns was apparently consistent with the existence of large areas each speaking a common language and observing a common system of law and custom, and it is likely that, by the beginning of our period, there were in existence several such large linguistic and cultural units, including Yoruba, Edo, Igbo, Idoma, Nupe, Hausa and Kanuri, each of which may have embraced a million people or more.

KANEM, BORNU AND HAUSA

Prior to the thirteenth century, the only one of these peoples to have created anything like an empire were the Kanuri of Kanem. Living in the north-eastern corner of the region, and speaking a language of the Nilo-Saharan family, these were essentially a people of the Sahel, the desert's edge. The northerners among them were pastoralists, keeping camels and horses as well as goats and sheep. The southerners were agriculturalists, growing sorghum, dry rice and other hardy grains. The reason for their early ascendancy over their neighbours was that they commanded the southern approaches to the shortest and least arduous of the trans-Saharan crossings, which led northwards through Kawar, with its inexhaustible salt mines at Bilma, to the oasis region of the Fezzan, where caravans could be rested and revictualled, before undertaking the final stage to Tripoli and the Mediterranean coast. The northern Kanuri, like other pastoralists, were warlike and mobile, and since early Muslim times, if not before, they had been the main suppliers of slaves to Ifriqiya and Egypt. The trade brought them in return the constantly developing weapons and accessories for successful conquest in Sudanese latitudes – the big Barbary horses, so essential to carry the armoured knight, the chain-mail for horse and rider, the harness and saddlery, the swords and shields, and heavy metal lances (above, pp. 46–7). To monopolise such a golden road to wealth and power, and to guard it from rivals to the east and the west, was an obvious incentive to empire.

Thanks to the merchants from Ifriqiya who travelled down the road, Kanem was also the first society in the region to benefit from the wider outlook conferred by a universal religion. Its Sefuwa dynasty, of which the kings carried the title of *mai*, converted to Islam in the eleventh century. The first of the Muslim mais, Hummay (1076–86), is said to have died in Egypt, presumably while on pilgrimage to Mecca. His son Dunama (1086–1140) is known to have made two pilgrimages, and to have drowned in the Red Sea in attempting a third. Along with the new religion, therefore, these kings would have learnt the geopolitics of the Islamic world and have seen the importance of literacy and education in governing effectively larger numbers of people. As one consequence of this concern, there survives a chronicle of the dynasty, written in Arabic, and, from the thirteenth century at least, kept up to date in each successive reign. Though laconic in style, it provides a reliable framework of chronology, not only for Kanem but for the main events of the surrounding region. It tells us that, following their conversion, the Sefuwa kings built a new capital at Njimi, some 100 miles to the north-east of Lake Chad, from which the mais of the twelfth and thirteenth centuries were able to conquer and lay under tribute most of the horse-owning and slave-raiding peoples of the northern half of the Lake Chad basin, stretching eastwards to the borders of Darfur – the Teda of Tibesti, the Zaghawa and Tomaghara of Ennedi, the Bulala of Lake Fitri – who were the potential rivals for the monopoly of the northern trade route. Kanem reached the peak of its power during the reign of the great Mai Dunama Dibalami (1210–48). His armies were said to number 40,000 horsemen. At all events, they were numerous enough both to maintain the military ascendancy over the Chad basin and to patrol the whole of the desert route as far north as the Fezzan, where a resident governor was installed at the little town of Traghen.

Significantly, it was during this reign that the kings of Kanem began to be described as also lords of Bornu, the region to the west and south of Lake Chad, inhabited thus far only by Chadic-speaking peoples – Hausa to the west, and smaller, more fragmented groups like the Kotoko, known collectively as Sao, to the south. It would seem that Kanuri colonists first entered Bornu round the northern end of Lake Chad, and settled in the valley of the Hadejia river, which flows into the lake from the west. The initial infiltration may have been peaceful, but as the numbers of immigrant Kanuri farmers built up, they began to encounter serious resistance from the native Chadic-speakers, which led to two centuries of warfare. It came at a time when the Kanem kingdom was weakened by dynastic divisions and when its suzerainty over the peoples to the east of it was being increasingly challenged, notably by the Bulala of Lake Fitri, who during the fourteenth century carried their attacks right up to Njimi and temporarily seized the mastery over the road to the north. At some point in the 1390s Mai 'Umar ibn Idris abandoned the former capital, and in the words of the chronicle, 'he took out his armies and all his possessions and his people into Kaga, and down to this day none of our rulers have ever returned to Kanem to re-establish their residence there'.[1] Four successive mais died fighting against the Sao, and it was not until the last quarter of the fifteenth century that conditions were settled enough to permit the building of a new capital at Ngazargamu, some 120 miles west of Lake Chad.

In the early sixteenth century Leo Africanus painted the picture of Bornu as a military kingdom, depending for its revenues on the slaves brought in by the annual dry-season campaigns of its 3000 armoured knights, who were accompanied to war by vast numbers of conscripted peasants armed with spears and bows. The regular

[1] Dierk Lange, *Le Diwan des sultans de Bornu* (Wiesbaden, 1977), p. 76.

slaving grounds were in Sao territory to the south of Lake Chad. However, a strong military power with few natural resources and little industry could not overlook the attractions of booty and tribute that might be taken from the prosperous cities which were emerging in central Hausaland. These, like Bornu though on a smaller scale, were dominated by horse-owning military aristocracies organised under rulers called *sarkis*. These, too, raided their weaker neighbours, taking tribute from the nearer ones and slaves from the more distant. Their ruling groups had mostly converted to Islam during the fifteenth century, under the influence of Dyula traders from Mali, who also supplied them with Barbary horses and fighting gear. Very likely, it was under Dyula influence that the Hausa developed their excellence in industries like weaving, dyeing and leatherwork. One of the first signs of grace expected of Muslim converts was that they should distinguish themselves from 'naked pagans' by the decency and cleanliness of their dress. The Islamised Hausa followed the example of Mali and Songhay by settling most of their war captives in slave villages around their walled cities, where they grew food, cotton and indigo, and prepared hides and skins for the industries of the free citizenry. Soon, the camel caravans which brought them the salt of Bilma departed northwards again, laden with Hausa robes and sandals destined for the markets of the Maghrib. Even more important for the survival of the Hausa cities was the influence of Islam on law and government, with the balancing of the military caste by one composed of clerics, many of them immigrants attracted by the patronage of the rulers for their knowledge of distant countries, their literacy and their expertise in an international system of law and justice. Some, notably Kano, had chronicles, like that of Kanem and Bornu. Muhammad Rumfa, sarki of Kano from 1463 till 1499, is remembered in the Kano chronicle as the great *mujaddid*, defender of the faith, who sought the advice of the celebrated jurist al-Maghili of Tuat in converting the old Hausa institutions of kingship into those of a Muslim sultanate.

These growing Islamic connections no doubt helped most of the Hausa to keep their independence when, in the sixteenth century, they faced interference from the great Muslim powers to the east and west of them. The earliest major incursion came from Songhay, probably in 1515, when the Askia Muhammad led a marauding expedition through the territories of Zaria, Katsina, Kano and Gobir, and on to the Tuareg capital at Agades. The motive seems to have been booty rather than conquest (above, p. 70), but the sarkis of Zaria, Katsina and Gobir all lost their lives, and it was said that as many as half of their subjects were marched away into slavery. Kano, however, was able to withstand a siege for long enough to be able to make terms. And at the end of the campaign Muhammad's allies among the western Hausa broke off the Songhay connection and built up the kingdom of Kebbi on the central Hausa pattern, which was henceforward to prove an effective bastion aganst Songhay attacks.

Much more significant was the threat to Hausa independence which came from the east, from Bornu. It led to the permanent occupation and settlement of eastern Hausaland and the neighbouring Chadic-speaking territories by Kanuri people, while all of central Hausaland remained subject to Bornu's tribute-taking attacks. Kano, only 250 miles up the Hadejia valley from Ngazargamu, was well within range and suffered repeated attacks. On one occasion, around 1561, the Bornu army penetrated as far west as Kebbi, more than 500 miles from its base. The general impression that emerges of these campaigns is that the Hausa cities themselves survived partly because of their defensive walls, but mainly because their inhabitants were fellow Muslims. The pagans of the countryside, however, especially those of the dependent slave villages, were fair game for the Bornu predators.

Bornu reached the zenith of its power and prestige between the middle of the sixteenth century and the end of the seventeenth. Although most of Kanem remained independent under the Bulala dynasty, the western part of the country around the old capital at Njimi had been reconquered and, with it, control of the great caravan route to the north, as far as the salt mines of Bilma. Bornu was thus the neighbour of Ottoman Tripoli, and it was in regular diplomatic relations with Morocco and Egypt. After the break-up of Songhay following the Moroccan conquest, Bornu was probably the most powerful state in black Africa. Unlike the Askiyas of Songhay, the Sefuwa mais had been wise enough to have their slave bodyguard, which was the core of their infantry forces, initiated into the use of firearms. These were imported from Tripoli, along with Turkish military instructors, by Mai Idris Aloma (1569–1600), whose biographer, Ibn Fartua, classed firearms high among the benefits which God in his bounty had conferred upon the sultan. They were probably not of much importance in the little wars against weaker neighbours by which Bornu made its living. However, they strengthened the monarchy in its relations with its own powerful subjects, and their greatest significance was perhaps as a deterrent against long-distance adventures like that of Morocco in Songhay. Against an army accustomed to the sight and sound of muskets, a surprise victory like that of Tondibi would have been impossible.

The ascendancy of Bornu established by Idris Aloma continued through most of the seventeenth and eighteenth centuries. Essentially it consisted in maintaining the military power to exact tribute from the neighbouring states, but it was reflected also in a cultural and religious hegemony which resulted from a closer relationship with the central currents of Islam. Hausaland had been converted from the west and remained, especially after the fall of Songhay and the decline of Timbuktu, on the periphery of an outer province of the faith. Its rulers did not go on pilgrimage or keep the company of scholars and theologians. In Hausaland the most active clerics were increasingly to be found among the Fulbe nomads infiltrating from the west, who did not belong to the official establishment and would one day take the lead in overthrowing it. The Islam of Bornu had, in contrast, come from Kanem, where it had been the religion of the state since the eleventh century. In Bornu it was the religion of the Kanuri conquerors, who saw themselves as warriors of the faith in a pagan land. There had been a long tradition of royal pilgrimages in Kanem which, following the tribulations of the conquest, was taken up again in Bornu. Idris Aloma returned from pilgrimage to build mosques of brick in the principal towns of his kingdom, and to appoint religious judges (*qa'ids*) to administer justice according to the shari'a law. His grandson, Mai 'Ali, who reigned in the later seventeenth century, made three pilgrimages, and was accompanied on each by thousands of his subjects. Between his many military campaigns he presided over a court famous for the high standard of its legal and theological disputations.

During the eighteenth century the military ascendancy of Bornu slowly faded, although the religious ascendancy survived. Armies could still be sent to the walls of Kano as of old, but the actively developing parts of Hausaland were now in the west, in Zamfara and Gobir, and they were beyond the effective range of Bornu – as were their trade routes, which passed northwards through Agades and Aïr. It was in the desert marches of northern Gobir that the Fulbe leader Usuman dan Fodio would in 1804 launch his great jihad for the overthrow of the Hausa kingdoms. The sarkis of central Hausaland – Katsina, Zaria and Kano – would appeal for help to their overlord the mai of Bornu, who was by then blind and senile and unable to take decisive action, even against the Fulbe rebels of his own country. Nevertheless, the Fulbe did not conquer Bornu, which was saved by a warrior cleric from Kanem, Muhammad al-Amin al-Kanemi, who proved himself a match for Usuman dan Fodio. A full circle thus turned in West Africa's most ancient empire, with Kanem coming to the rescue of Bornu.

THE WOODLANDS AND THE FOREST

South of Hausaland and Bornu, most people spoke languages of the huge Niger-Congo family, which owed its wide dispersion to the success of its early members in using woodland and forest environments for effective food production. It was a process which had started in the Late Stone Age, and had accelerated greatly with the availability of iron tools for clearing woodland and forest. It had received fresh impetus from the drier climatic conditions which set in during the early second millennium AD and which helped to cause a southward drift of the human population following the retreating rainbelt. Thus, Chadic-speakers had moved southwards from Aïr and the rest of the southern Sahara in sufficient numbers to impose their languages upon the northernmost Niger-Congo speakers who had previously predominated in Hausaland and in Bornu before the Kanuri conquest. There must have been a corresponding pressure of northern Niger-Congo peoples into the better-watered lands further south. The most favourable conditions for population growth were to be found on the margins of the lighter woodland and the denser forest. Here, the annual summer rainfall could be relied on. Here, even patchy clearing would admit sunlight enough for the vegetable crops, above all yams and oil palms, which were grown in these latitudes. Here, moreover, there was still plentiful hardwood for smelting, building and wood-carving, and a natural defence system against hostile intruders from the open savanna to the north, who were always reluctant to enter a well-wooded environment with its illimitable opportunities for concealment and ambush. Finally, the woodlands were ridden by the tsetse-fly and were therefore largely closed both to horses and to beasts of burden. Invasions by cavalry forces were thus excluded.

For all these reasons, the history of the woodlands developed rather separately from that of the northern savanna. Some trade contacts there were, for the woodland peoples were certainly importing both the copper of Aïr and the tin of the Jos plateau for their own metallurgical industries by the end of the first millennium, and doubtless there were some commodities, including slaves, which passed the other way. But the woodlands remained unvisited by the 85

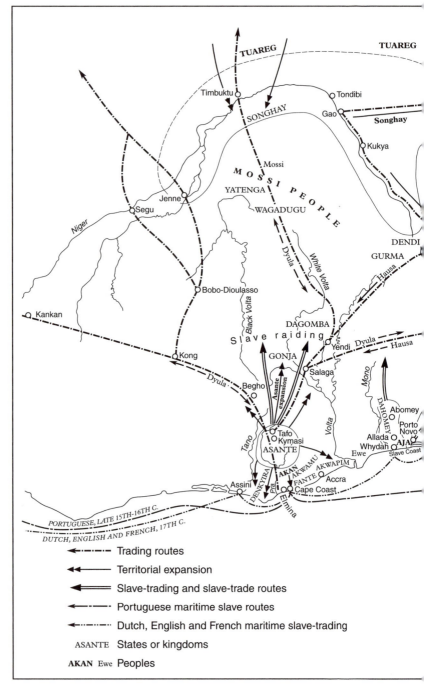

9 The central Sudan and lower Guinea, 1400–1800 (see also Map 8, pp. 74–5)

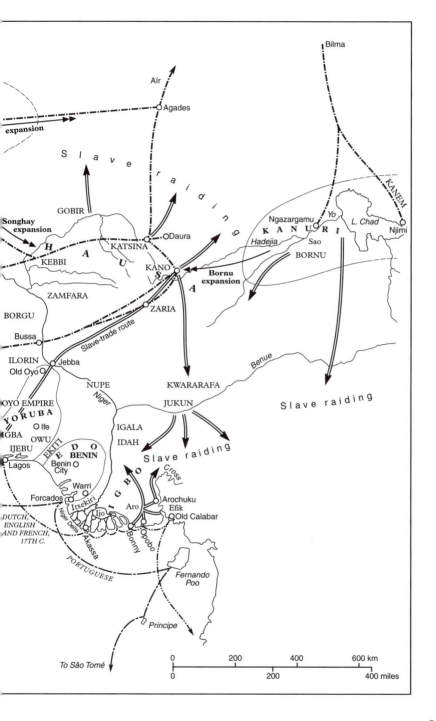

Muslim merchants and preachers who played so large a part in the history of the open savanna, so that Islam and Arabic learning, and distant travels for education and pilgrimage, came to the woodlands only at the very end of our period. One very positive consequence was that the woodland peoples were left free to develop their own highly naturalistic traditions of sculpture in wood, terracotta and brass, free from Islamic inhibitions about the portrayal of the human form. The most typical examples seem to have been concerned with the commemoration of ancestors in family shrines, and the best show a skill which has won the admiration of the world. Some of these objects, especially those made of metal, are of historical value when they have been recovered in a secure archaeological context. For the rest, historians have to try to evaluate the oral traditions gathered in a few places of special importance. For the period prior to the sixteenth century, this means in effect the dynastic traditions of Oyo, which have to stand for the whole of Yorubaland, and those of Benin, which are all that we have for the Edo. For the Ibo, who constitute the largest ethnic and linguistic grouping of the woodland and forest margin, we have no whisper of tradition that antedates the period of European contact.

The traditions of origin of the major Yoruba cities are unanimous in conceding the position of seniority to Ile Ife, and they follow a very common pattern of such traditions in asserting that history began with a great royal founder, by name Oduduwa, who ruled over all the Yoruba until, at the approach of death, he divided his kingdom among his sons, who then went out to govern its several parts. The son who went to Oyo was remembered as the founder of a line of twenty-three generations of kings, who ruled before the end of the nineteenth century AD, which seemed to indicate a starting-point around the thirteenth or fourteenth century. A parallel genealogy claimed by a twentieth-century Oba of Benin seemed to point in the same direction. However, the trend of recent archaeological research has been to show that the origins of town-building at both Ife and Benin are older by several centuries than the remembered genealogies of the royal dynasties. It has also questioned whether these origins need be attributed to the diffusion of dynasts from a single centre. The Nigerian archaeologist Ade Obayemi, for example, has argued the case for a 'predynastic' period characterised by autonomous small-town settlements, extending over the whole of Yoruba, Edo, Idoma, Nupe and Borgu. The most persuasive part of his argument rests on the survival, right into modern times, of small-town mini-states in the peripheral areas between the larger political systems which have evolved in their midst.[2] According to this view, the primacy of Ife was a primacy of wealth and culture rather than dominion. Situated just inside the forest limits, its iron, glass and ter-racotta industries were well supplied with hardwood fuel, and its glass foundries in particular specialised in the production of the blue *segi* beads used for the decoration of the royal crowns of all the main Yoruba cities. At latest by the thirteenth century, its metal-workers were becoming skilled enough to cast sculptures in zinc brass, using the sophisticated 'lost wax' process. The emergence of Benin to primacy among the Edo-speaking people was probably similar. Here, excavation has shown that the main city walls are but the nucleus of a vast system of defensive walling totalling perhaps 10,000 miles in all, which suggests that the city grew by encompassing a number of small, closely neighbouring towns, reflecting a growth of population around a successful industrial centre, rather than an expansion by military conquest.

In southern Nigeria as a whole, the enlargement of states by con-quest seems to have been a consequence of the southward spread of cavalry warfare and slave-raiding from Hausaland. In the Kano Chronicle we see the kings of the early fifteenth century supplying horses and armour to the Jukun people living along the Benue valley, who used them to raid for slaves in areas still further to the south. Zaria at the same period seems to have been engaged in a similar exchange with the Nupe. By the late fifteenth century Nupe was being reorganised into an aggressive, centralised state by a new dynasty from Igala which had grown up in the region to the south of the Niger–Benue confluence. Igala was taking slaves from northern Iboland, and by the early sixteenth century was engaged in major warfare with Benin. Meanwhile, Nupe was raiding into Yorubaland, and sometime around 1535 actually occupied the northern Yoruba kingdom of Oyo, forcing its ruling dynasty to evacuate the capital and take refuge in the neighbouring kingdom of Borgu. The exile lasted some eighty years and was followed by a reconquest in which horses and cavalry armour were applied to the reconstruction of a new, centralised and expansive Oyo kingdom, which was destined in the seventeenth and eighteenth centuries to incorporate or make tributary all the forest-free parts of Yoruba and Ajaland.

In their origins all of these important developments occurred quite independently of the activities of Europeans on the Atlantic

---

[2] A. M. Obayemi in J. F. A. Ajayi and M. Crowder (eds.), *A History of West Africa* (3rd edn, London, 1985), pp. 260–74.

coast. Here and there, indeed, some of the captives taken in the later stages of these wars were exported overseas, but it would seem that the main impetus of conquest and political consolidation was only incidentally concerned with the slave trade in any external direction. The new cavalry forces were dependent on the states of the savanna for a continuous supply of horses, and these were no doubt purchased mainly with slaves. The prime object of the new empires, however, was to produce concentrations of wealth and power by imposing tribute over the surrounding areas, and also by the forced transfer of populations into the neighbourhood of the new metropolises for agricultural and industrial reasons. It had long been the custom of the great Hausa cities to settle communities of slaves in agricultural villages around the urban areas. Benin strictly limited the sale of slaves from its metropolitan region to Europeans, because their labour was needed at home. The compulsory resettlement on somewhat more privileged terms of skilled men, especially blacksmiths, from conquered communities had been practised by many African states, including the empires of the western Sudan. Again, at the highest social level, slaves, and especially eunuchs, often became the intimate servants and officials of courts and kings, since they lacked the family connections which could lead to a conflict of loyalties. More generally, within West African societies the slave status of first-generation captives slid fairly easily into a difference of class or caste among their descendants. Servile origins were long remembered, but seldom alluded to. Similarly, it was taken for granted that the descendants of forced migrants would assume, for military purposes, the patriotism of their new societies.

Unfortunately, too little is known of the history of most of the city kingdoms of southern Nigeria for us to appreciate fully the significance of the enlargement of political scale which took place in the early centuries of our period. It appears, for example, that at a time of dissension among the ruling factions in the thirteenth century, Benin adopted a new ruling dynasty from Ife, traditionally the most ancient and ritually prestigious of the Yoruba cities, but this did not at once set the kingdom on the road to expansion. The new dynasty, despite its possession of state swords, a stable of stall-fed horses for use on ceremonial occasions, and a guild of royal brass-casters able to portray its gods and heroes in a manner fitting for the palace shrines, still took some two centuries to establish its ascendancy in the capital city. It was only in the mid-fifteenth century, a mere generation before the arrival of the Portuguese, that the throne was seized by a usurper, Eware, who became the first great conquering Oba, subjecting not merely his own Edo people, but a wide circle of Yoruba and Ibo towns to the east, the west and the north. Alan Ryder, the historian of Benin, suggests that Eware was responding to the general enlargement of scale that was taking place elsewhere in the region, especially in Igala and Nupe.[3] At all events, during Eware's reign Benin developed something like a standing army, and its metropolitan area became a regular recipient of war captives, which transformed the character of the state. The established citizens became courtiers and warriors, traders and skilled craftsmen, commanding large numbers of slaves, who grew the food and carried it into the city, and who transported the raw materials and the finished products of the important regional trade. When the Portuguese reached the Gold Coast, they found that cloth, beads and probably also slaves were already being imported there from Benin, and it is likely that it was the Akan chiefs, anxious to buy more slaves to dig for gold, who suggested that the Portuguese, with their superior shipping, should supplement the canoe traffic passing perilously through the creeks and coastal waters.

The Portuguese reached Benin in 1486, during the reign of Eware's son, Ozalua. By this time they were planning to colonise and establish sugar plantations on the islands of São Tomé and Principe, so their interest in a local supply of slaves was increased. Ozolua, a conqueror like his father, welcomed the newcomers, selling them slaves and cloth for the coastal trade, and peppers and a little ivory for the European market, in exchange for copper and brass for his metal industries, coral for his own ceremonial dress, and glass beads and European textiles with which to reward his courtiers. Individual Portuguese accompanied the Oba on his military expeditions and excited his interest in firearms. It was explained to him that these weapons could only be supplied to Christian allies of the Portuguese, and in 1514 he sent an embassy to Lisbon asking for both clergy and cannon. King Manuel sent the clergy, and also a letter promising that 'When we see that you have embraced the teachings of Christianity like a good and faithful Christian, there will be nothing within our realms with which we shall not be glad to favour you, whether it be arms or cannon and all other weapons of war for use against your enemies; of such things we have a great store, as your ambassador Dom Jorje will inform you.'[4]

But it was not to be. The priests sickened and soon withdrew. Ozolua died unbaptised, and his successor, Esigie, continued to

[3] Alan Ryder, *Benin and the Europeans 1445–1897* (London, 1969), p. 8.
[4] *Ibid.*, p. 47.

expand his frontiers without the help of European arms but with conspicuous success, defeating the great inland state of Igala and carrying his conquests westwards along the coastal lagoons to the island of Lagos. As Benin grew more powerful, it also grew more indifferent to the European trade. Higher prices were demanded for slaves, and the sale of male captives was forbidden from the metropolitan districts. The Portuguese, now firmly established on São Tomé and Principe, found it easier to do business with Benin's neighbours, especially those to the east, around the Niger Delta, where the military outreach of Benin was proliferating under a series of Edo princelings, who were founding little kingdoms among the western Ibo, which were too remote to be controlled from the metropolis.

Throughout the Delta region the coastline was masked by a belt of swamp and mangrove, intricately dissected by rivers and lagoons. Even the patches of dry land were sterile and uncultivable, and the Ijaw inhabitants of the coast had from time immemorial lived by fishing and by boiling salt, trading the produce of the brackish waters for the oil, yams, meat and iron tools of the the Ibo people of the lush, forested interior. Even the earliest of the Portuguese accounts, that of Pereira in 1505, describes the great canoes, 6 feet wide in the beam and large enough to carry eighty men, which came down the rivers from 100 to 250 miles inland, bringing vegetables, cows, goats, sheep and slaves. 'They sell all this to the natives of the village [in this case probably Bonny] for salt, and our ships buy these things for copper bracelets, which are here prized more than brass ones, a slave being sold for eight or ten of such bracelets.'[5] So far was the system already established that it needed only enlargement to meet the needs of the Atlantic traders as they came to the Delta in ever greater numbers.

There can be little doubt that the military pressure of Benin upon the western Ibo, and that of Igala upon those living to the north of them must have fuelled the flow of captives, especially during the sixteenth and early seventeenth centuries. However, it is certain that the decentralised pattern of Ibo society itself was also favourable to the trade in men. Living in stockaded villages amid their forest plantations, communities of 3000 to 5000 people regarded even their closest neighbours as foreigners. Kidnapping of individuals by one community from another was a recognised hazard of life. Only a few specialists – smiths, diviners and long-distance traders – could travel

[5] T. Hodgkin, *Nigerian Perspectives*, (2nd edn, London, 1975), p. 123.

abroad with reasonable security, and it was through such professional networks that kidnapped slaves passed into the international trading circuit.

So long as the Portuguese monopoly lasted, the trade seems to have been confined to the rivers actually connecting with the main Niger, roughly from Akassa to Bonny, and the number of slaves exported each year was probably less than 5000. With the advent of Dutch and British traders in the later seventeenth century, however, the system was extended eastwards to the Cross river, where the Efik of Old Calabar assumed the role of middlemen played further west by the Ijaw. The slaves exported down the Cross river were still mostly Ibo, and here kidnapping reached its most highly organised form under the priests of an oracular cult based at Arochuku on the Ibo border with the Efik. During the eighteenth century the Aro priests and their henchmen, armed now with guns, spread out widely over eastern and central Iboland and became the main inland suppliers of slaves to all the ports from Old Calabar to Bonny. It may be that during this century alone the Ibo sold nearly a million of their own people into slavery – none of them directly to Europeans, but to African middlemen who organised overland and river transport, and who brought back into the interior imports that were genuinely valued, such as iron, copper, hardware and cloth. Probably no Ibo village community would have sold its own members in exchange for such commodities, but members of other village communities were seen in a wholly different light. The Ibo in fact behaved like a vast assembly of tiny nations. On this premise, their participation in the trade was no more immoral than that of larger nations which raided their weaker neighbours. Nevertheless, the practical effect was to make Iboland a more prolific and enduring source of slaves than any comparable area of Africa.

To the west of Benin, the so-called 'Slave Coast', extending from Lagos to the Volta, acquired its evil name only in the late seventeenth century. Here, as the modern air traveller between Lagos and Accra can observe, the coastline is a narrow beach, pounded by heavy surf on one side and separated from the mainland by a wide stretch of marsh and lagoon on the other. Rivers flow to the lagoon, which empties to the sea only at Lagos. Elsewhere ships must ride at anchor and small boats must face the perils of the surf. It is no wonder that the Portuguese sailed by, noting that it was a coast where no business was to be done. Behind the lagoon, however, lay a unique region of coastal West Africa, where for meteorological reasons there was a break in the forest line and the savanna reached down to the coast. Here was the home of the Ewe and Aja peoples, the former living in independent village communities like the Ibo, the latter just beginning to experience the more ambitious state-building activities of small dynasties on the western Yoruba pattern.

As we saw in the previous chapter (p. 77), the isolation of the Ewe was brutally shattered by the eastward conquests of the Akan kingdom of Akwamu in the 1670s and 1680s, when thousands of Ewe captives were sold on the beaches of every fishing village from the Volta to Whydah. During the eighteenth century the Ewe passed into the raiding sphere of Asante, when many Ewe captives were resettled in the heartland of the empire around Kumasi. Meanwhile, the Aja were being drawn into a more direct and long-lasting connection with the Atlantic trade, most of which passed across the beaches of Allada and Whydah. Here, at least three new factors came into play almost simultaneously. The first was the Akwamu expansion, the captives from which were exported through the Aja coastal states. The second was the expansion from the north-east of the great Yoruba state of Oyo, which swept with its newly developed cavalry forces around the western fringes of the Nigerian forest belt, conquering the Egba and Egbado Yoruba and reaching the coast between Badagri and Porto Novo, on the eastern frontier of Ajaland. The third factor was the emergence, between the two great powers of Akwamu and Oyo, of the inland Aja kingdom of Dahomey.

In origin no more than an offshoot from the coastal kingdom of Allada, led by a branch of the ruling dynasty, who set out with a few hundred followers to conquer the stateless inhabitants of the Abomey plateau, Dahomey developed along centralised, military lines, and by the late seventeenth century was in command of the slave-raiding opportunities in the hinterland of the coastal states. Though itself frequently raided by the cavalry forces of Oyo, it was able to keep its autonomy by paying tribute when necessary, and finally to expand its territory back to the coast by conquering Allada and Whydah between 1724 and 1727. As in the Akan region further west, it was the expansion of the successfully militarised kingdoms at the expense of their weaker neighbours that supplied the tragic flow of captives to the sea-coast and thence to the New World. During the period of almost continuous warfare from about 1680 till about 1730 the export of slaves through Allada and Whydah reached some 20,000 a year. Thereafter, with the single, strong power of Dahomey in control of the beaches, the trade became a royal monopoly, and the supply fell to about one quarter of its former level, as Dahomey, having satisfied its territorial ambitions, was concerned only to maintain supplies of European firearms and court luxuries, and to provide the quota of these items required for its tribute payments to Oyo. It is significant that in the Dahomean savanna the cavalry of Oyo was able to maintain its ascendancy over the imported muskets of Dahomey.

The triad of cavalry warfare, tribute and forced migration which dominated so much of West African history during our period is perhaps most clearly seen in the meteoric rise of the Oyo empire. Its capital city at Old Oyo was sited far out in the savanna tip of northern Yoruba, in country that is today almost uninhabited, and which was probably only very lightly populated in the early seventeenth century, when the ruling dynasty returned from its long exile in Borgu. The new system of government then instituted was based squarely on a military hegemony, which demanded regular tribute from all within reach of its swift-footed cavalry squadrons. This hegemony was built up entirely within the seventeenth and eighteenth centuries. It started from very small beginnings, but at its zenith in the mid-eighteenth century it consisted of four concentric areas: first, the metropolis itself, which would have corresponded more or less with the site of the ancient city as it existed before the Nupe conquest; second, the immediately neighbouring Yoruba towns, which were the first to be conquered and were situated so close that their traditional rulers could be recognised as brothers; third, the country of the Egba and Egbado in south-western Yorubaland, where Oyo suzerainty was enforced by resident commissioners (*ajele*); and fourth, an outer periphery, mostly in Aja country, from which tribute was exacted by the threat of far-flung punitive expeditions. At every stage of its growth, the population of the metropolis increased, and soldiers and officials needed to be fed and serviced by larger and larger contingents of forced migrants brought in from the areas of military activity. During the later eighteenth century the army began to be neglected, perhaps, as Akinjogbin has suggested, because the rulers had found an easier road to wealth by acting as middlemen in a newly developed long-distance slave trade between Hausaland and the Atlantic coast, which crossed the Niger at Jebba and reached the sea at Porto Novo. In the longer term this was to prove a disastrous change of emphasis, when the Oyo empire broke up under the impact of the Fulbe revolution in the early nineteenth century.

It is noteworthy that for most of our period the kingdoms of the southern savanna remained very little influenced by Islam. The *alafins* of Oyo, the *etsus* of Nupe, the *attas* of Igala, the *obas* of Benin

95

and the *akus* of the Jukun were all in ceremonial and ritual matters old-style 'divine kings' – not in the sense that they enjoyed absolute powers, but in the sense that they were regarded as the natural points of contact with the unseen world. They inhabited the innermost courtyards of palace cities, surrounded by hundreds of wives and thousands of officials, soldiers and servants. They ate alone. They were seen in public only once or twice a year. In sickness or old age they were subject to ritual murder or suicide. They were buried together with sacrificial victims. In all these ways, and in everything implied by them, the kingdoms of the southern savanna were two or three centuries behind those of the northern savanna. They were less aware of the outside world. They were less adaptable to change. Nevertheless, when these systems finally yielded, it was, with the exception of Benin, to influences from the Muslim north and not to any emanations from the Atlantic trading frontier to the south.

7 Nubia, Darfur and Wadai

THE CHRISTIAN KINGDOMS AND THE ARAB PENETRATION

In the long middle stretch of the Nile valley south of Egypt, the thirteenth century saw the climax of the transition from a Christian tradition to a Muslim one in the two riverine kingdoms of Maqurra and 'Alwa, where Christian dynasties had ruled since their conversion by Byzantine missionaries during the fifth and sixth centuries AD. The Arab conquerors of Egypt in the seventh century had moved on quickly to mop up the other Byzantine provinces in North Africa, but they had seen no advantage in trying to extend their conquests beyond the Byzantine frontiers to the south. Instead, they had negotiated a pact (in Arabic, *baqt*) with the king of Maqurra, whereby in exchange for an annual payment of 365 slaves, they undertook not to attack the Nubians but on the contrary to keep them supplied with the wheat and wine needed for the celebration of the Christian eucharist. There was to be free passage for merchants and bona fide travellers, but fugitives from either side were to be arrested and returned. Prominent among the travellers were the pilgrims from both of the Nubian kingdoms and also from Ethiopia, who made their way to and from Jerusalem in large companies with drums beating and flags flying, and with frequent halts for Christian worship.

The Fatimids, who conquered Egypt from Tunisia in 969 with an army composed largely of black slave soldiers from the western Sudan, were naturally anxious to secure a comparable field of recruitment in the east. An envoy, one Ibn Salim al-Aswani, was despatched to both the Nubian kingdoms, and on the basis of his highly favourable report the *baqt* was renewed in 975, and remained in force through the two centuries of Fatimid rule. It was during these centuries that Christian Nubian civilisation reached its zenith. It was a civilisation based on the intensive cultivation of the narrow flood plain of the Nile, growing dates at its northern end and millet and sorghum further south. The agricultural surplus, produced largely by slave labour, was sufficient to support an urban population of traders and artisans, dominated in their turn by an equestrian aristocracy, given over to horse-breeding, hunting and warfare, whose military exploits into the back country brought in the slaves

for domestic use as well as for export. On the Egyptian frontier, the
Maqurran cavalry were renowned for their skill in mounted archery,
which helped to hold back the persistent attempts of Arab pastoralists from southern Egypt to infiltrate Nubian territory with their
flocks of camels, sheep and goats. Ibn Salim noted that, except for
the northern cataract region, which even then was being occupied by
Arab nomads, the only Muslims permitted to enter Maqurra or
'Alwa were merchants.

The Maqurran capital at Dongola, sited just above the Third
Cataract of the river, was described by an eleventh-century Christian
Armenian visitor as 'a large city on the banks of the blessed Nile'
which boasted 'many churches and large houses, set on wide streets.
The king's house is lofty, with several domes of red brick, and resem-
bles the buildings of Iraq.' The southern kingdom of 'Alwa was
reported by Ibn Salim to be richer and more powerful than Maqurra.
Its capital at Soba, some 12 miles up the Blue Nile from its confluence with the White Nile, possessed 'magnificent buildings and
churches overflowing with gold, all set in the midst of lush gardens'.[1]
Greek remained the liturgical language in both countries, and the
splendour of Nubian ecclesiastical art has been revealed in this
century by the archaeological recovery of the wonderful painted
frescos on the walls of the seventh-century cathedral at Faras, now
displayed in the National Museum in Khartoum. The foundations of
a brick-built, five-aisled cathedral, resembling that at Faras and likewise dating to the seventh century, have recently been excavated at
Soba, and the surrounding Christian town-site has been found to
cover an area of about one square mile.

When, in 1171, Egypt was conquered by the Ayyubids, who were
Sunni Muslims from Armenia, the black slave soldiers of the
Fatimids were naturally suspected of loyalty to their former masters.
They were abruptly disbanded and banished to upper Egypt, where
they made common cause with the Arab pastoralists pressing into
the borderlands of Maqurra. By 1260, when power in Egypt was
seized by the Mamluks, the situation on the Nubian frontier had got
beyond control. At first the Mamluk sultan Baybars tried to by-pass
Maqurra by occupying the Red Sea port of Suakin and developing
more direct trade links with 'Alwa and Ethiopia. King David of
Maqurra responded by raiding into Egyptian territory and capturing

[1] Ibn Salim's account of his journey is summarised by the fifteenth-century historian al-Maqrizi, trans. G. Vantini, *Oriental Sources concerning Nubia* (Heidelberg
and Warsaw, 1975), p. 613.

the pilgrim port of 'Aydhab. Baybars thereupon sent an army, composed largely of pastoral Arab levies, into Maqurra, where it defeated King David and, after plundering as far south as Dongola, installed a vassal ruler in his place. Further expeditions of the same kind were conducted during the reigns of sultans Qala'un and al-Nasir Muhammad, around the turn of the thirteenth and fourteenth centuries. Finally, in 1316 a Muslim candidate was placed upon the throne of Maqurra, and in the following year, as we know from an inscription on its walls, the former metropolitan cathedral of Dongola was converted into a mosque. Only in the inhospitable district around the Second Cataract, by this time by-passed by caravan trails running straight across the desert from Aswan to Dongola, did a small Christian principality, with its capital at al-Daw near the modern town of Wadi Halfa, survive for some time longer, by paying tribute to the Muslim rulers of Maqurra.

The long-term consequence of this sustained Mamluk intervention was not so much to extend Egyptian influence in Nubia, but rather, by destroying Maqurra's power of resistance, to let loose the pent-up flood of nomads from upper Egypt. Arab immigrants poured in, first the semi-sedentary Banu Kanz from the arid region between the First and Third cataracts, then purely nomadic groups like the Juhayna from the deserts of upper Egypt, who infiltrated the steppe on either side of the Nile valley. Many Arabs settled in the Dongola reach, dispossessing and enslaving the former Nubian farmers. The great historian and philosopher Ibn Khaldun, who was living in Cairo while these dramatic events were taking place 500 miles higher up the Nile valley, described their impact thus:

Clans of the Juhayna Arabs spread over their country and settled in it. They assumed power and filled the land with rapine and disorder. At first the kings of Nubia tried to repulse them by force, but they failed. So they changed their tactics and tried to win them over by offering their daughters in marriage. Thus was their kingdom disintegrated, for it passed to the sons of the Juhayna by their Nubian mothers, according to the non-Arab practice of inheritance by the sister and her sons. So their kingdom fell to pieces and their country was inherited by the nomad Arabs. But their rule presented none of the marks of statesmanship, because of the essential weakness of a system which is opposed to discipline and the subordination of one man to another.[2]

In these circumstances it was not possible, even for a Muslim dynasty, to hold together a kingdom of the size and shape of

Maqurra, which consisted of little more than an immensely long river line, broken by cataracts and backed by deserts on either side. The last reference to a Nubian king was in 1397, and thereafter Maqurra vanished from the stage of history. Such little written information as survives about the southern Christian kingdom of 'Alwa suggests that a comparable political breakdown occurred there also, sometime in the thirteenth century. At the beginning of that century, the Armenian traveller Abu Salih witnessed a prosperous kingdom, with a vibrant urban culture supporting 400 churches and a metropolitan cathedral. But in 1287 a Mamluk emissary, 'Alm al-Din Sanjar, reported on his contacts with nine apparently independent Christian warlords, ruling from a series of riverside fortresses, running from the Atbara confluence southwards to the Gezira, which probably represented the provincial centres of the former 'Alwa kingdom.

Geographically, most of 'Alwa lay to the south of the desert, with large areas of dry grassland on both sides of the Nile. By the fourteenth century, if not before, Arab pastoralists were penetrating the open countryside in significant numbers, some of them moving up the Nile valley from Maqurra, others following the line of the Red Sea hills southwards from upper Egypt, others again arriving directly by sea from the Hijaz. By the end of the fifteenth century large parts of the former kingdom were apparently united under the hegemony of a Muslim dynasty. According to traditional accounts, a semi-legendary Arab chief called 'Abdallah Jamma' defeated the last of the organised Christians of 'Alwa and captured Soba. His son, Shaykh 'Ajib al-Kafuta, a less shadowy figure, established a stronghold at Qarri, just below the confluence of the Blue Nile and the White Nile. His authority extended from the northern Gezira right across the Butana plain between the Blue Nile and the Atbara and in an unspecified way over the Arabic-speaking chiefdoms now established along the Nile valley to the Egyptian frontier. But the supremacy of the 'Abdallabi dynasty in the old 'Alwa kingdom was short-lived, for within a decade or two its ascendancy was to be challenged by invaders coming not from the north but from the south.

THE FUNJ SULTANATE

The origin of the Funj sultans who ruled over much of the Nilotic Sudan from the early sixteenth century until the early nineteenth is still a matter of debate among historians. No contemporary documents have survived, and the so-called Funj Chronicle was probably

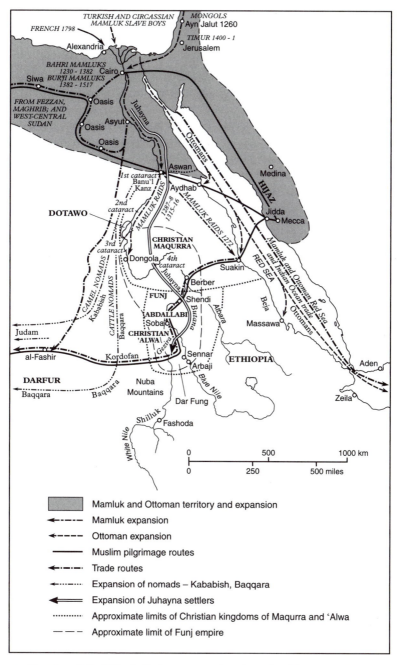

10 Egypt and the Nilotic Sudan, 1250–1800 (see also Map 3, p. 18)

compiled only just before the Turco-Egyptian conquest of 1821. One of its versions suggests that the early homeland of the Funj was to the south of the Blue Nile, around the area still known as Dar Fung. The traveller James Bruce, who recorded traditions of the kingdom in 1772, believed that the Funj were Shilluk, that is to say that they belonged to the northernmost of the Nilotic-speaking peoples, who in the seventeenth century had built up a considerable kingdom astride the White Nile with its capital at Fashoda. The two areas are not in fact so far apart, and if we bear in mind that Shilluk traditions tell of a long period when their ancestors were engaged in driving out the previous inhabitants of their country whom they called *ap-Funy*, the most likely conclusion would seem to be that the Funj came from the southern Gezira, and that they were black Africans and not Arabs. Quite possibly, they stemmed from one of the southern provinces of the old kingdom of 'Alwa, and their endeavour was to reconstitute that kingdom around a more southerly base.

At all events, their first appearance in history, around the turn of the fifteenth and sixteenth centuries, was as pastoralists and horsemen under the leadership of one 'Amara Dunkas. The account of David Reubeni, a Jewish traveller who claimed to have journeyed in disguise through the region with a merchant caravan in 1523, suggests that 'Amara was a Muslim, and it is possible that some at least of his followers had been affected by the penetration of Arabs before setting out on their conquests. In 1504, in a battle at Arbaji on the Blue Nile, the Funj defeated the Arab warriors of the 'Abdallabi. This suggests that, in the vacuum following the collapse of 'Alwa, the coincidental movement of Funj northwards and Arabs southwards met head-on in the central Gezira, in competition for some of the best grazing lands of the southern Sudan. The Funj henceforth occupied the Gezira, but contented themselves with a loose suzerainty over the 'Abdallabi, who continued as the overlords of the Butana plains and of the narrow riverine farmlands below the confluence of the two Niles. David Reubeni reported that the Funj dominions began to the north of Dongola. If so, they encompassed not only 'Alwa but also much of the old kingdom of Maqurra. Sinnar, some 80 miles up the Blue Nile, became the commercial hub of the new sultanate, but 'Amara Dunkas and his immediate successors lived further to the south, perhaps in a peripatetic tented capital like the Solomonid kings of Ethiopia. Reubeni described 'Amara as a black king, who maintained a barbaric court, but ruled over both white and black subjects. Whether or not 'Amara himself was a Muslim, it is clear that the Funj became rapidly Islamised, no doubt through contact with the Muslim societies among whom they settled. By the early seventeenth century at latest, the dynasty had settled permanently at Sinnar.

The power of the Funj sultans, as also that of their 'Abdallabi vassals, rested on the ability of their mounted soldiers to levy regular taxes from the settled riverain cultivators, and to exercise at least some control over the cattle nomads of the Gezira and the Butana plain. Most of these pastoralists had to move their herds between summer and winter grazing grounds, and so could be waylaid at river crossings and other narrow places, and forced to hand over some of their stock as tax or tribute. Again, the revenues of both Funj and 'Abdallabi rulers depended greatly on customs dues levied on trade. Essentially, they controlled a network of long-distance caravan routes leading to Egypt and the Red Sea ports, along which there passed commodities of high value, such as the gold and civet musk of south-western Ethiopia, the ivory and ebony of the White Nile, and the slaves captured from all the weaker communities of the southern frontier. By the eighteenth century, if not before, the trade routes running north and south were criss-crossed by new pilgrimage routes used by West African Muslims from as far afield as Senegambia and even southern Morocco, which would have been impracticable so long as the Nile Valley was ruled by Christians. Situated at the pivot of these lines of commercial and religious communication, Sinnar developed into a large and prosperous metropolis. As the missionary and traveller Theodore Krump described it in 1701:

In all Africa, as far as the Moorish lands are concerned, Sinnar is close to being the greatest trading city. Caravans are continually arriving from Cairo, Dongola, Nubia, from across the Red Sea, from India, Ethiopia, Darfur, Bornu, the Fezzan and other kingdoms. This is a free city, and men of any nationality or faith may live in it without a single hindrance. After Cairo, it is one of the most populous cities. Every day a public market is held on the public square [in front of the sultan's palace] in the best possible order.[3]

From the middle of the sixteenth century onwards, the main direction of Funj expansion was westward, into Kordofan and the Nuba mountains. But these were mainly slaving grounds. Funj rule there was never effective, and by the middle of the eighteenth century they had passed into the control of Darfur, the rapidly

---

[3] 'Sudanese Travels of Theodore Krump 1710–1712', trans. J. Spaulding, *The Heroic Age in Sinnar* (East Lansing, 1985), pp. 112–13.

expanding sultanate to the west of the Funj domains. To the east, the Beja people of the Red Sea hills, though converting gradually to Islam since the fourteenth century, remained politically almost independent. Beyond them, the Ottoman Turks controlled the Red Sea ports for most of the period. To the south-east, the Funj engaged in a series of fruitless campaigns with the emperors of Ethiopia for control of the trade route from Sinnar to Gondar and the grazing lands of Fazugli. These culminated in a resounding Funj victory on the banks of the Dindera near Sinnar in 1744, but changed little. To the south, the Nilotic-speaking peoples in and around the Nile marshes were untouched by the authority of the Funj sultans until the later seventeenth and eighteenth centuries, when the Shilluk and Dinka peoples pushed northwards down the White Nile and into the southern region of Funj. By the 1770s, when Bruce was in Sinnar, the Shilluk in their war canoes were raiding as far downriver as the great confluence.

During the sixteenth and seventeenth centuries the Funj sultanate seems to have provided its subjects with long periods of relative peace and prosperity, during which the recently settled Arabs mixed and fused with the descendants of the Christian Nubians to form a cohesive population with common religious beliefs and the awakening of a vaguely perceived Sudanese patriotism. Very largely, this was a process which followed as more and more people, whose ancestors had entered the Sudan as nomads, became sedentary farmers in the more favourable parts of the Nile valley. It was particularly marked in the riverine lands of the former kingdom of Maqurra between Dongola and the increasingly important river-port of Shendi near the Atbara confluence, and also in the ʿAbdallabi country around the confluence of the two Niles, where the term Jaʿaliyyun came to denote these riverside farmers. Further south, the Arab element was weaker and the black African element stronger. Here, in the Gezira and across the huge swathe of savanna between Kordofan and Darfur, the sense of being Arab depended much more upon the adoption of Islam, for religious conversion was usually accompanied by the invention of a fictitious Arab pedigree, or *nisba*.

Conversion in the early days was usually the result of involvement in trade with Muslim partners and was apt, during the first two centuries of contact, to be fairly superficial. Later, more genuine conversion was the work of holy men, most of whom came to the Sudan in the course of pilgrimage from countries further to the west. Thus it could come about that in the Funj kingdom the Islamic law, the shariʿa, was taught in the Maliki form prevalent in the Maghrib, and not in the Shafi'i form of Egypt. And the pattern of holy men and their descendants, each with his circle of enthusiastic disciples practising strict observance of the law alongside popular Sufi devotions, was likewise a feature of Maghribi Islam. In the Sudan the holy men, known as *faqi*s, came to wield immense power. They became closely involved with the Funj and 'Abdallabi rulers, advising, criticising and supplying moral support for political actions. Frequently they were rewarded with large grants of land, so that many became in time important proprietors and political authorities in their own right. Other faqis practised as merchants and penetrated the trading community. Even the nomads came in time to have their faqis, who moved around with them performing religious and magical services.

The Funj sultanate reached the height of its power during the long reign of Badi II (1644–80). A Funj garrison was established at Alays on the White Nile, as a check upon the Shilluk people, who were always trying to expand their territory downstream. Meanwhile, the Funj cavalry advanced across Kordofan and reduced the recently Islamised chiefdom of Taqali in the Nuba mountains to a tributary state. The Funj captured or purchased large numbers of non-Muslim Nuba, and resettled them in slave villages around Sinnar as the recruiting base for a slave army. In the long run this proved to be a destructive innovation, as it alienated the sultans from the old warrior families who had formed the aristocracy of the early Funj state. In 1718 these aristocrats deposed the reigning sultan and substituted a high officer of the royal household who did not even belong to the ruling clan. His son and successor, Badi IV (1724–62), was the last effective ruler of the sultanate. Although he reigned for thirty-eight years, he did so only by attacking the old Funj families and appointing royal slaves to their traditional offices and estates. After his death, the state fell apart into regional warlordships, governed by members of the old military families, known as the Hamaj. These found their chief support in the emerging middle class of rich merchants and landowners, known generally as the Jallaba, most of whom preferred to have an efficient tyrant on their own doorsteps rather than a distant one who could no longer provide them with the security they needed in order to manage their business affairs. During the second half of the eighteenth century the prevailing anarchy at the centre of the sultanate caused the long-distance trade to re-route itself through the more northerly river-port at Shendi in order to avoid the chaos at Sinnar. In 1814 the Swiss traveller J. L. Burckhardt found Shendi to be a hive of commercial activity, with caravan routes radiating in all directions, to Ethiopia, Kordofan,

Darfur and Suakin. And when, in 1821, the Egyptian forces invaded the sultanate, they met with scant resistance, and found to their dismay that Sinnar, which had once enjoyed a legendary reputation for wealth and splendour, was little more than a heap of ruins.

FROM THE NILE TO LAKE CHAD

Until the eve of our period the vast region between the middle Nile valley and Lake Chad remained the most isolated section of the whole Sudanic belt. Extending for some 1200 miles to the west of the Nubian kingdoms of Maqurra and 'Alwa, it consisted mostly of dry savanna, broken here and there by mountain outcrops like the Nuba mountains of northern Kordofan, the Tibesti massif in the north-west and the horseshoe of highland country which stretched from Ennedi, through Darfur to Wadai, and formed the watershed between the Nile drainage system and the huge inland basin of Lake Chad, of which the lake itself occupied only the south-western corner. At the centre of the horseshoe the volcanic massif of Jabal Marra rose to a height of more than 9000 feet above sea level, offering fertile soils and an assured rainfall to the Fur people who cultivated its southern slopes. Except for the Fur and their neighbours the Maba, who cultivated the highlands of Wadai, all the peoples of the region were primarily pastoralists, herding camels, horses and donkeys, sheep and goats, and, together with the Nubians, they constituted most of those who spoke languages of the Saharan division of the Nilo-Saharan language-family. They included such peoples as the Nuba and Berti of Kordofan, the Zaghawa of northern Darfur, the Teda and Daza of Tibesti and the Kanuri of Kanem to the north and east of Lake Chad.

Islam, as we have seen (above, pp. 80–1), had reached Kanem at least as early as the eleventh century, brought by traders from Ifriqiya, using the shortest of the trans-Saharan caravan routes from Tripoli and the Fezzan, but there is no indication of its spreading eastwards from there. At least in Darfur, and possibly still further to the west, there may have been outposts of Nubian Christianity, for Christian symbols occur as decoration on the potsherds found in the ruins of a burnt brick building identified as a church or monastery at 'Ain Farah in northern Darfur. If so, the connection could have arisen either from 'Alwa across Kordofan, or else, and more probably, by the desert trade route leading southwards from Dongola. At all events, for so long as Christianity remained the established faith of Maqurra and 'Alwa, the spread of Islam was evidently inhibited as

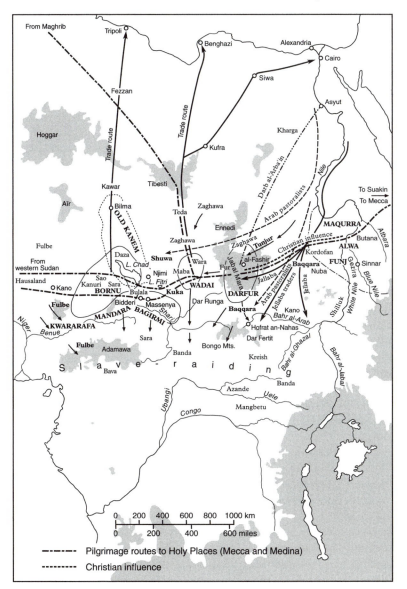

11 From the Niger to the Nile, 1400–1800

far west as Lake Chad. It was only in the thirteenth century that this situation began to change. And, as in Nubia, the prime agents of the change were the pastoral, nomadic Arabs pressing southwards from upper Egypt. The penetration of Arab pastoralists into Maqurra, which began in the thirteenth century, spread across northern Kordofan and Darfur and into the Chad basin by the end of the fourteenth century. In 1391 the king of Kanem, Mai Abu 'Amr 'Uthman, wrote to the Mamluk sultan Barquq complaining of the misbehaviour of the Judham and other Arabs, who were attacking people in Kanem and selling their captives to slave-dealers from Egypt. Without doubt, the arrival of these newcomers upset the whole balance of power around Kanem's eastern frontier. In the Lake Chad basin these warlike Arab pastoralists made common cause with the Bulala and Kuka around Lake Fitri, joining them in raids against Kanem, which were to result in the displacement of that kingdom from the north-east to the north-west of Lake Chad (above, p. 81). In the early sixteenth century Leo Africanus was to report the existence, to the east of Kanem, of a large and powerful kingdom of 'Gaoga', the ruler of which traded directly with Egypt, sending slaves and ivory northwards in exchange for horses, arms and armour. This account is best understood as referring to a greatly expanded kingdom of Kuka (Gaoga) under its Bulala rulers following the Arab penetration of the Chad basin. Certainly, we know that the fifteenth- and sixteenth-century kings of Kanem were constantly at war with the Bulala, which had by this time become a strong cavalry power. The special interest of Leo's account is the implication that the Bulala kingdom had become a major slave-raiding state with a direct trans-Saharan link to Mamluk Egypt, running in parallel with Kanem's route to the Fezzan.

In the highlands of Darfur and in parts of Wadai the infiltration of warlike Arab pastoralists roughly coincided with the advent of a new ruling group, the Tunjur, who displaced earlier ruling lineages of Eastern Sudanic-speaking Daju agriculturalists from southern Darfur. The Tunjur were not themselves either Arabs or Muslims. According to tradition they practised a form of ritual kingship which involved the building of stone-walled citadels, at Jabal Uri in Darfur and at Kadama in Wadai, each surrounding a stone palace with an audience platform reached by a nine-stepped stairway. It seems most likely that in origin they were a group of veil-wearing camel nomads, who had migrated from the Egyptian desert across Kordofan and northern Darfur, and who later invented a fictitious Arab ancestry. From their Fur and Maba subjects the Tunjur probably demanded little but tribute in the shape of labour, food and drink for their royal capitals and their standing armies of mounted cavalry. Significantly, Jabal Uri was situated at the southern terminus of the notorious Darb al-ʿArbaʿin, the Forty Days Road, leading to upper Egypt via the oases of Atrun and Kharga. No doubt from an early period of their rule, a pattern was established of trading slaves to Egypt and to the Nilotic Sudan. Every year the supplies of horses and armour came south from Egypt, and every year they were employed in slave-raiding expeditions against the defenceless populations further to the south. It was a pattern long familiar in the history of Kanem but now enacted later in time upon a more easterly stage.

ISLAM AND THE SULTANATES OF WADAI AND DARFUR

If an early result of the penetration of the central Sudanic regions by Arab pastoralists was the establishment of trading links with Egypt, a later one consisted in the religious and cultural integration of the region with the rest of Muslim Africa. Whereas the first was motivated by the development of new trade routes running north and south, the second was much more concerned with communications and influence running east and west. In this case the vital event was not so much the fall of Christian Nubia as the emergence during the early sixteenth century of the strong Muslim kingdom of the Funj. For West African Muslims, and particularly for the poor who needed to work their passage by farm labour or the exercise of a craft, the existence of a Muslim state in the Nilotic Sudan opened the possibility of making the pilgrimage without crossing the Sahara. The presence of pilgrims travelling slowly and cumbrously across the Sudanic belt had far-reaching consequences for the whole region. One such example was that of Ould Dede, a Fulbe Muslim cleric from the Senegal, who built a shrine at the tomb of his long-lost father at a place called Bidderi in the Bagirmi kingdom east of Lake Chad, which became a religious centre of great influence. Another is that of the Muslims of the Maghrib, accustomed as they were to desert travel and the care of camels, who habitually travelled across the desert fringes to avoid the expenses of Egypt and the other countries under Ottoman rule. Many passed through the Fezzan, and some of these now turned south-eastwards to the Tibesti highlands and across the Chad basin to Wadai and on through Darfur, Kordofan and the Butana to the Red Sea port of Suakin.

At some time early in the seventeenth century the Tunjur dynasty of Wadai was overthrown in a *coup d'état* by another Muslim cleric, 109

'Abd al-Karim, a Nubian Arab from the northern part of the Funj kingdom, who had travelled widely in the Hijaz and perhaps also in Morocco, and who may even have studied for a time at the religious school at Bidderi. He claimed to be a Sharif, a descendant of the Prophet, as did most of the respectable holy men of Muslim Africa. 'Abd al-Karim's military support came from Shuwa Arabs, who had been herding their camels and sheep for some two centuries in the northern part of the country, and who were probably anxious to expand from the desert margins into the lands of the Maba cultivators. Nevertheless, it appears that there was a ground swell of enthusiasm for Islam at this time, as there was in other parts of central Sudanic Africa, which no doubt proceeded from a genuine respect for the lives and teaching of the holy men who were spreading into the region from the longer-Islamised parts of the continent. Such holy men were tireless in preaching the necessity for Muslims to live under Muslim rule, and among their followers considerations of self-interest could go hand in hand with a real concern for justice and public morality.

According to the traditions, 'Abd al-Karim was himself not averse to blending political deviousness with religious fervour. He is depicted defeating the last of the Tunjur rulers by the stratagem of tying branches to the tails of the camels of his Arab allies and so raising enough dust to suggest a much larger host than that which he had. Another story shows him as benefiting from the very prayers he was advocating to the faithful. 'Then the sultan of the Tunjur gave him his daughter to wed, and said "Pray for me". But, instead, he prayed on his own behalf, and so the sultan died, but the sharifs rule Wadai till now.'[4] As a vignette of the transition from the pastoral way of life to that of the settled cultivator, the site of 'Abd al-Karim's capital in the mountain-enclosed defile of Wara was fortuitously discovered by his followers who were searching for some calves which had strayed while grazing. Around the brick-built palace and mosque a large town soon grew up, which was regularly visited by traders and clerics from many regions, but especially from Funj and upper Egypt. At the centre of the sultanate, 'Abd al-Karim and his successors maintained many of the rituals of pre-Islamic sacral kingship. The sultan's food and drink were carried into the palace secretly, and he ate alone. When in audience, he was seated behind a curtain, and his words were relayed by a spokesman. His authority was symbolised by royal drums

[4] H. R. Palmer, *Sudanese Memoirs* (Lagos, 1928, reprinted London, 1967), vol. II, p. 42.

and a royal fire, from which all other fires had to be rekindled at the new year. Elaborate sacrifices were made to the royal ancestors.

Outside the capital, the sultan was represented by four provincial governors and by some thirty military feudatories enjoying landed estates from which they had to raise both cavalry and foot soldiers. Tribute was paid by cultivators in foodstuffs; by pastoralists in camels and horses, sheep and cattle; by hunters in ivory and honey; by smiths in tools and weapons; and by other craftsmen in the products of their trades. The territory of Wadai was considered to stretch for some 170 miles to the south of the capital, to Dar Runga in the northern foothills of the Ubangi–Shari watershed. But all round the southern border-lands the non-Muslim peoples were required to pay tribute in slaves, on pain of military raiding for defaulters. The external necessities of the sultanate – chiefly horses, firearms and other weapons, armour and cotton textiles – were paid for in ivory and slaves. The trade in slaves was thus self-perpetuating, and it became increasingly destructive as the hunting grounds extended further and further from the capital. It was the same in all the other militaristic kingdoms of the savanna belt.

Darfur, which by the early nineteenth century was the largest and most powerful of the sultanates of northern Central Africa, passed under Muslim rule at about the same time as Wadai. Here, if the traditions are to be believed, the Tunjur rulers were first confronted by local Fur chieftains as early as the fifteenth century. But the founder of the main successor dynasty was Sulayman Solongdungu (meaning 'the Arab' in Fur), who in about 1640 finally drove out the Tunjur and conquered the country around Jabal Marra. Sulayman was said to be the son of an Arab woman. In the traditions his reign was remembered as one of constant warfare and conquest, in which the Fur established their dominance over the surrounding Arab nomads – both the camel pastoralists of the deserts to the north and the cattle-owning Baqqara Arabs living to the east and south-east of the Jabal Marra range. Sulayman's grandson consolidated the position of the dynasty by marrying a wife from the Zaghawa people of northern Darfur. The resulting expansion of territory brought the sultanate into conflict with Wadai, which continued until a peace was finally negotiated in the second half of the eighteenth century. Thenceforward, Darfur turned its warlike activities eastwards against the failing strength of the Funj, while Wadai turned westwards against Bagirmi.

By this time the religious and economic circumstances of the two sultanates had changed considerably, in processes similar to those which were affecting the Funj. The era of experiment was giving way to one of consolidation. Much permanent construction was undertaken, including schools, mosques and forts. In Darfur, right at the end of the eighteenth century, a new royal capital was built on the eastern side of Jabal Marra, which became known as al-Fashir (meaning in Arabic the open space in front of a royal palace). Muslim settlers were attracted from other lands, and not only from the Funj kingdom and Egypt, but also from Bagirmi, Bornu and other states to the west. Pilgrims from the western Sudan, known collectively as Takrana, or people of Takrur, stopped for long periods on their way to and from Mecca. Some settled there permanently to cater for those who passed through. Clerics from many countries were attracted to these outlying Muslim lands. Islam became much more widely accepted than previously among the general population, but in particular it became associated, as in Funj, with an emerging middle class of merchants, jurists and official administrators.

The ancient commercial links between Darfur and Egypt were greatly strengthened at this time, from which the sultan himself was the prime beneficiary. The Scottish traveller W. G. Browne, who visited Darfur between 1793 and 1796, wrote: 'The king is the chief merchant in the country, and not only despatches with every caravan to Egypt a great quantity of his own merchandise, but also employs his own slaves and dependants to trade with the goods of Egypt on his own account, in the countries adjacent to the Sudan.'[5] By this time the sultans had come to depend very largely on their slave troops, known as *kurkwa* or spearmen. This tended to isolate them from the traditional leadership groups based on ties of clan and lineage. While giving the royal administration a measure of independence, it went hand in hand with the growth of powerful chieftainships which were bound to the sultan by economic rewards rather than the loyalty of family connections.

Wadai, similarly, expanded its trading connections, especially to the west, with Bornu and with the great emporium of Kano. In the years just before and after 1800 the resourceful Sultan Sabun of Wadai helped members of the Sanusi brotherhood to forge a new and independent trans-Saharan trade route passing through Ennedi and the Kufra oasis to Benghazi on the coast of Cyrenaica, which by the nineteenth century was the most prosperous of all the desert links. Enterprising traders from the Nile valley, known as Jallaba, simultaneously spread into Darfur and Wadai, attracted by the rich trade in ivory and slaves from the indeterminate southern border-

[5] W. G. Browne, *Travels in Africa, Egypt and Syria from the Year 1792 to 1798* (London, 1799), vol. V, p. 109.

lands of both sultanates. Jallaba later became associated primarily with the slave trade, but also acted more generally as the middlemen and financiers of long-distance trade.

To the south of Jabal Marra and beyond the wide valley of the Bahr al-Arab, in the broken, hilly country of the Nile–Congo watershed, lay the region known as Dar Fertit, inhabited by Kreish and other peoples speaking the eastern group of Central Sudanic languages. According to Browne, the peoples of Dar Fertit had within the period of living memory enjoyed both political independence and material prosperity. Their country was well watered and rich in iron and copper ores. There were excellent blacksmiths producing tools and weapons of the highest quality. Copper from the many small mines of Hofrat en-Nahas, near the headwaters of the Bahr al-Arab, was cast into ingots and exported through Darfur and Wadai, where it doubtless played an important part in the process of political centralisation and the enhancement of royal authority. Copper from Hofrat en-Nahas also found its way to the great market at Kano. By the time of Browne's visit, however, the people of Dar Fertit had been reduced into vassalage and were forced to pay tribute, mainly in slaves. The Darfur sultan sent out annual tribute-collecting expeditions, called *salati*, which were in effect slave-raids. Meanwhile, the Jallaba traders, operating their own salati under licence from the sultan, ranged even further afield than the royal expeditions, especially over the vast swampy plains of the Bahr al-Ghazal, which supported great herds of elephants.

As we shall see (below, pp. 155–6), Dar Fertit was not the only country of the southern borderlands of Islam to have undergone profound changes by 1800. The southern frontiers of Wadai between the river systems of the Shari and the Ubangi-Congo, inhabited by speakers of languages belonging to the Ubangian group of the Sudanic family, were known to the Arabic-speakers as Dar Runga and Dar Banda. Here, in the late eighteenth century, the trade in slaves and ivory operating from Wadai collided with that working up the Congo river system from the European trading stations on the Atlantic coast. Thus, it is no exaggeration to say that all the many peoples, from the inland basin of the Logone-Shari to the equatorial White Nile, were caught up in a pincer movement of largely destructive trading activities from the north and the southwest. By the late nineteenth century, many of these borderlands had become practically uninhabited, the survivors from a century or more of slave-raiding having retreated south-eastwards, into the comparative safety of the equatorial forest.

8   The north-eastern triangle

In north-eastern Africa two great cultures, one Christian and the other Muslim, had by the middle of the thirteenth century long been expanding their influence over the Semitic- and Cushitic-speaking peoples of the region. The Christian element, planted from Egypt and Syria between the fourth century and the sixth, had its base in the central highland area extending from Tigre in the north through Wag and Lasta to Shoa in the south. It was an area of high plateaux with rich, volcanic soils, which supported a dense and steadily growing population of mountain farmers, who cultivated a whole variety of cereal crops, using ploughs and keeping cattle, horses, mules and donkeys. The Christian clergy were almost entirely monastic, following Monophysite (Coptic) doctrines about the person of Christ, but using the canonical books of the Old and New Testaments, translated from Greek into Geʿez, the old Ethio-Semitic language of the northern highlands, which still remains the liturgical language of the Ethiopian Orthodox Church. Despite its monastic base, or perhaps because of it, Ethiopian Christianity was capable of inspiring large numbers of ordinary lay people to lead lives of great piety. Although few kept the marriage laws, many prayed and fasted and did penance, and sent their children to be taught to take part in a liturgy of music, hymnody and sacred dance.

The Muslim element, dating from the eighth and ninth centuries, was based in the coastlands of the Red Sea and the Indian Ocean, where the only closely settled communities were those of the seaport towns, around which fishermen, seafarers and merchants practised some vegeculture to support their other activities. It was among them that Islam had first spread from their trading partners on the Arabian side of the Red Sea. The arid lowlands behind the coast were sparsely inhabited by camel pastoralists, who lived from the milk and meat of their beasts, but also used them to transport their only other source of wealth, which was the salt from the pans formed in the little lake-filled depressions in the desert behind the coast. The salt of the lowlands was the most essential commodity traded to the highland farmers, and the camel nomads thus became the human intermediaries linking the coast and the interior. Like their counterparts in the Arabian and Saharan deserts, they assimilated Islam more easily than

Christianity and became the means of its spread to the southern parts of the region which were not yet Christian.

The southern populations belonged to two main groups, divided geographically by the Rift Valley. To the east of it, the mountains of Bali and Sidamo were the homeland of the Oromo, who spoke an Eastern Cushitic language akin to that of the Somali. Basically they were mountain farmers who cultivated cereal crops on the highland plateau, but they also kept large herds of cattle, which were pastured by their young men and boys in the grasslands of the Rift. Like other pastoralists, as their herds increased, they became land-hungry and warlike, and their northern neighbours on the Shoan plateau had to develop a system of frontier garrisons to contain them. In the sixteenth and seventeenth centuries, when these defences broke down, the Oromo pastoralists were to spread out over the grasslands of the upper Awash valley and up the eastern flank of the Shoan plateau, until they became the most widely distributed of all the ethnic groups in the region.

Meanwhile, in the wetter and more forested country to the west of the Rift, there lived a diverse group of Sidama peoples, speaking Omotic languages and practising some ancient and interesting forms of vegeculture alongside the keeping of stall-fed cattle, the hunting of wild animals for their skins and tusks, and the breeding of civet cats for their musk. It was to this part of the region that the caravan traders of the Muslim coastlands directed their efforts. Sidama communities were prone to raid each other for slaves, and Sidama women were famed for their beauty in Arabia and throughout the Middle East, as were Sidama boys castrated as eunuchs especially for the export trade. The great merchants settled their agents at collecting points along the northern edges of Sidama country, and these took wives from the local ruling families and soon sent for Muslim clerics to teach their children. Thus, by the thirteenth century there had emerged a chain of petty sultanates running all the way from Zeila on the Red Sea coast, up the line of the Awash valley to the eastern corner of the Shoan plateau in Ifat, and so on through Dawaro to Hadya and Fatagar, thus encircling the southern marches of the Christian kingdom expanding from the north. To the Arab historian al-Maqrizi, writing in the early fifteenth century, this was the southern 'fringe' of Islam.

THE SOLOMONID ASCENDANCY

The southward shift in the centre of power of the Christian kingdom from its original base at Aksum in Tigre to the heartland of the modern Ethiopia on the Shoan plateau some 900 miles further south is to be seen primarily not as a migration of people, but as a slow process of colonisation, assimilation and nation-building. In its heyday, from the second until the seventh century, Aksum had flourished by controlling a web of trade routes along which the produce of the interior – including gold, ivory and slaves – was conveyed to the Red Sea port of Adulis on the bay of Massawa, to be fed into the intercontinental shipping lanes linking southern Europe and southern Asia. When the trade of the Red Sea was disrupted by the Arab conquests of the seventh century, Aksum lost most of its strategic significance. But there is also evidence that by this time the local environment was suffering from overexploitation by an urban population which it could no longer support. Soils were becoming eroded. Tree cover had been felled for fuel. As we know from the inscriptions left by Aksumite kings, much of the local produce was obtained in the form of tribute from subordinate rulers. This required constant enforcement by the royal armies, which could no longer be fed or fuelled in the neighbourhood of Aksum. In these circumstances the imperial system soon disintegrated. Aksum became the victim of its former tributaries, above all from the Cushitic-speaking Agau kingdom of Damot, which overran and sacked what remained of the capital city in the tenth century. The Church, by now based upon a growing network of rural monasteries and nunneries with little to pillage but their books, survived the crisis, but the royal dynasty, which had already fled from the old capital, shrank into insignificance.

Somewhere around the middle of the twelfth century a new centre of Christian power emerged in the province of Lasta, some 450 miles to the south of Aksum. The new Zagwe rulers did not even speak the same Semitic language as their Aksumite predecessors. They were Christianised Agau, in origin probably local warlords, whose legitimacy depended solely upon their recognition by the authorities of the national Church. They were, at all events, devout Christians, who established their capital beside the monastic centre at Roha, where they set their war captives to the excavation of the subterranean, rock-hewn churches which made it a place of pilgrimage for the whole surrounding region. The greatest of the Zagwe kings was Lalibela, who ruled during the first quarter of the thirteenth century and gave his name to the completed complex, where people have ever since come in their thousands to celebrate the great festivals of the Church, camping out on the mountainside within sound of the
liturgical drumming and chanting rising from the churches below

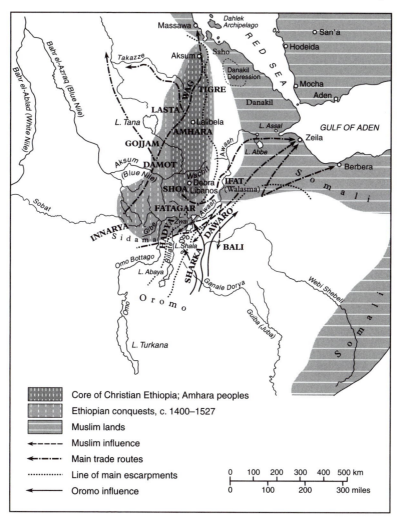

12 The Horn of Africa in the age of the Solomonids

ground level. During the period of Zagwe rule Christianity spread from new monastic centres both westwards into the Agau country north of Lake Tana and southwards among the Semitic-speaking Amhara of the Shoan plateau.

It was from the Amhara that there emerged the third imperial dynasty of Christian Ethiopia, known to historians as the Solomonids, from their claim to descend from the former Aksumite kings, and through them from the mythical union between the biblical King 117

Solomon of Judea and the Queen of Sheba who came to visit him from the land of Ophir and bore him a son, Menelik, who later stole the Ark of the Covenant from his father and carried it away to Ethiopia. It was an old story, concocted many centuries earlier in Arabic versions, and probably designed to explain the puzzling survival of many Jewish practices in Ethiopian Christianity. Now, it was revived and elaborated in Ge'ez translation by the monastic supporters of what was probably in origin no more than an ambitious family of frontier warlords, who were presenting themselves as a Semitic-speaking alternative to the Cushitic-speaking Zagwe. It was a claim well calculated to appeal to the ecclesiastics of Aksum and the northern monasteries who would need to co-operate in a lawful coronation. And so, in 1270, Yekunno Amlak, having defeated and killed the last of the Zagwe, was crowned *negus negasti*, 'king of kings'.

The advent of the new dynasty inaugurated a period of 250 years during which the Christian kingdom dominated the whole surrounding region and reached its pinnacle of prestige and power. The Solomonids soon abandoned the fixed capital of their Zagwe predecessors and lived as military leaders in vast, tented camps pitched for a part of each year near the scene of the season's campaigning or for as long as the local food supplies lasted. As Amharic-speakers from the southern marches of the old kingdom, their first concern was to extend and consolidate this southerly base. Their early aims were thus primarily territorial, to make room for the further settlement of Christian Amhara on the western side of the Shoan plateau and in the adjoining highlands of Gojjam situated within the great bend of the Blue Nile. Their early campaigns were directed westwards, against those Agau-speaking people who had not been incorporated into the Zagwe kingdom. These were largely assimilated into Amharic Christian culture by a combination of expropriation, deportation, resettlement by Amhara colonists and evangelisation by clergy trained at the monastic schools of the islands of Lake Hayq and at Debra Libanos near the Gojjam frontier.

With armies strengthened by contingents from the conquered territories, the second Solomonid emperor, Amda Siyon (1314–44), shifted the main direction of expansion to the east and the south. Henceforth, the emphasis was less on settlement and assimilation and more on economic and political control. In pre-Solomonid times the main caravan routes to the outside world had been the northern ones descending the Eritrean escarpment to the Red Sea or else down the valley of the Atbara to Nubia and Egypt. But from Shoa the shortest access to the sea was down the valley of the Awash to Zeila, which was controlled at its steepest and narrowest section by the long-established Walasma dynasty of Ifat. It was inevitable that a Christian kingdom growing in strength on the Shoan plateau would attempt to lay hands on this route. At the very beginning of his reign, then, Amda Siyon passed on from destroying the last remnants of the Agau kingdom of Damot to the conquest of Hadya, the nearest of the Sidama sultanates to his own southern borders and that most famed for its trade in slaves. Soon, however, he was picking quarrels with Ifat for interfering with his coastbound caravans. Finally, in a great campaign in 1332, his armies invaded Ifat and swept through Dawaro, Bali and Sharka, the provinces situated at the head of the Rift Valley. Basically, these conquests were to endure for two centuries. Hadya, like the Agau provinces, was fully annexed and was to become a major centre of Christian evangelisation. But the other Sidama states continued to be ruled by their own dynasties, paying tribute which had to be enforced by periodic military expeditions.

The most sustained resistance, however, came from Ifat, where Islamisation had gone furthest, and where, because of its strategic position on the trade route, Christian influence was greatest. Throughout the fourteenth century the Solomonid kings employed the classic tactics of the powerful neighbour, by inviting Walasma princes to their court and supporting in the periodic succession struggles those candidates who promised political loyalty and Christian conversion. The result was to split the dynasty, one party ruling a puppet state in old Ifat, the other retreating south-eastwards with the hardcore of the Muslim community to the Chercher mountains and the Harar plateau beyond. There they set up the sultanate of Adal, which in time unified most of the Muslim groups in the region of the Horn. In particular, the rulers of Adal developed a system of alliances with the warlike Somali nomads of the Haud plains, which provided the new state with military muscle. Aided by these Somali war-bands, the Walasma princes conducted fierce raids upon the Rift Valley tributaries of the Christian emperors. Only for one brief moment was the Christian kingdom able to excise this thorn from its eastern flank. This was in 1403, when King Dawit led a series of military expeditions up into the Harar plateau, and then pursued the fleeing Walasma ruler all the way to Zeila, where he was at last captured and killed. The rest of the Walasma family retreated to the Yemen, only to return some twenty years later to rebuild their African fortunes with the help of Arab soldiers supplied by the king of Yemen. There, they reoccupied the mountain fastness from which they had been driven and from which, a century later, they would break out and overrun the Christian kingdom.

THE HALCYON YEARS OF THE CHRISTIAN EMPIRE

During the whole course of the fifteenth century the empire of the Solomonids enjoyed long periods of stable government, of economic prosperity, and of religious and cultural activity unparalleled in any part of Africa south of the Sahara. Dawit was succeeded by able and energetic emperors, of whom the most outstanding was Zara Ya'qob, who ruled for thirty-four years (1434–68). In particular, Zara Ya'qob was praised by the royal chroniclers for his personal piety and his ardent support for the Ethiopian Church. Even the weaker rulers who followed him, up until the reign of Lebna Dengel (1508–40), managed to hold their vast domains more or less intact. Towards the end of this period, the country was visited and described by a number of European travellers, notably by the Portuguese embassy of 1520–6. As a result, we can supplement the chronicles of the Solomonid court, with their inevitable concentration on military and diplomatic affairs, with the observations of literate outsiders which offer at least some picture of the economic and social life of the country as a whole.

To these men from Western Christendom medieval Ethiopia seemed strikingly lacking in the close-built towns of Europe and the Middle East. Only Aksum, the ancient capital in the far north, still used by the Solomonid kings for their coronation rituals, was a town in this sense, although a little later Harar, which in 1520 became the capital of the sultanate of Adal, more than rivalled Aksum in size. On the other hand, the Ethiopian countryside, extending for around 1000 miles from north to south, along the line of the central highland massif, struck them as unusually populous and well husbanded. The rich volcanic lands were tilled with ox-drawn ploughs to yield harvests of wheat, barley and millet. Herds of cattle and sheep grazed the mountain pastures. Horses, donkeys and mules carried produce to weekly markets, where cotton and coffee, beeswax and honey were exchanged for the salt carried up on camel-back from the Danakil desert.

Even to Portuguese visitors, whose own society was barely emerging from feudalism, it was obvious that Christian Ethiopia was a land where every man had a master. Francisco Alvarez, the chaplain of the embassy of 1520, commented that there would have been 'much more fruit and tillage if the great men did not ill-treat the people'.[1] In fact, most peasant farmers were near to serfs, bound to the land and compelled to yield at least one-third of their crops, together with many other services, to the feu-holder, who might be the king or a chief, a monastery, a regiment or an individual knight or soldier. More still of the peasant's production was taken for the tribute which flowed from every province to the royal court. From Shoa and the southern provinces much of the tribute was delivered in kind – in food and drink, mules and cattle, honey and wax. Some provinces had access to gold or ivory, which could be accumulated in the royal treasure chests. But much of the external trade of the northern provinces must have arisen from the need to convert country produce into portable wealth for delivery as tribute to the distant capital. Some of the agricultural surplus of the highlands was no doubt carried down the escarpment to the coast and sold as provisions for the Red Sea shipping and food for the pilgrims to Mecca. Thus the lords of Eritrea and Tigre were able to pay their tribute in Arabian horses and Indian silks and cottons, in swords and coats of mail from Syria and Turkey, and in gold, some of which may have come from as far away as West Africa. Yet the inequalities observed by Alvarez have to be balanced by the high ideal of Ethiopian society, expressed in the notion of the *tellek saw*, the man born to greatness, who had to prove himself to the populace by deeds of valour or of kindness, and who was, at least in theory, democratically accountable and electable. It was almost a society open to the talents, aspiring and therefore dynamic.

Treasure and luxuries apart, the royal encampment, with its officials and ecclesiastics, its nobles and their retinues, its military commanders and their troops, its artisans and armourers, its cooks and grooms and herdsmen, represented a huge agglomeration of people, which quickly drained the resources of the surrounding country. At its centre were pitched 5000–6000 tents for the king and the nobility, and the attendant population probably numbered ten times as many. The Ethiopians told Alvarez that they were unable to understand how Europeans could live in permanent cities, seeing that their own capital had to move every three or four months in order to solve the problems of supply, and that an area once occupied in this way could not be revisited for at least ten years. The same pattern was repeated on a smaller scale at the courts of provincial governors and local grandees. When the royal court moved from one site to another, Alvarez described the scene thus:

---

[1] C. F. Beckingham and G. W. B. Huntingford (eds.), *The Prester John of the Indies* (Cambridge, for the Hakluyt Soc., 1961), vol. II, p. 515.

The tenth part of them may be well-dressed people, and the nine parts common people, both men and women, young people and poor, some of them clothed in skins, others in poor stuffs, and all of these common people carry with them their property, which consists of pots for making wine and porringers for drinking. If they move short distances, these poor people carry their wood with them, which are some poles. The rich bring very good tents. I do not speak of the great lords and gentlemen, because each of these moves a city or a good town of tents, and loads and mule-teers, a matter without number or reckoning. The court cannot move with less than fifty thousand mules, and from that upwards the number may reach a hundred thousand.[2]

At the centre of all this activity, his great white tents shielded from the public gaze by a double enclosure of high curtains, there lived and worked the Christian king. He was surrounded by many of the trappings and ceremonies of other African monarchs. The greatest in the land appeared before him bared to the waist, and he inter-viewed them from behind a gauze curtain, communicating always through an intermediary. Individuals were promoted or destituted at a nod. Even the most religious kings kept at least three official queens, and the complex network of royal kinship was a vital factor in the affairs of state.

There were important ways in which the long-established Christian culture of the country gave the Ethiopian kingdom a very different world view from those of its Muslim or partly Muslim neighbours. The world of Islam was all around, and national security no less than trade demanded a wide knowledge of its strengths and weaknesses, its doctrinal divisions and its political rivalries. The *abuna*, the bishop of the Ethiopian Church, was always an Egyptian Copt, and this fact in itself demanded a working relationship with the Muslim rulers of Egypt. But the king's subjects also went on pilgrimage to Jerusalem, where they met with European Christian pilgrims and sometimes accompanied them to their home countries. In this way numbers of Ethiopians became scattered over the northern Mediterranean lands. In time, some returned home carrying letters from European courts, or even with European ecclesiastics or artificers in their train. When the Portuguese embassy arrived in 1520, they found a Florentine painter, Brancaleone, who was on friendly terms with the king, and there was no difficulty at all in finding an interpreter fluent in Latin, so that Alvarez could be subjected to minute investigation on matters of doctrine and liturgy by Negus Lebna Dengel himself.

[2] *Ibid.*, vol. I, pp. 320–1.

This concern with religious matters reflected the intense hold of Coptic Christianity upon the core populations of the kngdom. No more than their rulers did most Ethiopians find it easy to observe Christian marriage laws, with the result that full communicant membership was largely confined to the very young, the very old and the very sick. Nevertheless, there was a steadily growing recruitment to the monastic life among both men and women, accompanied during the fourteenth and fifteenth centuries by a notable revival of biblical studies, as distinct from the mere copying of biblical texts, and by the emergence of a religious literature written in Amharic rather than Geʿez. In this revival the Old Testament found especial favour and helped to give religious education a nationalist slant. Ethiopians identified themselves with the people of Israel, observing the Sabbath as well as Sunday and adopting the Jewish dietary laws. The children of the royal house and those of the great nobles shared in this education, and at least one of the great kings of the fifteenth century, Zara Yaʿqob, lent the whole weight of his office to the reorganisation and consolidation of the national church. Divergent monastic traditions were reconciled, if need be by force. The monasteries were given tribute-bearing lands for their support and territorial spheres in which to exercise their influence. The king's soldiers accompanied the abbots on their visitations, and all Christians were enjoined to carry signs of their faith on their persons, on their dress and even on their ploughs. Churches, consisting of large thatched rondavels, each inside a circular fence, were supposedly built within the reach of all Christian communities, and attendance at Saturday and Sunday worship was made compulsory. While it may be that Zara Yaʿqob in his zeal was far in advance of the mass of his subjects, it is evident that Alvarez and his Portuguese companions felt themselves to be travelling in a deeply Christian country.

THE LEFT-HANDED CONQUEROR: IMAM AHMAD AND THE HUMBLING OF CHRISTIAN ETHIOPIA

The fall of Christian Ethiopia from the position of strength and security which it had built up over two and a half centuries at the heart of the North-East African region was extraordinarily sudden and swift. No doubt with the eye of history it is possible to see that the collapse was at least in part the result of a process of decline which had set in with the death of Zara Yaʿqob sixty years before, with the growth of factions at the royal court, with the repeated election of kings who were minors, and with the mounting power of the 123

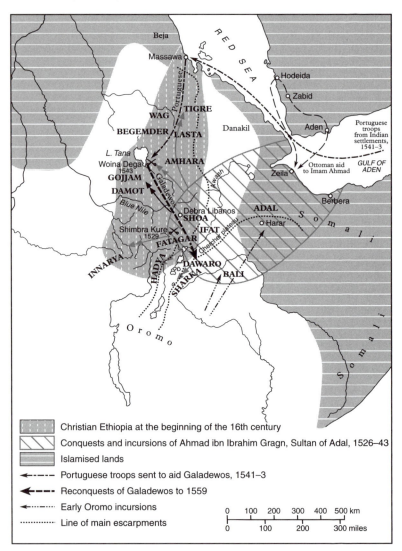

13 The Muslim counter-offensive in the Horn

provincial nobility over against the royal officials. In practice, however, the system had not been severely tested, and therefore it had endured. Following a number of defeats on the Adali frontier during the reigns of his two predecessors, Negus Lebna Dengel had in 1516 won an important victory over Imam Mahfuz, the military commander of the sultanate of Adal. Hence, from 1520 till 1526, he dallied with the Portuguese embassy like a man who had no need of an ally from the Christian West. Yet only a few years later he was to suffer a crushing defeat at the hands of a young Adali general, Ahmad ibn Ibrahim, who was to spend the next fourteen years laying waste the Christian kingdom from Bali in the south to Tigre in the north, from Gojjam in the west to the Awash gorges in the east.

Ahmad, nicknamed *gragn*, the left-handed, by his opponents and given the honorific title *al-Ghazi*, the conqueror, by his fellow Muslims, was one of those rare individuals who combined at an early age the talents of a soldier and a statesman. Born in one of the minor emirates bordering on Ifat and Adal, he came to the fore as a cavalry knight on the Christian frontier and in the faction-fighting between the various allies of the Walasma dynasty which made up the internal politics of Adal. While still in his teens he assumed the leadership of a group which overpowered the ruling sultan and reduced him to a figurehead in his capital city of Harar. The real rule passed to Ahmad, who assumed the title of imam and built up an effective alliance of Danakil and Somali clans from the coastal lowlands, with jihad against Christian Ethiopia as the uniting theme. The nomads were spurred on by the expectation of booty, above all in cattle and slaves, and in his opening campaigns Ahmad led these fierce horsemen to the lush pastures of Dawaro at the head of the Rift Valley escarpment, and on westwards to Fatagar in the broad valley of the upper Awash. A counter-expedition led by Lebna Dengel's governor in Bali was crushed and all its members enslaved. Then, in 1529, at Shimbra-Kure in Fatagar, Imam Ahmad faced the assembled might of the Christian heartlands. Despite the arrival of armies summoned even from the far northern provinces to confront him, he won a decisive victory. All the southern provinces of the Christian empire were now in his hands, and he devoted a year to dismantling their defences, mopping up their garrisons and replacing their Christian rulers with Muslims.

For any previous sultan of Adal this would have been more than enough. But Imam Ahmad was intent upon the complete destruction of the Christian state. In 1531 he was back in Shoa, with plans to take over and administer every province in the kingdom. When Lebna Dengel retreated westwards into Gojjam, the Imam followed him as far as the Blue Nile gorges, where he burnt the celebrated monastery of Debra Libanos. His biographer described the monks hurling themselves into the flames like moths into a lamp. Then, turning north-eastwards, he circumvented the high redoubts of the central watershed by passing through the coastal lowlands into

Tigre, and so westwards again to Begemder, Lake Tana and northern Gojjam. Thus, by 1535 Imam Ahmad had encircled the northern heartlands of the Christian kingdom. All along his terrible path Christian governors had been replaced by Muslims. Even the cliff-top prison on Mount Gishen, where the royal princes eligible to succeed to the throne were confined to keep them out of political mischief, had been emptied of its inmates. But the main thrust of the destruction in the Imam's holy war was naturally against the structures of the rival religion. Countless numbers of the Christian clergy were put to death. The ancient cathedral of Aksum was pillaged of its treasure. The island monastery of Gelila in Lake Tana and several other leading monasteries were burned to ashes, and their illuminated manuscripts and pictures destroyed. Even the rock-carved churches of Lalibela and those of central Tigre were attacked and their wall-paintings disfigured.[3]

For several years during the mid-1530s Imam Ahmad consolidated his power over the Christian highlands. Nevertheless, not everything went well for him. With the flow of booty diminishing, his nomad followers, Somali and others, drifted home to their warmer plains, leaving him to govern his conquests with the aid of renegade Christians of dubious loyalty. In the highlands the end of open opposition marked the beginnings of covert guerrilla resistance. The emperor remained at large, and refused Ahmad's overtures for a peaceful settlement. When Lebna Dengel died in 1540, he was succeeded by an able warrior prince in Galadewos (1540–59), who was free from the stigma of his predecessor's defeats. In 1541 the Portuguese from their eastern capital at Goa at last responded to Christian appeals by landing a small force of matchlockmen at Massawa, whose firearms put courage into the Christians of Tigre. The Ottoman governor of Zabid in the Yemen countered by sending a parallel force of Turkish troops equipped with firearms and light cannon. Thus, the global contest between the Ottoman sultans and the monarchs of western Christendom spilled over into the north-eastern triangle of Africa. The Portuguese suffered heavy losses, but when, in 1543, they at last joined forces with those of Galadewos, they met the Muslim armies in battle at Woina Dega near Lake Tana. In the course of a desperately fought battle on 22 February the Muslims were defeated and the great Imam killed. It was the end of the Adali occupation of the highlands, but the fourteen years of jihad had left a Christian kingdom demoralised and in ruins, which would

[3] Taddesse Tamrat, in *CHA* III, p. 175.

not until the late nineteenth century recover either its medieval territory or its political and cultural ascendancy.

THE PRIMACY OF THE PASTORALISTS: OROMO MIGRATIONS AND SETTLEMENT

The long-term result of Imam Ahmad's occupation of the Christian kingdom was that it fatally undermined the whole system of frontier defences against the nomadic, pastoral peoples by whom Ethiopia was almost surrounded. These defences had consisted of standing militia, of which each unit was supported by the dues and services arising from a particular area of land. Most of the regimental lands were situated near the frontiers, and the majority of them near the eastern escarpment, where lowland pastoralists constantly attempted to raid the crops and cattle of the highland peasantry, and where in the absence of military resistance raiding was always liable to develop into conquest and settlement. In the far north the pastoral neighbours were Beja and Arabs. In the Red Sea plains from Massawa to Zeila they were Danakil. To the east of the Rift Valley provinces they were Somali, with the Oromo to the south of them. In the event, it was the Oromo who broke in.

To the peasant Oromo who had remained in their old homelands in the mountains of Bali, the jihad was as much of a disaster as it was to other settled populations in the central highlands. But their pastoral offshoots had been able to move southwards with their herds to avoid the fighting. There, both they and their cattle multiplied, causing them to divide into two segments, the Borana and the Barentu. The land becoming too confined to hold them, they dispersed, the Barentu moving towards the eastern part of the region, that is, into areas that were mainly Muslim. The Borana expanded both northwards and southwards along the line of the Rift. Those who went south crossed the dry savanna of what is today northern Kenya and thence descended the valley of the Tana river, reaching the Indian Ocean coast early in the seventeenth century, displacing some of the North-Eastern Bantu-speaking peoples as they did so.

The northward movement of the Borana Oromo was chronicled in some detail by an Ethiopian monk in the late sixteenth century, and from his account it is clear that there was nothing cataclysmic about their expansion. They became aware of a power vacuum on their northern frontier and gradually they filled it by driving their cattle some tens of miles further up the Rift Valley than they had ventured before. It was an encroachment rather than an invasion, for

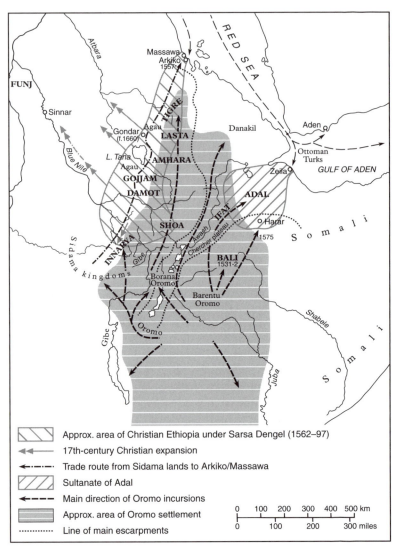

14 The impact of the Oromo in North-East Africa

they lacked any central organisation. It was the members of the
warrior age-group (*gada*) of the day who pushed the cattle camps
northwards, operating in bands of a few thousand at most. They
were armed with spears and at this stage had no horses. Even a vesti-
gial relic of the former imperial garrison could have stopped them in
their tracks. Such was the state of insecurity around the frontier as a

whole, however, that the Oromo were able to drive in their wedge. They began their penetration in the southernmost province of Bali, and they did it around 1531–2, at the precise moment when the imperial garrisons had been wiped out by Imam Ahmad, and when Ahmad himself had moved on to the conquest of Shoa.

After his eventual victory over Imam Ahmad in 1543, Negus Galadewos was still very much preoccupied with the sultanate of Adal and its Somali allies, who, although they had evacuated the central highlands, had not abandoned their attempt to occupy Dawaro, the province at the head of the Rift Valley. This area was the scene of severe fighting for many years. In 1559 Imam Ahmad's successor, Amir Nur, attempted to revive the jihad, and a large Muslim army from Harar advanced towards the Christian highlands. Galadewos assembled an army to withstand this invasion, but was defeated and killed in another battle in Fatagar province, on the Shoan side of the Awash. His death marked, according to a modern historian of the Oromo, a turning-point in the history of the region.[4] The new emperor, Sarsa Dengel (1563–96), withdrew to the west of the Blue Nile, where a permanent capital was built, thus in effect abandoning the central provinces of the old kingdom to defend themselves as best they could. Meanwhile, sections of the Barentu Oromo were overrunning Adal, causing Amir Nur to withdraw in order to defend his own home territory around Harar. The spread of the Barentu over most of the old sultanate of Adal virtually brought to an end Muslim political activity in the Horn of Africa until the nineteenth century. Immediately, however, it enabled Borana groups to push northwards up the eastern margins of the Shoan plateau and to occupy parts of Angot, Amhara and Begemder. By the end of Sarsa Dengel's reign more than one-third of the old Christian kingdom had been occupied by them.

From the end of the sixteenth century on, the Oromo had become too numerous and too widely spread to be stopped. Put in the simplest way, what they achieved during the century that followed was to occupy most of the land between 3000 and 5000 feet above sea level. In terms of rainfall and vegetation, these were the intermediate lands, too dry to be reliable for settled agriculture, but admirable for transhumant pastoralism combined with a little wet-season farming. Geographically, they were disposed in the form of a cross dividing the three main mountain massifs of the region. The main axis was

---

[4] Mohammed Hassen, *The Oromo of Ethiopia, a History 1570–1860* (Cambridge, 1990), p. 25.

formed by the Rift Valley in the south and the foothills of the great eastern escarpment in the north. The crosspiece consisted of the Chercher highlands to the east and the broad plain of the Awash and Gibe watershed in the west. Many of these areas were only lightly populated before the coming of the Oromo, and the most lethal fighting practised by them was probably against fellow pastoralists such as the Somali and the Danakil. Elsewhere, the settlement of the Oromo often contributed a new and complementary feature to the economy. It was an infiltration comparable to that of the pastoral Fulbe among the sedentary farmers of the western Sudan, with the same liability to sudden bursts of violence, especially from the most recent arrivals.

Still, even if the Oromo incursions were less terrible than they used to be painted by historians looking at events mainly from the Amharan viewpoint, there is no denying the problems which they posed to the rulers of the Christian kingdom, whose southern provinces were now lost beyond any hope of recovery, and whose eastern frontier, from Tigre south to Shoa, was soon to be thrown into a state of the utmost chaos. Sarsa Dengel was probably the last emperor to have any chance of restoring stability even within greatly reduced frontiers, and his policies have been increasingly questioned by historians. Certainly he devoted much effort to rebuilding a central army to counterbalance the local loyalties of the feudal militias. But the direction in which he employed his forces was not that most directly threatened by the Oromo. Instead, writing off the southern trade route to Zeila, he concentrated on reopening the older routes leading down to the Sidama country from the north. His main campaigns were fought in the Agau-speaking region around Lake Tana, and further south in Gojjam, Damot and Innarya. These gave him a full treasury, especially from the trade in Sidama slaves, of whom some 10,000 were sold each year to the Ottomans, based since 1557 at Arkiko on the Red Sea coast and soon to seize Massawa and Zeila. But he left his south-eastern frontier unguarded, for the Oromo to penetrate in ever greater numbers. In the withering judgment of Merid Aregay, 'Sarsa Dengel contributed to the dismantling of the system of defences by using the soldiers to ravage peaceful provinces, thereby clearing the way for the [Oromo] to enter.'[5] Once settled in the lush countryside of the Gibe valley, many of the Oromo reverted from pastoralism to sedentary farming.

[5] 'Southern Ethiopia and the Christian Kingdom 1508–1708', unpublished Ph.D. thesis, University of London, 1971, p. 230.

This transformation reached its climax in the early nineteenth century, when five Oromo kingdoms emerged in the Gibe valley in place of the former Sidama polities.

THE SEVENTEENTH AND EIGHTEENTH CENTURIES

The emperors of the seventeenth and eighteenth centuries had narrower options than had Sarsa Dengel and his predecessors. Susenyos (1607–32) set a new pattern by incorporating Oromo groups from the eastern frontier as units of his imperial militia (*chewa*), enjoying the right to receive tribute and services from the local Tigrean and Amhara peasantry. In one sense, this amounted to legitimising the occupation of lands which Oromo groups had already seized. In another sense, however, it gave the longer-settled Oromo an interest in resisting further incursions by newcomers. It was an age-old expedient of empires facing barbarian pressure on their frontiers. It meant that some of the Oromo became 'amharicised' and Christian, but at the cost of no one any longer knowing quite what he should be defending.

Faced with the alienation of large territories to the east and south, and with perennial disturbances even in the heartlands of the old empire, in Shoa, Lasta, Angot and Tigre, it was natural that the seventeenth-century emperors should concentrate their attention increasingly on the west and the north. This was not historically Christian territory. Its people were Cushitic-speaking Agau. Before the sixteenth century the Christian empire had largely passed them by, with only an occasional nibble at their eastern fringes. These were the areas regularly raided by Sarsa Dengel, and where Susenyos and then Fasiladas (1632–67) built their capital cities at Dunqaz, Enfraz and finally Gondar. Here, the Christian kings became increasingly divorced from their former Amharic nobility and clergy, their households served by Agau slaves and protected by Oromo mercenaries. It was in these circumstances that Susenyos began to cultivate the friendship of the Portuguese Jesuit missionaries, who had been present in the country since 1557 and who probably led the king to believe that he could best re-establish his authority with the help of the Christian West. Susenyos announced his own conversion to the Roman Catholic Church in 1612. Ten years later, on the advice of an overzealous Portuguese bishop, he made it the official religion of his kingdom. The great majority of his people were opposed, and revolt followed revolt. For ten more years Susenyos succeeded in crushing these, but finally in 1632, while riding with his son and heir Fasiladas across one such battlefield in which his troops had inflicted heavy casualties on the dissenters, Fasiladas reportedly pointed to the bodies of the slain, saying to his father 'These were once your loyal subjects.' At this, the emperor, whose confidence had been failing for some time already, broke down and abdicated in favour of his son. Fasiladas on his accession restored the traditional Monophysite faith and deported the Jesuit missionaries, who lived on in Ethiopian legend as 'the wolves from the west'.[6]

The Oromo by this time were sated in their territorial ambitions and the momentum of their expansion had run down. They were still seen at their most characteristic within the cruciform area best suited to their pastoral life. Within that area their own culture remained dominant. Beyond it, Oromo groups were in military control of wide territories where they imposed themselves as overlords, but where their own culture tended to succumb to that of their subjects. The Christian kingdom was by now confined almost to the north-western quadrant of the region, where Oromo occupied a privileged status as feudal militias, although at the price of some cultural assimilation. In the north-eastern quadrant the Oromo had acquired a similar standing in relation to the Muslim population living around Harar. In the south-eastern quadrant, which included their ancient homeland in the mountains of Bali, the Oromo continued to be most themselves, observing their traditional religion and the succession of age-sets within the gada system. In the south-western quadrant, Oromo ruled in most of the Sidama provinces, trading through Harar to Zeila, and through this contact becoming increasingly Muslim in religion.

Throughout this period the Christian kingdom was becoming more and more a shadow of its former self, confined within a shorter and shorter radius of Gondar. Whatever thrust remained in imperial politics was directed still further northwards in campaigns against the Funj sultanate of Sinnar in the gold-bearing region north and south of Fazogli. Its main trade routes led northwards to Massawa, now in Ottoman hands. For long periods the empire was rent by political and military anarchy, the main beneficiaries of which were the by now ubiquitous Oromo. By the middle of the eighteenth century, according to one recent account, Ethiopia had a king who was half Oromo by birth and depended on Oromo soldiers and administrators. The Oromo language even replaced Amharic as the everyday language of the court.[7] The period from 1769 until 1885 is

[6] C.f. E. Haberland in *General History* V, p. 732.   [7] M. Abir in *CHA* IV, p. 569.

known to Ethiopian historians as the *Zamana Masafent* – the time of the biblical 'Judges', to distinguish it from that of the biblical 'Kings'. It was a period when provincial autonomy became institutionalised. Only the Christian Church retained a wider ambit, maintaining its hold over the old provinces in the central highlands, which had long ceased to pay more than a nominal allegiance to the dynasty at Gondar. It was around the local Christian nobility of Tigre and Shoa that the Ethiopian empire of modern times was eventually to be reconstituted.

Meanwhile, Islam continued its slow but relentless expansion among the pastoral peoples surrounding the Christian highlands, and most significantly perhaps among the Somali living in the dry steppe country between the eastern highlands and the Indian Ocean coast. So much is this the leading theme of Somali historical tradition, with every clan seeking to identify itself with some remote ancestor who crossed the sea from Arabia, that it has often been presented as a wholesale migration of Somali from north to south. In reality, however, it has to be attributed to the peregrinations and intermarriages of an essentially nomadic population across a vast and remarkably uniform landscape, which had already witnessed the growth of an unusually large community of language and custom without any corresponding development of centralising political institutions. Islam, it would seem, was early planted in the seaport towns of the north coast, where merchants from both sides of the Aden Gulf handled the trade in livestock, slaves and the precious resins of myrrh and frankincense gathered on the sparsely forested hilltops between Berbera and Hargeisa. Somewhat later, around the ninth and tenth centuries, Muslim trading communities developed around the widely spaced harbours of the Indian Ocean coast, notably at Ras Hafun, Mogadishu, Merca, and Kismayu, where the more southerly Somali brought their produce for trade. By the thirteenth century at latest, Mogadishu was the seat of a Muslim sultanate, with a Friday mosque of stone and schools serviced by clerics and other holy men, of whom some would doubtless have accompanied their nomadic visitors into the interior. All down their western margins, the Somali bordered with the long-settled Oromo, whose cult centres in the eastern highlands were most easily approached by following the valley of the Webi Shebele river, which flowed into the Indian Ocean between Mogadishu and Kismayu. It was very likely by this route that Islam finally reached most of the Borana migrants dispersed through the Sidama lands to the west of the Rift Valley, in a movement dating to the eighteenth century. During the nineteenth century these would carry it into the borderlands of the Egyptian Sudan, thus completing the religious encirclement of the Christian centre of the region. It was a predicament which few could have thought that Christianity was likely to survive.

9 The upper Nile basin and the East African plateau

Between northern Central Africa on the west and the Ethiopian highland region to the east lay the great basin of the upper Nile. At its centre, extending for nearly 300 miles on either side of the White Nile, was the Sudd, a vast, swampy region most of which lay under water for half of every year and which set a natural limit to the southward expansion of the great kingdoms of the middle Nile – first Meroe, then the Christian kingdom of ʿAlwa, then the Muslim sultanate of the Funj. The Sudd was inhabited by Western Nilotes (sometimes called Rivers and Lakes Nilotes) speaking the closely related Dinka, Nuer and Lwo languages. Though practising some agriculture, these were primarily pastoralists and fishermen, who congregated during the wet season on the low ridges which rose above the flood waters, and during the dry season spread out with their cattle to take advantage of the floodland grazing. Beyond them to the east and the south, the drier periphery of the upper Nile basin was inhabited by another set of Nilotic-speaking peoples known as Eastern (or Highland and Plains) Nilotes, who were the easternmost of all the Sudanic-speaking peoples.

Until shortly before the start of the second millennium AD, all these Nilotic peoples seem to have lived to the north of the Imotong mountains, within the modern frontiers of the Sudan Republic or in the lowland margins of south-western Ethiopia. Northern Uganda was occupied mainly by Central Sudanic-speakers, with Bantu to the south of them. Northern and central Kenya was occupied by Cushitic-speakers, who made a deep wedge into the northern reaches of the Bantu world, separating the North-Eastern Bantu of eastern Kenya from the Interlacustrine Bantu around Lake Victoria. During the second millennium, however, there occurred a great expansion of Nilotic peoples southwards. In northern Uganda, Central Sudanic languages were reduced into a few pockets, all to the west of the White Nile. In Kenya, Cushitic languages were eliminated from the western highlands and the Rift Valley. Only in north-central Tanzania did a handful of Southern Cushitic languages survive as remnants, surrounded by Bantu languages to the west and south and by Nilotic languages to the north and east. Moreover, there is ample evidence of Nilotic cultural influences spreading far to the south of Nilotic language frontiers.

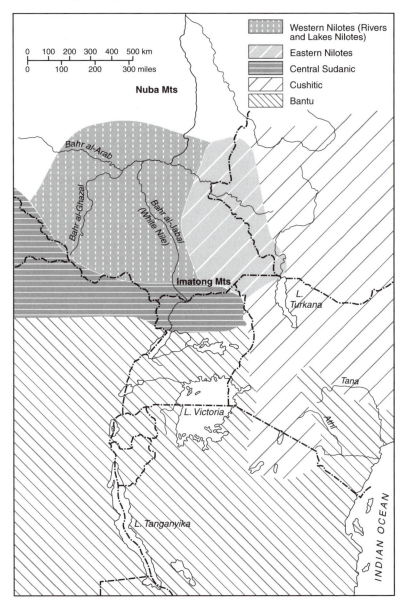

15 The upper Nile basin and the East African plateau: the distribution of language-families, *c*.1250

We do not know the reasons for this long-lasting overspill of Nilotic populations from the upper Nile basin on to the East African plateau. One reason may have been zoological, in the sense that the Nilotic peoples were strongly pastoral, and it may have been the increase of herds rather than of people which provided the main dynamic of expansion. If so, such movements may have been triggered by climatic variations. We know from the careful records kept in Egypt that there were great variations in the Nile flood, which may have had their most catastrophic effects in the Sudd region, where the waters were most dispersed and most subject to evaporation. Another reason may have been that Eastern Nilotes at least had developed hardier cereals and a more effective pattern of mixed farming than their southern neighbours, so that they were able to infiltrate the drier areas which had not previously been used for food production. Yet another reason may have been technological, in that the Nilotic peoples were more proficient as iron-workers, and so were better armed and more practised in warfare than their neighbours to the south. What we do know is that in southern Uganda, Rwanda, Burundi, eastern Congo (Zaïre) and north-western Tanzania a uniform early Iron Age culture, which had lasted for more than a millennium, was succeeded by a later Iron Age culture, with a totally different pottery tradition and with a pattern of farming which used much more of the land area than the early Iron Age people had done. In western Kenya this later Iron Age culture, associated with an essentially similar pottery tradition of northern origin, was introduced directly into a region hitherto very little affected by any kind of early Iron Age culture, where mainly pastoral, Cushitic-speaking farmers had continued to use neolithic equipment until after the beginning of the second millennium AD.

THE EARLY EASTERN NILOTES AND THEIR IMPACT

The archaeological evidence for this transition in western and central Kenya has been neatly surveyed by John Sutton, who shows that the earliest Iron Age culture practised in this region was that associated with the hillside hollows, frequently lined with dry stone walling, which are commonly known as 'Sirikwa holes'.[1] These were the stock pens of Eastern Nilotic Kalenjin peoples, who occupied the whole area of the western highlands and the adjacent parts of the

[1] J. E. G. Sutton, *The Archaeology of the Western Highlands of Kenya* (Nairobi, 1973), pp. 5–33.

Rift Valley until they were dispossessed by the Maasai in the eighteenth century. The starting-date of their occupation is uncertain, but is likely to have been at a period corresponding with the earliest Eastern Nilotic incursions into Uganda, where later Iron Age pottery was certainly in use by the eleventh century. In western Kenya the distribution of later Iron Age sites would suggest that the Eastern Nilotic immigrants were mixed farmers who tilled the higher and moister slopes of the western highlands, using the deep, rich soils around the forest margins, but sending out their young men and boys to pasture the herds on the lower, drier grasslands of the Uasin Gishu plateau and in the central section of the Rift Valley. The large proportion of Cushitic loan-words surviving in their language would suggest that the Kalenjin mixed with and absorbed their Stone Age predecessors, while their social organisation into age-sets and their adoption of certain Cushitic customs and taboos, such as the prohibition against eating fish, would indicate that cultural influence worked both ways.

It is to be hoped that one day we shall know much more about this early Eastern Nilotic infiltration into western Kenya, for its potential significance is very great. We need many more chronological data, and more evidence about the southward spread of the pattern of mixed farming which resulted from the mingling of Nilotic and Cushitic people in this region. Geography would suggest that a way of life based around expanding herds of cattle would spread more easily through the dry uplands of central Tanzania and north-eastern Zambia, which were still at the beginning of the second millennium populated mainly by hunters and gatherers, than through regions further to the west where agricultural populations had long been established. For the present our lack of information forbids us to do more than pose the question. What is certain, however, is that the later Iron Age culture associated with the Eastern Nilotic Kalenjin in western Kenya had its counterpart in Uganda and other areas to the west of Lake Victoria. As in the east, its archaeological hallmark was a coarse, poorly fired, roulette-decorated pottery, which here ousted the handsomely grooved and bevelled Urewe ware of the early Iron Age. Not only did a new pottery style supersede the old, but it was also used in areas where no pottery had been used before, because they were too arid for the methods and crops of early Iron Age farmers. Running diagonally across Uganda from north-east to south-west, and on southwards through eastern Rwanda and Burundi, is a corridor of fairly dry grassland, well suited to cattle-raising and grain agriculture, but much less so for the vegecultural farming practised by the early Iron Age Bantu. It would seem highly

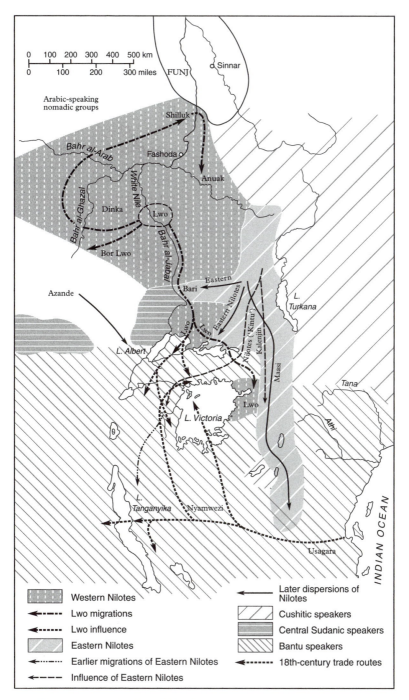

Legend

Western Nilotes	Later dispersions of Nilotes
Lwo migrations	Cushitic speakers
Lwo influence	Central Sudanic speakers
Eastern Nilotes	Bantu speakers
Earlier migrations of Eastern Nilotes	18th-century trade routes
Influence of Eastern Nilotes	

16 The upper Nile basin and the East African plateau: languages and
cultures, c.1400–1800

likely that fairly specialised pastoralists moving in from the direction of the Eastern Nilotic homelands became the first effective food-producers in these dry areas. They would have included the ancestors of the specialised pastoralists later known as Hima in western Uganda and Tutsi in Rwanda and Burundi. In so far as they remained in the grassland belt, their peculiar way of life and their milk diet would have encouraged a large measure of endogamy and the persistence of a characteristic pastoral physiognomy. But of course there would always have been blurring around the edges, where pastoralists and cultivators interacted, and at least in the field of language it would seem that the Bantu speech of the early Iron Age cultivators everywhere triumphed over that of the later Iron Age immigrants.

In fact, we can be sure that the later Iron Age immigrants into Uganda included many who were by no means specialised pastoralists. The distribution of later Iron Age pottery covers every type of soil, vegetation and rainfall, from the lush islands and coastlands of Lake Victoria to the cold, high valleys of the Ruwenzori range and the mountains of the Nile–Congo watershed which run through western Rwanda and Burundi. Moreover, the earliest layers of oral tradition preserved in the eastern part of the region – between Mount Elgon and the northern shores of Lake Victoria – paint a convincing picture of primarily agricultural immigrants coming from the north-east and settling in country already occupied by Bantu farmers and fishermen. The stereotypic, mythological figure of such traditions is called Kintu ('the superman'), and everywhere from eastern Busoga to central Buganda he appears as the leader of incoming migrants, whom he settles by agreement with the local clan-heads, dividing the land between the clans of the migrants and those of the earlier residents. Everywhere Kintu stands as the founding father of a series of small kingdoms, who welds clan-heads into his service by installing them in ceremonial positions at his court and being careful also to marry their daughters. Everywhere, likewise, Kintu is a culture hero, who introduces new crafts and new crops which improve the quality of life. Having carried out his mission in one small area, he leaves a regent in charge and moves on to repeat it in another, performing incredible feats of statesmanship and procreation. Until quite recently historians, with only the suspect genealogies of the longest-surviving royal dynasties to work from, have tended to place the Kintu period around the fourteenth or fifteenth century AD. Nowadays, thanks to the contributions of Iron Age archaeology, the Kintu myth has to be thought of as summarising the developments of several hundred years, starting with the appearance of later Iron Age pottery around the eleventh century.

It is clear from the traditions that the kingdoms of the Kintu period were very small, each comprising no more than a few hundred square miles and a few thousand subjects. The first hints of any larger polity come from the western grasslands between Lake Albert in the north and the Kagera river in the south. In traditional history this was the kingdom of Kitara, established by a pastoral dynasty of the Chwezi clan at a period roughly contemporary with the Kintu kingdoms further to the east. According to traditions recorded in the early twentieth century, the first capital of the Chwezi kingdom was at Mubende, on a striking hilltop midway between Lake Victoria and the Ruwenzori. The second and terminal capital was 40 miles to the south, in the famous earthwork site of Bigo bya Mugenyi. Although insignificant by comparison with the defensive systems of some West African cities, Bigo is the largest earthwork in eastern or southern Africa. An inner trench about a mile in circumference encloses a typical royal residence of later times. An outer trench some 7 miles long closes the angle between the confluence of two rivers: it is punctuated every hundred yards or so by a wide gateway through which cattle could be driven from the surrounding pastures. The pottery found on the site includes a roughly painted variety of the typical later Iron Age rouletted ware, which reoccurs at five other earthwork sites running from Bigo to Lake Albert. If all of these sites were comprised within a single jurisdiction, which is far from certain, the Kitara kingdom may have extended for some 90 miles from north to south and some 50 from east to west. In grassland country this might have comprised some tens of thousands of people and some hundreds of thousands of cattle. Radiocarbon tests indicate a period of occupation from about the fourteenth to about the sixteenth century. Since the excavations at Bigo during the early 1960s, however, the centre of archaeological interest has shifted to the neighbouring site at Ntusi only 6 miles away. Although undefended by earthworks, Ntusi has proved to be a site of urban dimensions, which lived not only by cattle but by grain agriculture, and which was also a centre of iron-working. Its refuse middens show that it was occupied continuously from the eleventh until the sixteenth century. Ntusi is best interpreted as the effective capital of an early kingdom, of which Bigo later became the royal residence and the focus of the royal herds. Here, once again, the earliest layer of tradition is shown to have telescoped rather than extended the true chronology of events.

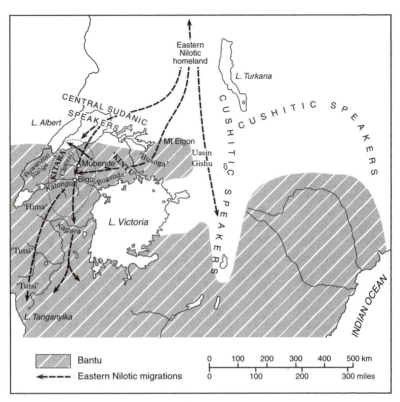

17 The upper Nile basin and the East African plateau: later Iron Age
population movements, *c.*1400–1700

THE WESTERN NILOTES AND THEIR IMPACT

On the East African plateau the kingdom of Kitara remained, so far as
we know, unique at any time between the eleventh and the sixteenth
century. Other kingdoms were numerous, but all quite small, and
their rulers are probably to be thought of, as Christopher Wrigley suggests, as 'sacred authority figures', whose original functions were of a
mainly ritual kind, which could be exercised almost at village level.[2]
By the late sixteenth century, however, Kitara had disappeared, and in
its place there had arisen a new configuration, based not on the central
grasslands, but upon the more mixed agricultural areas to the north,

---

[2] C. C. Wrigley, *Kingship and State: The Buganda Dynasty* (Cambridge, 1996),
p. 232.

the north-east and the south. It would seem that the impetus for these changes was given by the irruption of a new wave of Nilotic migration, coming this time from the Western Nilotes of the Sudd region. Significantly, only one of the three main components of this linguistic grouping was involved, namely the Lwo, whose original homeland was probably to the south of the Dinka and Nuer. The first effect of the Lwo dispersion was to redistribute the Lwo tribes into a rough circle around the Dinka–Nuer nucleus. The ancestors of the Bor Lwo settled to the west of the nucleus, around the lower Bahr al-Ghazal. The ancestors of the Shilluk settled to the north of the nucleus, on the White Nile around Fashoda, driving out an earlier set of riverain people, the Ap-Funy or Funj, who probably retreated to the north to conquer the Gezira triangle between the Blue and White Niles, and so found the kingdom of Sinnar on the ruins of the former Christian kingdom of 'Alwa (above, pp. 100–2). From Shillukland the ancestors of the Anuak moved up the Sobat and settled to the east of the nucleus around the modern frontier between Ethiopia and the Sudan.

Whatever touched them off, all these movements seem to have developed through a temporary militarisation of Lwo people into the role of riverain pirates – rather like the Vikings of European history – who lived for the space of two or three generations mainly by plundering their neighbours. Their boats were of the flimsiest, but they provided the mobility which enabled small bands of warriors to make daring raids upon the cattle, crops and persons of less warlike communities. Like other martial hordes – for example, the Oromo of Ethiopia (above, pp. 127–32) or the Mane of Sierra Leone and Liberia (above, pp. 73–6) – the Lwo were adept at incorporating captives into their societies, so that their numbers increased at a staggering rate. Numbers added to military strength, but also to the mouths that had to be fed, and this in turn quickened the pace of territorial expansion. At length, for reasons almost as obscure as those of the original disturbance, there would come the decision to abandon the military way of life and to settle as a ruling group in the midst of a subject population. Here again, the Lwo were very adept. They incorporated their new subjects into their own clans, drawing only a distinction between the *jo-kal*, the people of the chief's enclosure, and the *lwak*, or 'herd' of conquered clients. It was through their women that the lwak merged gradually with the kal, with polygamous chiefs begetting enormous numbers of children by conquerors and conquered alike.

The same pattern was followed by what was probably the main body of Lwo migrants, which moved southwards and right out of the 143 former Nilotic sphere, into Central Sudanic-speaking territory in northern Uganda, and on into Bantu territory still further south. Here, the initial penetration ascended the White Nile towards Lake Albert. A great military encampment was established beside the river at Pubungu, some 10 miles below the river's exit from the lake. This was in the heartland of the Madi people, who occupied both banks of the White Nile from Lake Albert to the Dufile rapids astride the frontier between the Sudan and Uganda. From Pubungu, Lwo expeditions radiated in all directions, bringing in booty and captives from the Madi and other Central Sudanic peoples such as the Lugbara and the Lendu. The captives were incorporated into the Lwo formations, and this swelled the appetite for further adventure and conquest. In this way there began a long process of assimilation which in the course of two centuries was to transform all but a tiny remnant of the Madi people, and other peoples living to the north of Lakes Albert and Kyoga, into Lwo-speaking Acholi, Alur, Lango and Kumam.

Unfortunately, no Iron Age archaeological research has yet been carried out in northern Uganda, and we can therefore only guess at the reasons why the peoples of this region were able to be absorbed linguistically and culturally by the Western Nilotic immigrants. It may have been just that this region was the closest to the Western Nilotic homeland and therefore received the largest proportion of Lwo immigrants. Or it may have been that the social and political organisation which grew from the Lwo war-camps, in which the chief acted as a major redistributor, first of booty and later of tribute, was positively attractive to peoples who had hitherto lived in much smaller and more dispersed communities. At all events, there was a fundamental difference between the political and cultural impact of the Lwo on the Central Sudanic peoples of northern Uganda and their impact on the Bantu peoples further south. For, in general, when the Lwo came into contact with the Bantu, even as outright military conquerors, it was the Bantu language which prevailed and Bantu social organisation towards which Lwo rulers made large compromises. It was only among the Bantu of western Kenya, living around the Kavirondo Gulf of Lake Victoria, that Lwo migrants were able to establish distinct communities of Lwo-speaking people.

The most significant of the Lwo conquests into Bantu territory was that which destroyed the Chwezi kingdom of Kitara. In Lwo history it probably followed soon after the establishment of the war-camp at Pubungu. It was probably carried out by a war-leader called Olum Labongo, remembered in Bantu traditions as Rukidi ('the naked man from the north'), the founder of the Bito dynasty of Bunyoro and the founding ancestor of a whole circle of lesser Bito dynasties which gradually came to rule over much of southern Uganda. Tradition tells us that the Chwezi ruler and his followers fled from Bigo and Ntusi at the approach of the Lwo armies and that Rukidi occupied for a time the capital of the Chwezi kings. The archaeological excavation of Bigo has, in fact, demonstrated that the centre of the site was radically reconstructed so as to include a large, hemispherical mound reminiscent of those made at Shilluk capitals and elsewhere. Nevertheless, traditions make it clear that in the long run a capital in the grasslands proved unsuitable for a Lwo dynasty, which soon moved its headquarters to the region round and north of Mubende, where agriculture could be practised on a larger scale. It was here, in the northern half of the old Kitara kingdom, that the new kingdom of Bunyoro developed. It is said that the bodies of the first three Bito kings were carried north to the neighbourhood of Pubungu for burial. This may be some indication of the period for which the Bito and their henchmen remained Lwo-speaking foreigners in a Bantu world. Thereafter, we may suppose, the Bito spoke the Nyoro language of their Bantu subjects, and intermarriage between Lwo and Bantu had gone so far that there was no longer any sense of racial difference.

Meantime, as was only to be expected, there had taken place in the southern half of the old Kitara kingdom a regroupment of the more distinctively pastoral population which had fled southwards with their cattle at the time of the Lwo invasions. Here, leadership came from the Hinda clan, which claimed a relationship with the Chwezi, and which succeeded in establishing a loose-knit hegemony on either side of the Kagera river, in Karagwe to the south of it and in Nkore to the north. The Hinda dynasty was in its way as significant as the Bito one. Its scions spread in all directions, and soon there were a dozen or more small, Hinda-ruled kingdoms, reaching from south-western Uganda through north-western Tanzania to the southern confines of Burundi. The Nyiginya dynasty, which in the early seventeenth century planted the nucleus of what was to develop into the important kingdom of Rwanda, probably derived from the same source. Although the ideology and rituals of small-scale kingship were already in existence among the older Bantu agricultural communities inhabiting the land, the impetus towards expansion and centralisation in all these kingdoms was connected with the management of cattle in relation to the needs of cultivators. Whereas the earlier pastoralists in the region had lived a life largely

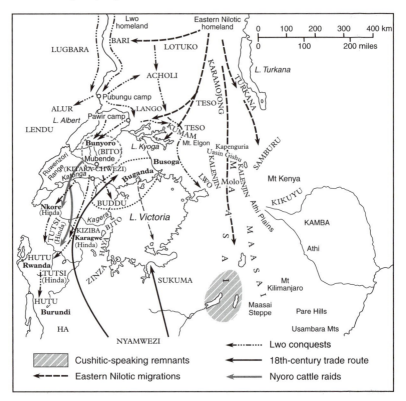

18 The upper Nile basin and the East African plateau: settlements of the
Nilotes, *c.*1700–1800

separate from that of the cultivators living to the east and west of
them, the next phase was one in which some pastoralists interpene-
trated the surrounding farmlands, lending out their cattle in twos
and threes to cultivators, who valued them for their milk and even
more for their manure, and were prepared to pay for their loan with
gifts of food and drink, and other services of a feudal kind.
Naturally, as it spread, this system invited the intervention of political entrepreneurs, men of power who were able to enforce the observance of the contract. This seems to have been the dynamic for the
spread of Hinda dynasties in the farmlands of the Haya and Zinza
peoples living between the Karagwe grasslands and Lake Victoria. In
Rwanda and Burundi a similar process occurred with the westward
penetration of Tutsi pastoralists from the eastern grasslands into the
rich mountain valleys of the Nile–Congo watershed, with their dense

146

populations of Hutu cultivators. At first the penetration was peaceful, but later the payment of tribute was enforced by military means and the successful kingdoms grew in size. The emergence of large, centralised kingdoms based on conquest was only the last stage in the process, gathering momentum only during the seventeenth century in Rwanda and the eighteenth century in Burundi.

During the first century after the Lwo conquest of Kitara the northern Hinda kingdoms had to endure the attrition of an aggressive and expanding Bunyoro. Whenever Bunyoro needed cattle, it raided Nkore, and sometimes also Karagwe and eastern Rwanda. Though the direct rule of the Bito kings never extended far to the south of Mubende, tributary sub-kingdoms, some ruled by Bito dynasties, stretched to the shores of Lake Victoria, including what later became the Ganda province of Buddu and the Haya kingdom of Kiziba south of the lower Kagera. According to the traditional history of Bunyoro, even the nuclear heartland of Buganda was ruled by a Bito dynasty descending from the twin brother of the Lwo conqueror, Rukidi. Even if this claim now looks dubious, there can be no doubt that during most of the seventeenth century the Ganda kingdom suffered repeated attacks from Bunyoro armies. Only in the late seventeenth century did Buganda recover its poise. When it did so, however, it was to the accompaniment of a new political policy of resounding significance. It was that conquered territory must be fully integrated, not by recognising a local dynasty as tributary, but by the imposition of appointed governors and by the deliberate absorption of the conquered populations into Ganda clans. Thus, when Buganda began to extend its territory, the result was a lasting access of power, which made the next step easier than the previous one. By the early eighteenth century Buganda had recovered all the territory lost to Bunyoro. By the end of that century it controlled the shores of Lake Victoria from the Kagera to the Nile. It was still a smaller country than Bunyoro and its tributary sub-kingdoms, but politically and militarily it was far more coherent. All important appointments were held at the king's pleasure. A network of well-kept roads linked the capital with the provinces. Royal commands flowed outwards, and tribute and services flowed in. By the late eighteenth century Buganda was already directly involved in trade with the coast and the outside world. The king's ivory hunters ranged widely around the peripheries of the kingdom. His caravans travelled regularly to the south of the lake, and were soon to be augmented by a fleet of long-distance canoes. Imported cotton textiles were already in use at the royal court, along with cups and saucers, 147 plates and cutlery, which would before long be followed by firearms and the preachers of world religions. Thus, although the direct impact of the Western Nilotic infiltration was felt most directly in northern Uganda and, within the Bantu world, in Bunyoro, the indirect results were much more widely spread. The Hinda states were one kind of response. The transformation of Buganda into a centralised, expansive and outward-looking polity was another response to the same challenge.

THE LATER EASTERN NILOTES AND THEIR IMPACT

It was no accident that during the eighteenth century the long-distance trade routes connecting Buganda with the Indian Ocean coast had to make a wide detour through central Tanzania instead of passing directly through the Kenya highlands. The reason was the presence, right across the central highland region of Kenya and northern Tanzania, of specialised pastoralists pursuing a highly mobile and predatory way of life, which would have posed an impossible threat to the passage of trading caravans. These people were Eastern Nilotes, but of a later dispersion than the Kalenjin. Sometimes called the Plains Nilotes in order to distinguish them from the Highland Nilotes of the earlier dispersion, they included such peoples as the Bari and Lotuko of the Sudan–Uganda frontier region, the Karamojong and Teso of north-eastern Uganda, the Turkana and Samburu of north-western Kenya; but the most important and widespread of their ethnic sub-groupings were the Maasai, whose arena eventually extended right down the Rift Valley from north-western Kenya to the plains of central Tanzania.

Of the origins of these people it is only possible to say that they must have been relatively close to the ancestors of the Kalenjin and relatively distant from those of the Western Nilotes. Probably they emerged from the same hilly borderland between the southern Sudan and southern Ethiopia as did the Kalenjin, but some centuries later. Perhaps the Eastern Nilotic homeland was particularly liable to climatic fluctuations, so that in times of extended drought migration was the only alternative to disaster. At all events, the second Eastern Nilotic dispersion seems to have begun somewhat later than that of the Western Nilotic Lwo. The westward movement of the Bari is placed by tradition later than the first southward thrust of the Lwo, but somewhat earlier than the final stages of Western Nilotic incursions into northern Uganda. Again, it is clear that Lwo-speakers were at one time spread right along the northern shores of

Lake Kyoga, but that many of them were later absorbed by Eastern Nilotic Teso moving in from the north-east, while even a group like the Lango, which kept its Lwo speech, was much penetrated by Eastern Nilotic influences. All this suggests that the period from the late seventeenth century until the early eighteenth was one of great movement, and probably it was at this time also that the ancestors of the Samburu and the Maasai, followed by those of the Karamojong and the Turkana, began to encircle the Lake Turkana basin to the west and the south.

Like other migrants who set out to seize country already settled by others, the later Eastern Nilotes could succeed only by force of arms. In so far as they were specialised pastoralists, however, interested only in cattle and the monopolisation of scarce grasslands, they were destroyers, or at the least extruders. The Maasai, especially, were conquerors of this destructive kind. They believed that cattle had been put in the world for their own exclusive use. Their social organisation was essentially military and based on an age-set system which made it the duty of boys to herd cattle and of young men to plunder and defend cattle, so that the middle-aged and elderly might enjoy the possession of cattle and plan the strategy for obtaining more and more. The impact of the Maasai can be seen most clearly in relation to the western highlands of Kenya, where the distribution of abandoned 'Sirikwa holes' shows that the Kalenjin were once in possession of the whole plateau. The Maasai intrusion left them clinging to the outside edges of their former territory. The Uasin Gishu Maasai occupied the central grasslands from Kapenguria to Molo, with half of the Kalenjin survivors to the west of them and the other half to the east. Probably it was the same story in the Rift Valley, the Athi Plains and the Maasai Steppe. The Maasai could enjoy excellent relations with some kinds of neighbours, particularly those practising a different mode of economic life in a different ecological setting, such as the Kikuyu in the forested foothills of Mount Kenya or the Pare in the hills to the east of the Maasai Steppe, with both of whom the Maasai regularly traded their hides and their surplus women in exchange for iron tools and weapons. But to inhabit the same kind of territory as the Maasai was to invite attack, and the main significance of their occupation of the eastern grasslands was that it erected an impenetrable screen across the natural and direct routes between the rich region to the west of Lake Victoria and the Indian Ocean coast.

Hence the growing importance towards the close of our period of the region to the south of Lake Victoria, inhabited by a series of fairly closely related peoples of whom the Nyamwezi formed the   149 central group. This was not on the whole a rich land capable of supporting a dense population. Most of it was rather dry country covered with thorny bush, in which agricultural communities had constantly to divide and subdivide, sending out colonies to considerable distances to find suitable land on which to settle. Kingship remained on a small scale: there was no economic basis for the elaborate court life or the hierarchies of officials found in Buganda, Rwanda and the larger interlacustrine kingdoms. In small communities separated from each other by large tracts of uninhabited bush, hunting remained an important part of the economy, and it may be that the availability of ivory and rare skins was what turned the minds of the Nyamwezi and their neighbours to the possibilities of long-distance trade. So far as we know at present, it was only during the eighteenth century that migrants from Usagara and other districts near the coast began to settle among the Nyamwezi, bringing with them such curiosities as conus-shell discs and ivory horns, which were soon adopted as forms of regalia. Thus the connection between coast and interior was established, and the response of the Nyamwezi seems to have been electric. Within two or three generations of the breakthrough, they had created a near-monopoly of the long-distance carrying trade, to the deep interior as well as to the coast. In their societies prestige came to be associated with distant travel, and in the mid-nineteenth century the explorer Richard Burton was to report how in the Nyamwezi villages every boy carried about with him a tusk of ivory proportionate to his strength, so that when older he would be prepared for a man's most serious employment as a caravan porter. By this time Nyamwezi caravans linked the coast with the interlacustrine region, the whole vast region around Lake Tanganyika and the Copperbelt of Congo (Zaïre) and northern Zambia, and some had even penetrated as far west as Angola. At the end of the eighteenth century the system was probably still confined to the region south of Lake Victoria and east of Lake Tanganyika. Even on that scale, its existence made possible, in some of the larger interlacustrine kingdoms, the outward-looking attitudes which assisted their nineteenth-century development.

10   The heart of Africa

The least accessible region of Africa, and therefore the one most neglected by historians and archaeologists alike, is that comprised by the equatorial rainforest and the belt of woodland savanna immediately to the north of it. Until quite recently, the forest was penetrable only by its rivers, and these were well guarded from the outside world by the cataracts leading down from the inland basin to the sea, to the extent that even three and a half centuries after the Portuguese established regular communications with the Congo estuary, no European had set eyes on Lake Malebo or the 4000 miles of easily navigable waterways that lay beyond. The woodland savanna to the north of the forest was tsetse-infested and therefore closed to the baggage animals which operated further north, so that the only means of travel was on foot. Here, then, was an area as large as the entire United States and lying geographically at the very heart of the African continent, at the crossroads between north and south, east and west, which apparently lived almost unto itself. Not quite so, however, because with human populations there is always seepage at the edges, and people exchange ideas and technical innovations that affect every aspect of life. While we still face the fact that less is known about the history of this region than any other, what information exists cannot be just passed over in a few glib, negative generalisations.

The rainforest of Central Africa used to be viewed as so inhospitable that only a very few, very primitive people could possibly have lived there. But, thanks very largely to the work of Jan Vansina, it is today recognised that, even if much of it was inhabitable only by hunter-gatherers, there existed within it countless riverine and intercalary savanna micro-environments capable of supporting vigorous food-producing populations. In Vansina's perhaps somewhat overstated opinion, 'Contrary to the stereotype, rainforests are desirable environments, and the ancestors of the western Bantu-speakers, seeking an easy living, certainly thought so.'[1] Today it is likewise accepted that the Bantu languages spoken in the forest are the oldest members of this subdivision of the Niger-Congo language-family,

---

[1] J. Vansina, *Paths in the Rainforests* (Madison, 1990), p. 46.

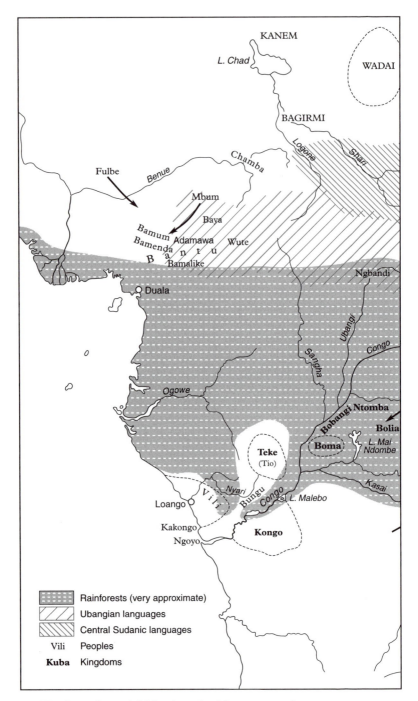

KANEM

L. Chad

WADAI

BAGIRMI

Logone

Shari

Chamba

Fulbe

Benue

Mbum

Baya

Bamum Adamawa Wute

Bamenda Bantu

B a Bamalike

Ngbandi

Duala

Ubangi

Congo

Sangha

Ogowe

Bobangi Ntomba

Bolia

Boma

L. Mai
Ndombe

Teke
(Tio)

Kasai

Nyari

Bungu

Congo L. Malebo

Vili

Loango

Kakongo

Ngoyo

Kongo

	Rainforests (very approximate)
	Ubangian languages
	Central Sudanic languages
Vili	Peoples
Kuba	Kingdoms

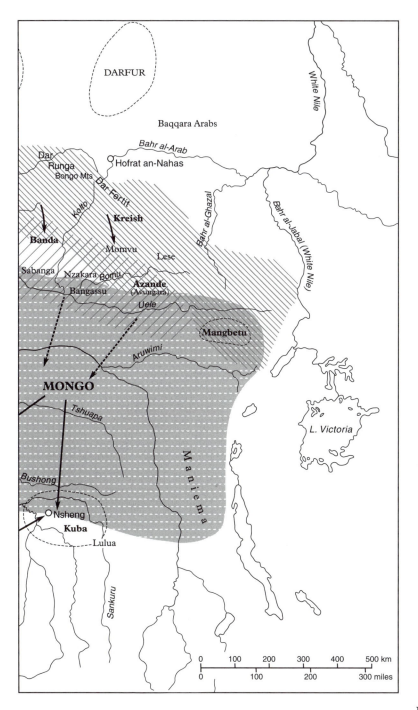

whose penetration of the rainforest must have begun in neolithic times, 3000 or even 4000 years ago. Nevertheless, occupation by Bantu-speakers was never more than partial, for throughout all this long period a physically and visibly different population of hunter-gatherers survived in nearly equal numbers to the food-producers and continued to occupy at least half of the actual territory. The food-producers remained largely confined to the river valleys and lakeshores, where enough sunlight could penetrate the forest cover for food plants to ripen, and where vegetable foodstuffs like yams, palm-oil and, later, bananas could be supplemented by fishing. Throughout the centuries the two populations interacted, and apparently quite peacefully, since their ways of life were complementary and not competitive, and to the point that everywhere the hunter-gatherers have adopted the language of the nearest community of food-producers. All this argues not only a very long but a very slow development of the food-producing occupation. It was only when the outer fringe of Bantu-speakers at last reached the much more favourable environments provided by the lakes and mountain valleys of the Western Rift and the Nile–Congo divide that the Bantu expansion became a fast-moving and dynamic process, giving rise to a whole new set of much more closely related, and therefore much younger, eastern Bantu languages.

While the Bantu-speaking food-producers were developing symbiotically with the hunter-gatherers of the equatorial forest, the speakers of two other linguistic groupings were expanding more competitively in the woodland savanna to the north of it. To the north-west were speakers of the Ubangian languages, which, like the Bantu languages, were a subdivision of the great Niger-Congo language-family. The largest individual languages in this sub-family were those of the Mbum, Baya, Wute and Banda peoples, who lived strung out along the highlands of the Benue–Logone and Ubangi–Shari watersheds, leaving the lower, drier plains to the north and east of them to the speakers of the Central Sudanic languages, like Sara and Momvu, Lese and Madi, whose wider linguistic affiliations were with the Nilo-Saharan language-family.

As in the West African 'middle belt', all these peoples of the woodland savanna between the Cameroon highlands and the eastern tributaries of the White Nile were cereal farmers, largely self-sufficient, and organised either in very small kingdoms or, more usually, in village or extended family groups with few or no political linkages between one and another. From the early centuries of the second millennium onwards, their northernmost representatives were increasingly harried by the horse-borne slave-raiders of the savanna states to the north of them – Bagirmi, Kanem, Wadai and Darfur. For this reason, and also perhaps because of a general southward shift in the climatic belts that occurred at this time, there was a slow drift of population from north to south, which is clearly reflected in the traditions of many of these peoples. It is certain that over these centuries many of their southernmost representatives drifted southwards into the equatorial forest, adopting Bantu speech and becoming culturally absorbed by their Bantu hosts.

In the west of the region, the Mbum, the Baya and the Wute seem to have been settled for many centuries on the highlands to the south of the Benue–Logone watershed, until towards the end of the eighteenth century, when they moved south into the Cameroon grasslands, to escape first from the raids of their fierce Chamba neighbours, and next from the Fulbe expansion into Adamawa. The Mbum migrants soon turned from refugees into conquerors on their own account, and settled down as the rulers of the stateless Bantu communities of the Bamenda plateau, taking the new name of Tikar. In the course of time some thirty small kingdoms emerged, each ruled by a *fon* of Mbum origin. Tikar or related dynasties also gave rise to kingdoms among the Bantu-speaking Bamum who were their neighbours to the south-east, and very likely also among the Bamileke, famed as highly skilled craftsmen in wood, ivory, brass and raphia. In all these cases the incoming Tikar conquerors adopted the languages of the conquered. Altogether, the Mbum migration offers a splendid example of how easily new kingdoms could arise where none had been before.

Further to the east, the slow drift of populations southwards from the Ubangi–Chari watershed into the forest margins had probably been going on in response to the gradual desiccation of the climate for several centuries before the Muslim sultanates of Wadai and Darfur turned to large-scale slaving in the seventeenth and eighteenth centuries (above, pp. 111–13). Possibly from as early as the eleventh and twelfth centuries, Nilotic peoples moving slowly up the Bahr al-Ghazal tributary of the White Nile had pushed Central Sudanic-speakers southwards and westwards towards the Ubangi basin. It is also likely that Ngbandi communities moved south from the Dar Runga to escape the attentions of the fierce, pastoral Baqqara Arabs, who began to settle the plains to the north of the Bahr al-'Arab around the beginning of the fourteenth century. By the end of our period the Ngbandi were living far to the south, astride the great bend of the Ubangi river.

But undoubtedly the most positive result of the attrition of the Muslim sultanates in the eighteenth century was to cause a consolidation of political structures among the peoples to the south. This was not just a simple process of challenge and response, for around the southern periphery of the Muslim states there were those who accepted the role of tributary slave-hunters for their powerful neighbours. Such were the Runga to the south of Wadai and the Fertit to the south of Darfur. Beyond the tributaries was the area of active raiding, which tended to become depopulated as some of its inhabitants were seized and exported, while others retreated out of range of the raiders. Thus, most of the Banda, who originally lived in the Dar Banda and the western foothills of the Bongo massif, drifted southwards into the country of the Ubangian-speaking Sabanga and Nzakara, while the majority of the Kreish retreated south-eastwards along the line of the Nile–Congo watershed into the country of the Momvu and Lese peoples. The smaller groups living in the direct path of such migrations tended to be absorbed by them, joining one or other of the many small Banda or Kreish chieftainships. Some, however, moved away, and followed the usual condition of such independence by making themselves the rulers over others.

It is in this kind of way that we have to see the origins of the Azande and Mangbetu hegemonies of the eighteenth and nineteenth centuries – the first as an indirect consequence of the pressure of Wadai on the Banda, the second perhaps following from the pressure of Darfur upon the Kreish. People speaking Mangbetu dialects of Central Sudanic had been in the rainforest south of the upper Uele for a thousand years or more, thriving on a banana-based economy, but it was not until the mid-eighteenth century that pressure from Azande raiding inspired a self-made petty ruler named Manziga to weld many small groups of Ubangian, Central Sudanic and Bantu peoples, along with their attendant hunter-gatherers, into a far-flung kingdom. The Mangbetu kingship was of the heavily ritualised kind, with vast palace installations and a tremendous display of royal insignia fashioned in burnished copper. 'The midday [light] of the equatorial sun', wrote the German traveller Georg Schweinfurth during a visit to Munza, the fourth and last Mangbetu ruler, 'shed a blinding light over this concentration of the red-gleaming metal, and a glow, as of burning torches, flickered on each ceremonial spear-blade, the serried rows of which provided a gorgeous background for the ruler's throne.'[2] The

---

[2] Georg Schweinfurth, *The Heart of Africa* (London, 1873), cited in D. Westermann, *Geschichte Afrikas* (Cologne, 1952), p. 171.

copper was surely that of Hofrat en-Nahas in the borderland of south-western Sudan, and paid for with the ivory of the Ituri forest. Schweinfurth noted that Munza was the middleman for the exchange of northern and southern produce over a region much wider than his own kingdom. It was probably from the same population layer as the Sabanga that there emerged, in the early eighteenth century, the Bandia group of militarised ivory hunters, who established three quite substantial conquest states among the Nzakara people living around the confluence of the Uele and Mbomu rivers, of which the largest was the kingdom of Bangassu. Also, somewhat later, there emerged a similar group known as the Avungara, whose members created a series of much smaller kingdoms extending eastwards into the basin of the White Nile. The Avungara chiefs lived without display in compounds little larger than those of their Azande subjects. All the independent rulers of Azandeland were descendants of Ngura, the leader of the original conquering horde, but despite the persistence of a close family feeling among them, it was accepted that there would be a segmentation of authority in each generation, mostly arising from the expansion of the hegemony at its peripheries. Under the Avungara royals there functioned a class of tribute-collecting officials, likewise often descending from members of the original horde. At the level of village chiefs, the petty rulers of the conquered peoples were often left in position. The most remarkable feature of Azande rule, however, was the system of cultural assimilation practised upon the young. Boys were removed from their parents at puberty and assigned, first as servants and later as armed retainers, to the Avungara rulers or to members of the Azande-speaking aristocracy. When they eventually returned to their villages to marry, they felt themselves to be Azande like their former masters, and so in three or four generations a new nation was built up, more effectively and certainly more lastingly than by the Mangbetu method of more centralised monarchy.

SOCIETIES OF THE EQUATORIAL RAINFOREST

The food-producing, Bantu-speaking population of the rainforest mostly lived, as we have noted, strung out along the rivers in highly mobile 'households', each ruled by a 'big man', who was always pictured as rich and beneficent. At any given moment, a household was normally settled alongside other households in a village. But fisher-folk like to be free to move to wherever the fishing appears to be best, 157 and they have their canoes which can quickly be packed with their few possessions and moved up- or downstream to another village of their choice. To illustrate the social ideals of such a way of life, Vansina quotes the words used by a 'big man' in addressing an initiate at a puberty ceremony in south-eastern Cameroon. 'This elephant [ivory bracelet] which I put on your arm, [let it help you to] become a man of crowds, a hero in war, a man with [many] women, rich in children, [possessing] many objects of wealth. [May you] prosper within the family and be famous throughout the villages.'[3] The basic socioeconomic system of 'households', which was probably in place throughout most of the rainforest by the beginning of the second millennium, was nevertheless capable of extensive transformations, particularly of scale. A great variety of real or imagined social relationships, and of ritual and political symbols, were either adopted or invented, usually with the object of establishing the legitimacy of the 'big men', and enhancing their power. But, even when larger and more complex political and military structures developed in response to the challenges of recent centuries, they still retained many features of the older and more egalitarian institutions.

The forests of the inner basin, south of the great bend of the Congo river, were the home of the large group of Bantu-speaking people known as Mongo. According to tradition, they had once had a matrilineal system of succession and egalitarian political institutions. But during the course of the second millennium they absorbed a whole series of migrants drifting southwards from the northern savanna, under whose impact conflict between villages turned into serious struggles to conquer and dominate. New types of iron weapons were introduced by the northerners, in particular a short stabbing spear used in hand-to-hand fighting. The newcomers likewise introduced more complex modes of economic exchange by the use of an iron and copper currency. Matriliny was replaced by patriliny, and this social and familial transition helped superior households and villages to dominate their less successful neighbours, since patriliny encouraged large-scale polygamy by the rich and successful and the increase of military manpower available in their households.

As a result of all these changes and the increase of population following from them, the Bolia, Ntomba and Jia sections of the Mongo moved from their traditional habitat on the banks of the Tshuapa tributary of the Congo to the dense forests around Lake Mai-Ndombe, in a migration which probably occurred several centuries

³ Vansina, *Paths in the Rainforests*, p. 73.

before the inner basin of the Congo became linked to the Atlantic trade with the coming of the Portuguese. The Bolia traditions say that the sacred symbols of kingship, in particular a lump of white kaolin mixed with the cement-like deposit found in the gigantic ant-hills of the woodland savanna, were carried along by the newcomers in their migrations from their northern homelands. 'As the size of successful households swelled, institutions supporting the ideology of chieftaincy, the key to the whole dynamic process, swelled as well and in the end produced a richly sacred kingship.'[4]

Vansina may very well be right in suggesting that the authoritarian revolution begun in central Mongo, and carried westwards by the Bolia in their migration to Mai-Ndombe on the western edge of Mongo territory, was likewise communicated in embryo still further westwards to the Teke (or Tio) settled on the sandy plateau north of Lake Malebo, and thence to the progenitors of the Kongo kingdoms to the north and south of the Congo estuary (below, pp. 161–3 and 166–7). One of the fruits of this relentless pursuit of centralisation by the Mongo people was the emergence, quite early in our period, of the long-lasting Boma kingdom, just to the west of Lake Mai-Ndombe, which reached the peak of its power in the sixteenth and seventeenth centuries.

In the opposite direction, another major trend in the history of the Mongo was their expansion southwards in a slow drift, which must have lasted for a millennium or more. On the southern border of the equatorial forest, one of the most creative manifestations of this Mongo expansion was the emergence, between the Kasai and Sankuru tributaries of the Congo, of the Kuba kingdom, renowned to this day in museums around the world for the artistic achieve-ments of its woodcarvers, metal-workers and weavers of raphia. Kuba emerged as a federation of several different peoples, including Lulua from the woodland savanna to the south of the forest as well as Mongo from the north. The ethnic group which came to dominate the rest was that of the Bushong, a Mongo sub-group, whose wealth and prestige came from their enterprise as fishermen and boat-builders, who explored and exploited the waters of the Sankuru. Their traditions speak first of an early period of settlement, when the component peoples of the later kingdom still maintained most of their original independence of each other. It was during this period of settlement and expansion that the singular political and ideologi-cal rituals of the later kingdom were developed, partly by borrowing

---

[4] *Ibid.*, p. 122.

from a common fund and partly by local innovation. It seems likely that the emergence of the Bushong ascendancy was based on a cluster of ideological devices that came from the north, up the rivers and along the paths of the rainforest.

According to Kuba tradition, the peoples of the Sankuru and Kasai valleys were welded together early in the seventeenth century by an extraneous adventurer, Shyam, who entered the Bushong country from the west, at the head of quite a modest band of followers. Perhaps rather too much emphasis has been placed by Kuba ideologues and by outside scholars on Shyam's work in creating the Kuba kingdom, but there can be no doubt that his name is associated with profound economic and political changes in the region. It is Shyam who is said to have set in motion an agricultural revolution by initiating the Bushong into the cultivation of the American plants, especially maize, cassava and tobacco, brought by the Portuguese to the Atlantic coast of western central Africa. This resulted in a rapid increase of population, which enabled Shyam to centralise his kingdom around a greatly enlarged capital city, fed and supplied by the surrounding peasantry, which attracted traders and craftsmen, as well as warriors, from all the neighbouring kingdoms.

During the eighteenth century Shyam's successors further centralised their kingdom by building a complex of political and ritual institutions, many of them quite unique. So secure and prosperous had the kingdom become by the end of our period that its kings could pick and choose in their dealings with the Atlantic trading system, for example by importing slaves and exporting ivory. In 1892, some 250 years after Shyam's reign, the Kuba capital was an impressive sight. It was surrounded by an outer wall, consisting of a palisade 10 feet high, within which was a rectangular grid of well-laid-out streets, squares, houses and compounds, with still higher palisades enclosing the royal palace. This included the king's meeting halls, storehouses, harem, personal dwelling, slave quarters, courtyards used for large assemblies and special houses for the royal drums. A new capital was built at least once in each reign, but always within the same small area of the kingdom, between the Lacwaddy and Lyeekdy tributaries of the Sankuru. The Kuba story is well worth more detailed study in Jan Vansina's outstanding monograph, *The Children of Woot* (1978), which embodies the fruit of some twenty-five years of reflection on his pioneering fieldwork carried out in the early 1950s. Its main lesson for the African historian is to demonstrate first how it was possible for ideas of political centralisation to percolate through the filter of the Congo forest, and secondly how large a part of the process of kingdom-building could be inspired by the sheer inventive genius of local leadership.

But Vansina also warns his readers against too ready an acceptance of the notion that the growth of territorial centralisation from the scale of 'big man' to 'king' was the norm for state-formation in this or any other part of Africa. The forests and wooded uplands of Maniema, for example, situated between the inner basin of the Congo river and the volcanic mountains along its eastern rim were some of the last lands to be settled by the western Bantu farmers before they spilled out towards the east. This was a region rich in diverse environments and resources, where there is evidence for considerable trade between the different farming communities. Yet here no large polities emerged. The nearest centralised kingdom to the Kuba, that of the Central Sudanic Mangbetu, which only came into being towards the end of our period, had its centre in the depths of the forest, far away to the north (above, pp. 156–7). In between, there developed a profusion of 'houses', of 'big men', of chiefdoms, of small kingdoms, of powerful ritual associations and brotherhoods existing for healing or initiation, which can be seen as alternative pathways to social and political cohesion.[5]

THE RED GOLD OF BUNGU

The western segment of the equatorial region, stretching from Duala southwards to the Congo estuary and inland as far as the Sangha river, the most westerly of the major tributaries of the Congo, comprised some of the most difficult terrain for food-producing settlement in the whole of the equatorial latitudes. The coastal plain was narrow, sandy and infertile, and the interior was mountainous, steep and densely forested. Most of it was suited only to a hunting and gathering existence. The Bantu inhabitants of the coast, the ancestors of the Vili and the Mpongwe, lived mainly by fishing in the sea and the coastal lagoons. Later, in their capacity as boilers and distributors of sea salt, they established trading centres up the valley of the Niari and the smaller rivers flowing westwards out of the forested interior. Here, along the watershed between the Nyari and the Congo estuary, was a comparatively small area north and south of the modern mining town of Mindouli which contained rich deposits of copper and iron ore. And this, most significantly, was the heartland of the Kongo-speaking people, who in their later dispersions remembered it as Bungu.

The ancestors of the Kongo people had no doubt been long settled in this general region – probably, in fact, since the penetration of the great forest by the first western Bantu cultivators using polished stone tools during the first millennium BC. The knowledge of iron-working, as also that of seed agriculture, had reached them only much later, probably around the fourth century AD, as the result of influences spreading through and round the forest region from the areas of eastern Bantu settlement. Nevertheless, by the beginning of our period the Kongo had become a nation of miners, with an aristocracy of smiths and traders in metal goods, which gave them an economic and political significance which spread far beyond their own ethnic homeland. Those who possessed the purest iron ores could produce the best tools and weapons, and not merely for their own use, but as objects of trade. Still more so, those who possessed sources of the much rarer and more widely admired mineral, copper, could be the jewellers to a whole region, supplying the emblems of wealth and authority as well as the items of personal adornment distributed by 'big men' to their households and by rulers to their loyal subjects. Metal goods constituted storable wealth, which could be hoarded and used to buy wives and other dependants, both from within the community and outside it. Many wives meant many children, a growing population and an incentive to colonise.

The economic and social stages leading from household to chiefdom, and then to paramount chiefdom and finally to kingdom, can be traced linguistically among the Kongo and Teke societies by the introduction of new political terminology and by the development of royal rituals. As Vansina has frequently reminded us, every western Bantu language had a word for 'big man' (normally, *mfumu*), which was used for heads of houses and village heads. Only later and more sporadically did there appear words for 'chief of a district' (*nkani*), and 'chief by conquest' or 'king' (*mwene* or *mani*). From such evidence, it seems that both communities had seen the emergence of kingdoms by early in the second millennium AD. With the offices of 'chief' or 'king' there went, as the principal item of regalia, the 'royal bell', made of welded iron, which could be struck in different ways so as to convey messages by reproducing the tones of the spoken language: it was thus the western Bantu equivalent of the 'royal drums' of eastern Africa. Such emblematic, clapperless bells were used in societies throughout the rainforest, and beyond it in a zone stretching from Nigeria southwards to Zambia, with a 'single bell' as the symbol of chiefly power and a 'double bell' that of a king. The occurrence of

The heart of Africa

these bells in archaeological sites yields a rough chronology, from which Vansina has concluded that paramount chiefs or kings had emerged among both the Teke and the Kongo by about 1200 AD. Obviously, the mere existence of terms for kings and their regalia did not imply that the kingdom concerned was necessarily a large one. As in the rest of Africa, even the largest kingdoms had sprung from small beginnings and had grown larger through the accumulation of small conquests. As the Kongo-speaking chiefdoms increased in size and complexity, and as their capital towns grew larger, so did the need for increased trade in food and other products. 'With increased trade came a set of innovative commercial institutions, such as market regulations, commercial law, the four-day week which regulated the periodicity of markets, and a monetary system based on iron, copper, and raphia-square units.'[6] And so, well before the advent of the Portuguese to the coast towards the end of the fifteenth century, some principalities had coalesced to form much larger and more militaristic kingdoms, to wit, the Vili polities along the coast north of the Congo estuary, the Teke kingdom on the dry plateau north of Lake Malebo, and the principality which became the great kingdom of Kongo by moving its centre from the north to the south bank of the Congo and conquering and progressively assimilating its Mbundu inhabitants (below, pp. 166–7).

At least by the fifteenth century, and possibly much earlier, the territory of the Vili people had been incorporated within three small kingdoms ruled by Kongo dynasties, of which the northernmost, that of Loango, was by far the largest and most resourceful. By the period of the earliest European contact with the region, the rulers, known as *maloango*, were practising a whole gamut of royal rituals, most of which could be paralleled in other widely scattered parts of Africa. For example, each maloango at his accession kindled a sacred fire, which would be extinguished only at his death, and torches from which were carried to the provincial centres, where they were kept burning as symbols of the royal authority. Again, the maloango presided over the annual rain-making ceremonies, at the conclusion of which, standing on his throne, he would shoot an arrow skywards to encourage the rain to fall. Likewise, to foster belief in his superhuman status, the maloango had to be invisible while performing any natural function. When he drank, all those present had to prostrate themselves and bury their faces in the ground. The maloango ate his meals alone, lest anyone who witnessed him in this activity should

[6] *Ibid.*, p. 155.

163

cause him to die. The common weal of the Vili people depended on the king's good health and physical perfection. None of these ideas and rituals was unique to Loango. All were borrowings from a common stock of African royal custom and protocol, which seemingly could be drawn upon whenever and wherever it was needed.

The people of Loango had compensated for their poverty in food production by developing manufactures, especially the weaving of cloth from raphia and other palm fibres, which they gathered from the local forests, and later from the extensive groves of palm trees which they planted on the coastal plain. These textiles they traded, along with the sea salt which they filtered and boiled from the coastal lagoons. They used their skills as boatmen not only in the coastal trade, but by planting relay stations at intervals up the valley of the Nyari, by which the copper and iron of Mindouli could be brought down to the coast with only a short overland portage over the intervening watershed. During the fifteenth and sixteenth centuries, when Atlantic commerce was dominated by the Portuguese, its main impact was on the African coasting trade, in which European shipping increasingly displaced that previously carried in short relays by sea-going canoes. By the mid-seventeenth century, however, Dutch merchants were doing a brisk trade in copper from Loango, and they noted how, in the September of each year, a large caravan of Vili smiths and labourers travelled the 90 miles up the Nyari valley to Bungu. While the labourers extracted the ore, the craftsmen smelted it and cast it into ingots for transport back to the coast at the onset of the next dry season. In the 1640s a Dutch trader estimated that the port of Loango could supply up to 80,000 pounds of copper annually. The copper ingots cast in the lower Congo, identifiable by their tiny size, were very widely dispersed across the whole surrounding region. Eugenia Herbert, the historian of copper production in Africa, has speculated on the convergence in the rainforest of copper from all three of the major sources in the continent. She writes that, by the nineteenth century, 'the zone supplied with copper from the Lower Congo must have come close to meeting that supplied by Katanga. Similarly, if copper from the Lower Congo was reaching the Uele, it may well have complemented that diffused south from Hofrat an-Nahas.'[7]

Similarly, the trade in ivory expanded to meet the Dutch demand, with the ivory frontier advancing as far as the Teke plateau in the east and the Ogowe basin in the north. Normally, sea salt was offered in

[7] Eugenia W. Herbert, *The Red Gold of Africa* (Madison, 1984), pp. 20 and 161.

exchange for tusks, and large-scale enterprises were set up to head-load goods from the coast to the interior and vice versa. At first, there was little or no trade in slaves with the Europeans, but by the end of the seventeenth century and on into the eighteenth, when Dutch and Luso-Brazilian demand for slaves greatly increased, and as supplies of copper and ivory dwindled, Loango became one of the most important slaving areas on the whole Atlantic seaboard, with 10,000 or more captives shipped out each year. Guns, cotton textiles, iron goods, beads, alcohol and tobacco were traded for slaves captured from wide areas of the inner Congo basin, the Kongo kingdom and Angola. For a time, Loango was the chief beneficiary from the trade, but later in the eighteenth century the trading advantage passed to its southern neighbours in the kingdoms of Kakongo and Ngoyo, which were closer to the Congo estuary and to the main sources of supply.

As the Atlantic trade developed, first in copper and ivory, and later in slaves, so the mercantile system of the Vili linked up with the trading chiefs of the Teke, who controlled their access to the Malebo Pool. But by the end of the eighteenth century the Vili had learned to by-pass the Pool altogether, using instead the Alima tributary of the upper Congo to reach the Bobangi 'people of the river', who lived and traded along the stretch of the river between the Pool and the Ubangi confluence. By the early nineteenth century these had become the main middlemen for the trade of the whole interior basin of the great river, and their tongue had become the trade language of the whole complex trading system which fed into the European ports along the coast. In the rapid expansion of economic horizons, these equatorial societies were by no means just static spectators. As Robert Harms has written, 'the Europeans could do no more than come to the coast; it was African initiative that forged trade routes seventeen hundred miles into the interior and developed the marketplaces and diplomatic machinery for long-distance trade'.[8] It was by means of Bobangi canoes plying the upper Congo and its great Ubangi tributary that the peoples of the northern savanna woodlands first came into contact with the coast-based commercial network of the European trading companies. The Muslim states of the open savanna further to the north had their first experience of foreign commercial imperialism when Egypt conquered the Nilotic Sudan early in the nineteenth century. The two systems were to meet explosively in the previously isolated region of the equatorial forests in the latter half of the century.

[8] Robert Harms, *River of Wealth, River of Sorrow* (New Haven, 1981), pp. 23–4.

11   The land of the blacksmith kings

As we saw in the previous chapter, the last, and the largest, of the conquering migrations from Bungu was that which was directed southwards across the lower Congo river and on to the iron-rich northern edge of the Angolan plateau. Here, the war-leader, using the title *Nakongo* or *Manikongo*, established his initial settlement, which was to become the permanent capital of the new kingdom, at Mbanza Kongo, the future São Salvador. All this was the country of the northern Mbundu, and the conquering settlers are said to have married the daughters of the Mbundu and to have recognised the spiritual authority of their chiefs (*kitome*). However, the Kongo asserted their own political predominance, and no doubt the centres of their excellent iron-working industry soon became the natural markets to which the Mbundu farmers of the surrounding area brought their produce for the purposes of trade and tribute. The numbers of the immigrants and their cultural impact were together strong enough to secure the prevalence of their Kongo language, in which the word 'Mbundu' came to denote only the unassimilated people of the remoter areas, who could lawfully be taken into slavery.

Meantime, the concentration of population around Mbanza Kongo soon resulted in a shortage of cultivable land. Famines occurred, and organised bands of colonists were sent out under Kongo chiefs to establish new settlements in the surrounding regions. From the central district of Mpemba, some expeditions went north-east to Nsundi and Mpangu, the provinces between Mpemba and Lake Malebo. Others went eastwards to Mbata. Others again went westwards to Soyo and Mbamba, the provinces between Mpemba and the Atlantic coast. Each expedition was led by a chief selected by the Manikongo, who was accompanied by representatives from each of the main Kongo clans, consisting of an elder and his wives and children and his Mbundu clients. From the historical boasting-songs handed on from father to son in these clan segments, the Belgian missionary Van Wing was able, some six or seven centuries later, to reconstruct a vivid picture of the dispersal. 'On our departure from Kongo', goes one account, 'there were nine caravans under nine chiefs with their staffs of office. We brought with us the basket containing the relics of our ancestors, which are used in the installation of chiefs. We brought the grass rings for the chiefs' roof-tops. The paths we travelled were safe. We kept all together. We were careful not to separate . . . The villages we built were peaceful.'[1]

Although some accounts suggest the opening up of new agricultural land, previously occupied only by hunter-gatherers, much of the expansion must have repeated the circumstances of the original settlement, with Kongo settlers and their assimilated adherents forcing their authority upon older Mbundu populations. Above all, it was evidently a structured expansion, in which the migrants maintained their links with the central monarchy. Tribute flowed to the capital, and the principal chiefs were appointed by the king, each of them taking as a symbol of his allegiance a brand from the royal fire and passing it on down the line of authority from his own provincial headquarters. When the Portuguese reached the region in the 1480s, the western provinces of Soyo and Mbamba had already been extended to the sea coast, and at the opposite end of the kingdom the royal armies were fighting the Teke on the frontiers of Nsundi. From the genealogical evidence about the central dynasty recorded somewhat later, it would appear that the Manikongo who was ruling at the time of the Portuguese contact was either the fourth or the fifth of his line. It is therefore reasonable to date the conquest of Mpemba at least to the fourteenth century.

The Kongo kingdom was not, however, the only one to have developed to the point of having a hierarchy of chiefdoms paying tribute to a central dynasty. In the north-east the Teke had, as we have seen, probably evolved something similar at an even earlier date, which may have been the ritual prototype for the early Kongo development in Bungu. The three coastal kingdoms to the north of the Congo estuary grew likewise into hierarchical structures, owing allegiance to conquering Kongo-speaking dynasties which claimed to have special expertise in the mysteries of smelting and forging metals (above, pp. 161–3). Finally, all down the eastern side of the main Kongo kingdom, and curving round it to the ocean coast to the south, lay a region that was pervaded by mobile groups of blacksmiths, which showed a propensity to develop into ruling dynasties wherever conditions were favourable.

In his study of the history of the southern Mbundu, Joseph Miller has shown that the earliest layer of political authority in central Angola was one based on ruling clans, each supposed to be descended from the first agricultural settlers of a particular small locality. For

[1] J. Van Wing, *Etudes Bakongo* (Brussels, 1921), pp. 78–80.

regalia, the ruling clan-heads employed cult objects carved in wood called *lunga*, which were essentially immobile, each being connected with a particular unexpandable piece of territory. However, the next layer of political authority was one introduced by groups of blacksmiths, who always arrived from the north and used regalia made of iron, called *ngola*, which symbolised a type of authority which was essentially mobile, expansive and hierarchical. Ngola emblems could be carried about from place to place. They could be used to wean people away from their local, lunga-based loyalties into new and wider groupings. As itinerant craftsmen, smiths were necessarily traders, interested in the security of the paths connecting one small community with another. They were also armourers, making weapons vital for successful hunting and warfare. They were ideally placed to organise warrior bands and to become the military patrons of small communities of settled farmers. Miller postulates a period of central Angolan history when rival organisations of ngola-bearing warrior smiths were competing for political authority over groups of lunga-owning territorial chiefdoms among the southern Mbundu. At about the same time as the Kongo kingdom was expanding its authority over the country of the northern Mbundu, one of the several ngola-bearing chieftainships was emerging supreme in the contest for control of the southern Mbundu. Its ruler assumed the title of *Ngola a kiluanje* (the conquering Ngola), and it was from this title that the early Portuguese navigators applied the name Angola to all the country south of Kongo. By the early sixteenth century the Ngola's kingdom had become the centralised, tribute-imposing kingdom of Ndongo, with a hierarchy of chiefs at several levels, and an army that was capable of blocking any further southward expansion of Kongo.[2]

THE PORTUGUESE AND THE OPENING OF THE ATLANTIC

Such in outline was the situation in western Central Africa when in 1483 a Portuguese caravel captained by the famous navigator Diogo Cão, sailing southwards on a voyage of exploration from Elmina, encountered muddy water several miles offshore and turned eastwards to investigate. Thus Cão reached the estuary of the Congo, called by the local people Nzadi (whence Zaïre), and made contact with the subjects of the Manikongo, Nzinga a Nkuwu. In the course of a later voyage in 1485–6 Cão visited the capital, twenty-three days' march inland, and then sailed home carrying a party of Kongo

[2] Joseph C. Miller, *Kings and Kinsmen* (Oxford, 1976), pp. 59–80.

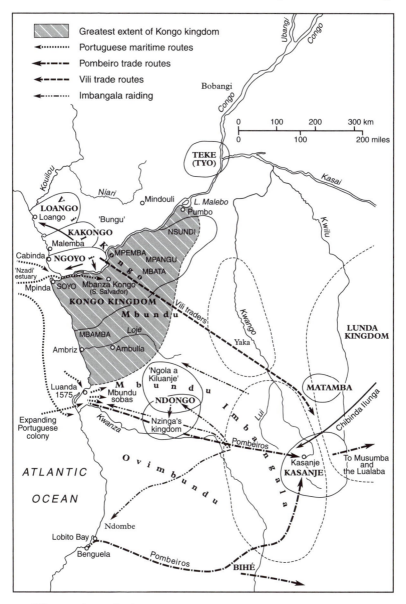

20 Western Central Africa

emissaries, who on their arrival in Lisbon were baptised into the Christian faith and placed in a monastery for initiation into Western ways. They were returned to Kongo in 1491 in a fleet of three caravels, carrying Portuguese priests, masons, carpenters and soldiers, a selection of domestic animals including horses and cattle, samples of European cloth and other manufactures, even a printing-press complete with two German printers. The ships anchored at Mpinda in the Congo estuary, and after a brief halt to baptise the provincial governor of Soyo, who was an uncle of the Manikongo, the expedition proceeded to the capital, where Nzinga a Nkuwu and five of his leading chiefs were baptised on 3 May 1491. A thousand of the Manikongo's subjects were detailed to assist the Portuguese masons in the building of a church. Meanwhile the Portuguese soldiers accompanied the armies of the king in a campaign to defend the north-eastern province of Nsundi from Teke raiders, in which European firearms contributed to a decisive victory and to the taking of many war captives. Most of the Portuguese then departed, carrying away a valuable cargo of ivory and slaves. The priests and craftsmen remained in Kongo, where the king's profession of their faith proved short-lived. However, that of his son Nzinga Mbemba, the governor of Nsundi, baptised as Afonso in 1491, developed into a lifelong commitment to Christianity and the Portuguese alliance. On the death of Nzinga a Nkuwu around 1506, Afonso won a disputed succession struggle and reigned until about 1543. These years marked the zenith of Portuguese influence in Kongo.

From the very beginning of his reign Afonso made serious efforts to transform his loose-knit African empire towards what he understood of the pattern of a Christian state of the Renaissance period in Europe. He sent for more missionaries and technicians, of whom the first contingent arrived in 1512. He stepped up the flow of Kongo students to Lisbon. He himself studied the laws of Portugal, which were sent to him in five great volumes, and informed himself in detail about the etiquette of the Portuguese court and the ranking system of European society. Soon his provincial governors were known as dukes, and his military leaders and court officials as counts and marquises, while the sartorial fineries sent from Lisbon were distributed to the inner circles of the Kongo aristocracy. It should not be assumed that such changes were merely superficial. Probably they symbolised a general hardening of the social structure in Kongo, whereby members of the conquering clans which had spread out from Mpemba into the surrounding provinces now became increasingly consolidated into a ruling class. Likewise, the early spread of

Christianity probably helped the process of social differentiation. It was a classic case of 'conversion from the top'. In 1513 Afonso took an oath of obedience to the pope, and three years later a Franciscan missionary wrote ecstatically of the king's Christian qualities. 'It seems to me from the way he speaks as though he is not a man but rather an angel, sent by the Lord into this kingdom to convert it; for I assure you that it is *he* who instructs *us*, and that he knows better than we do the Prophets and the Gospel of our Lord Jesus Christ and the lives of the saints and all the things concerning our Holy Mother the Church. For he devotes himself entirely to study, so that it often happens that he falls asleep over his books, and often he forgets to eat and drink in talking of the things of our Lord.'[3]

However, within Kongo society, the spread of the faith seems to have followed aristocratic channels, affecting the court at São Salvador and diffusing from there by a transformation of the traditional system of educating the sons of chiefs in the households of the great. Seen from the Kongo end, Christianity was the route to royal favour, the badge of the successful faction within a ruling group. Its connections with the universal Church were very slender, depending upon a dozen white missionaries, a few uncertainly motivated European craftsmen and a handful of Kongo students returning from Portugal, among them a son of Afonso who had been priested in Lisbon and consecrated to the episcopate in Rome. Like the ngola hierarchies among the Mbundu, the new religion was perhaps seen by the populace at large in the light of a powerful secret society introduced from abroad.

Of course, despite his Christian piety, Afonso was throughout his reign deeply involved in the capture and sale of slaves to the Portuguese. It was the inevitable price which he had to pay for his European advisers and for the material luxuries with which he rewarded his chief subjects. Without doubt, his slaving wars gave a military impetus to his kingdom and consolidated his authority in the border regions to the east and the south. The condition of success in these adventures was, however, that the trade should remain a royal monopoly. Hence his growing disquiet with the Portuguese sea-captains, who tried to trade directly with his subjects and even with his enemies. The official trading expeditions were soon supplemented by those of Portuguese colonists, many of them transported convicts, who had been settled since the 1490s on the

---

[3] Letter from Rui d'Aguar to King Manuel of Portugal, 25 May 1516, in A. Brasio, (ed.), *Monumenta Missionaria Africana*, vol. I (Lisbon, 1953), p. 361.

islands of São Tomé and Principe, and whose sugar plantations required large numbers of agricultural slaves. These men felt no obligation to support the alliance between Portugal and Kongo. They sailed up and down the coast, trading with the subordinate chiefs of the Manikongo and with others beyond his sway. They discovered the Kwanza river and sailed up its slow-flowing waters to make contact with the Ngola a kiluanje. Indeed, it is highly likely that the final emergence of the Ngola as the supreme power among the southern Mbundu was due to wars of conquest stimulated by the demand for slaves of the São Tomé settlers. At all events, the unofficial Portuguese were now in touch with the Manikongo's most powerful rival, and a series of official missions, beginning in 1520, all failed to bring the situation under control. So long as Afonso lived, there was no direct confrontation, but thirteen years after his death, in 1556, there was war on the frontier between the armies of the Manikongo and those of the Ngola, in which Kongo forces suffered a severe defeat. It was not the end of the Portuguese alliance with Kongo, but certainly it marked the moment when the civilising mission of Portugal was overtaken by the economic interest of the Atlantic slave trade, now centred on the growing sugar plantations of Brazil. The situation between the kingdom of Benin and the principalities of the Niger Delta had been reproduced in western Central Africa.

THE YAKA, THE PORTUGUESE AND THE IMBANGALA

It was in conection with the war of 1556 between Kongo and Ndongo (the kingdom of the Ngola) that the Portuguese first heard of people whom they called 'Jaga', who lived in the far interior and who sent warrior bands of extreme ferocity to fight alongside the Mbundu of Ndongo. Though the Portuguese later applied the term to other peoples using similar methods of warfare, there can be little doubt that at this stage it referred to the Yaka people who inhabited the middle reaches of the Kwango valley and who were the eastern neighbours of the Mbundu and the Kongo. Along with the Teke, who lived to the north of them, the Yaka had probably been among the main victims of the slave-raids conducted by the Kongo since the opening of the Atlantic trade. With the weakening of the Kongo kingdom following the death of Afonso, the raided became the raiders, joining forces with the Mbundu, not only for the defence of Ndongo but in many subsequent invasions of Kongo territory. These began during the reign of Afonso's grandson, Diogo (1545–61). His successor,

Bernardo (1561–7), was killed while fighting the Yaka on the eastern frontier. The next king, Henrique (1567–8), died in a war against the Teke. His successor, Alvaro (1568–87), had barely acceded when the whole eastern side of the Kongo kingdom was laid waste by a great invasion of Yaka war-bands, which swept through the provinces of Mbata and Mpemba, capturing and sacking São Salvador itself in 1569. Alvaro fled with his courtiers to an island in the lower Congo and sent desperate appeals for help to his Portuguese allies. Meantime the Yaka made profitable contact with the São Tomé traders at the ports of the Congo estuary, to whom they sold thousands of their Kongo captives, including members of the royal family and other notables.

So far as the Portuguese were concerned, it seemed at first that, once again, São Tomé had triumphed over the metropolis. However, when news of the disasters in Kongo at last reached Lisbon in February 1571, it provoked a revolution in Portuguese policy towards western Central Africa as a whole. On the one hand, an expeditionary force of some 600 Portuguese matchlockmen was quickly despatched to help Alvaro to regain his throne. On the other hand, the decision was taken to abandon further attempts to negotiate a peaceful relationship with Ndongo, and instead to grant a royal charter to Paulo Dias, the grandson of the great explorer Bartholomew Dias, permitting him to conquer the territory between the southern frontier of Kongo and a line 35 leagues to the south of the Kwanza, of part of which he would be the hereditary Lord Proprietor, and of the rest governor for life on behalf of the Portuguese Crown. The unspoken premise of the charter was that there would be perpetual warfare between the colony and the Ngola of Ndongo, at whose expense all conquests behind the coastal belt would have to be made. The preamble to the charter stated that conquest would promote the spread of the Christian faith, and it clearly envisaged that this would be mainly achieved by the conversion of war captives prior to their despatch as slaves to the New World. In Kongo, the Portuguese expeditionary force was successful in restoring Alvaro in 1574. The Yaka, unnerved by their first experience of firearms in trained hands, were soon driven back to their bases on the eastern frontier. The Kongo kingdom entered upon a second long period of stability, lasting till the mid-seventeenth century, during which the slave trade centred upon the markets on the Teke frontier, above all that at Pumbo near the southern shore of Lake Malebo. The traders who organised the caravan traffic to this market became known in Portuguese as *pombeiros*, and so dominant was 173 their role that the term was later applied to all traders operating in the far interior of western Central Africa. Meanwhile, in 1575 Paulo Dias carried out the occupation of Luanda Island. In the following year a bridgehead was established on the mainland, in the neighbourhood of the modern town.

For nearly 200 years the colony of Angola developed essentially as a gigantic slave-trading enterprise. The garrison seldom numbered more than 1000 European troops, armed only with matchlocks and scattered in half a dozen small forts in or near the Kwanza valley. To these were gradually added some thousands of slave soldiers, who fought with bows and spears. The strategy was to conquer first one and then another of the small Mbundu chieftainships, forcing the local rulers (called *sobas*) into a state of allegiance in which they paid tribute in slaves, whom they obtained by attacking their still independent neighbours further inland. Those most inclined to resist migrated into the interior and placed themselves under the protection of the Ngola of Ndongo, who soon began to mount major campaigns against the advancing frontiers of the colony. The territorial expansion of the Portuguese was thus slowed, but the slave trade was still fed by the captives made in this frontier warfare. Already by the last quarter of the sixteenth century the export of slaves from Luanda to Brazil averaged between 5000 and 10,000 persons a year. Alongside the purely military activity there grew up a commercial enterprise based on the local cabotage trade of the Portuguese up and down the coast of western Central Africa. The pombeiros who traded into the interior of Kongo with the salt and sea-shells of Luanda returned not only with slaves but with tens of thousands of the fine raphia cloths of the forest margins, which were in high demand with the Mbundu. Other pombeiros accompanied the military expeditions of the colonial garrisons and traded in the intervals of warfare.

Besides the direct trading and warfare between the Portuguese and the Mbundu, the Angolan slave trade was augmented by a third and more gruesome factor. This was the activity of nomadic bands of people who had entirely abandoned the food-producing way of life and who lived by raiding others, consuming their crops and their cattle and felling their oil palms for palm wine, before moving on to repeat the process elsewhere. Because of the similarity of their operations to those of the Yaka bands which raided the Kongo kingdom in the 1550s and 1560s, the Portuguese described these people indiscriminately as 'Jaga'. In point of fact there may have been no connection at all between the Yaka, who spoke a language closely akin to

Kongo, and the more southerly bands who operated among the Mbundu and their neighbours to the south, who later came to be known as Imbangala. These represented in some sense the extreme fringe of the westerly migrations of older Lunda lineages and political titles away from the reorganisation of Lunda society by the dynasty descending from the Chibinda Ilunga (below, p. 183). But although many of these groups maintained the tradition of their Lunda origins and of their long march to the west, only a small fraction of them could have had Lunda blood in their veins, because the migrants had incorporated fresh elements at every stage of their journey. Indeed, taken at their face value, Imbangala traditions appear to relate how, after crossing the Kasai, the main body had adopted the singular custom of destroying their own children at birth and of keeping up their numbers by adopting adolescents from the peoples whom they conquered on their travels. In reality, as Joseph Miller has shown, the so-called destruction of children referred to a system of military initiation known as the *kilombo*, in which lineage ties were utterly renounced, and children, whether born in the group or adopted, were brought up communally in quasi-military formations.[4] At all events, the elimination of family life was the ultimate adaptation to an economy of militaristic parasitism. Even more effectively than the Nguni migrants from southeastern Africa in the early nineteenth century, the Imbangala 'cultivated with the spear'.

The first written description of an Imbangala band was made by an English sailor, Andrew Battell, a war captive of the Portuguese, who employed him as the captain of a coastal trading vessel operating out of Luanda. Around 1600 Battell sailed southwards to Lobito Bay to buy foodstuffs for the colony. He found that the local community of Ndombe people had been destroyed by a band of some 16,000 Imbangala, who were living in a stockaded war-camp, eating and drinking the fruits of their victory. On at least some ritual occasions, human flesh was consumed with relish. Battell painted an intimidating picture of the leader of the band, one Kalandula. 'He weareth a palm-cloth about his middle, as fine as silk. His body is carved and cut with sundry works, and every day is anointed with the fat of men. He weareth a piece of copper cross his nose, two inches long, and in his ears also. His body is always painted red and white. He hath twenty or thirty wives, which follow him when he goeth abroad; and one of them carrieth his bows and arrows; and

<hr>

[4] Miller, *Kings and Kinsmen*, p. 234.

four of them carry his cups of drink after him. And when he drinketh, they all kneel down, and clap their hands and sing.'[5]

As befitted a desperado of his period, Battell ferried a detachment of Kalendula's followers across the Kuvu river to attack another Ndombe settlement, living on the site of the future Portuguese town of Old Benguela, and in due course sailed back to Luanda with the first of many cargoes of very cheap slaves. When, five months later, the band moved away into the interior in search of fresh victims, Battell and fifty other Portuguese merchants followed in their train. It was the beginning of a long partnership between Portuguese slave traders and Imbangala bands, which were soon operating around all the frontiers of the colony and of Ndongo.

THE SEVENTEENTH AND EIGHTEENTH CENTURIES

Thanks to the military and commercial activity of the Portuguese and to the operations of the Imbangala bands in the interior, the mainspring of historical change during the seventeenth and eighteenth centuries lay in the southern half of the region. The first crucial issue concerned the survival of Ndongo, and it centred on the astonishing career of a female ruler, Nzinga Mbande, who succeeded to the Ngolaship in 1624. Nzinga appreciated that the best hope for her kingdom, beset by the Portuguese on the west and by the Imbangala on the north and south, lay in establishing the position of an intermediary in the slave trade, whereby Ndongo would become an ally of the Portuguese, and the main source of slaves would be transferred from her own dominions to those of her eastern neighbours. Already before her accession, Nzinga had travelled as an envoy to Luanda, where the outlines of such an arrangement were agreed and were sealed by her own solemn baptism as Dona Ana Nzinga, the Portuguese governor standing as her godfather. The honeymoon proved, however, of short duration. During the second year of her reign Dona Ana appealed for Portuguese help against the Imbangala invaders of her kingdom. Forces were sent, but soon turned to slave-raiding on their own account. Western Ndongo was overrun, and refugees converged upon Dona Ana's headquarters in the east of the country. From there she led them north-eastwards to conquer and settle the region of Matamba, between Ndongo and the middle Kwango. Abandoning all her Christian connections, and

[5] E. Ravenstein (ed.), *The Strange Adventures of Andrew Battell* (London, 1901), pp. 31–2.

adopting much of the military organisation of the Imbangala, she succeeded in building up a powerful slave-raiding and middleman state, which remained of importance until the second half of the eighteenth century. After flirting briefly with the Dutch, who captured and ruled Luanda from 1641 till 1648, Dona Ana renewed her treaty relations with the Portuguese in 1656, and died, once more in the arms of the Church, in 1663, at the age of eighty-one.

Meanwhile, to the south of Matamba, the Imbangala bands were at last beginning to settle down. In some sense, the process may be traced back to the second decade of the seventeenth century, when several Imbangala bands closed in on both sides of the Kwanza valley in order to be in regular touch with the Portuguese frontier and the main trade route to Luanda. In these circumstances the bands started to treat the local Mbundu less as temporary victims and more as long-term subjects. On the one hand Mbundu youths were initiated into the *kilombo* formations, and on the other hand the Imbangala masters became progressively Mbunduised, taking Mbundu wives and adopting Mbundu lineages. As the Portuguese pushed their advanced posts further into central Ndongo, the Imbangala followed Dona Ana's example by retreating further into the interior in order to maintain their independence. Some time around 1630, one large group reached and conquered the region lying in the angle of the Lui and the Kwango rivers, henceforward known, after the leadership title of the conquering commander, as Kasanje. The original settlers were soon joined by others, and there emerged a new and powerful kingdom, and one which enjoyed an even more strategic situation than that of Matamba to the north of it, for across the Kwango from Kasanje lay the western frontier lands of the great kingdom of Lunda (below, pp. 182–8). Until around the 1680s the slave trade of Kasanje was supplied mainly by the captives from its own wars of conquest. Thereafter, an increasing proportion came from the frontier wars of the Lunda. Kasanje became the crucial broker state of the region, trading with the Lunda on the Kwango frontier and with the Portuguese pombeiros at marketplaces on its western borders. In the words of David Birmingham, 'the Portuguese now needed to play a much less active military role in Angola; they organised the final purchase and shipment of slaves, but most of the actual capturing of slaves passed out of their hands'.[6]

The rise of Angola, Matamba and Kasanje was accompanied during the late seventeenth and and eighteenth centuries by the

[6] David Birmingham, *Trade and Conflict in Angola* (Oxford, 1966), p. 132.

disintegration of the kingdom of Kongo. During the fifty years which followed the restoration of the monarchy after the Yaka invasions, as many as 1000 Portuguese traders had settled in the main towns of the kingdom, marrying local wives and founding a Luso-African bourgeoisie, whose descendants formed the core of a mercantile and nominally Christian community. The Church was still served by missionaries from Europe, but there were also some native clergy, and in the capital a small literate class of secretaries and bureaucrats helped the kings to collect their revenues and to conduct their relations with Luanda and São Tomé, Lisbon and Rome. Nevertheless, the expansion of the Portuguese colony and of the Imbangala bands operating around its fringes proved an increasing threat to the security of the southern provinces. In 1622 frontier disputes suddenly flamed into war, and the Kongo armies were soundly defeated by a combination of Portuguese and Imbangala forces. On the death of the king during the same year, faction fighting broke out within Kongo itself, and six rulers held the throne for brief periods during the following nineteen years. Stability was briefly restored under a king named Garcia II, who reigned from 1641 till 1661, largely thanks to the interval of Dutch rule at Luanda. With the return of the Portuguese, hostilities were resumed, culminating in 1665 in a great battle at Ambuila, when a Kongo army said to number 70,000 was virtually wiped out.

After the battle of Ambuila the Kongo kingdom broke up. The Manikongo Antonio had perished on the field, and none of the contenders for the succession was able to establish his authority over more than a limited area. The coastal province of Soyo had already been independent for some years. The southern province of Mbamba was overrun by slave-raiding bands. In the north, two rival dynasties competed indecisively until 1709, when one of them succeeded in reoccupying the capital, though with a greatly reduced territory. In these circumstances the old trade routes fell into disuse. The trade of the regions to the east of Kongo was tapped from Matamba to the south and, increasingly, from the rising commercial system of the Vili people from the three Kongo-ruled kingdoms north of the Congo estuary (above, pp. 163–4). From the late seventeenth century onwards the accent in the export trade shifted increasingly to slaves, and here the Vili distinguished themselves by developing a remarkable system of canoe transport, using the Nyari and its tributaries to reach the slave and ivory markets around the shores of Lake Malebo, thus undercutting the Portuguese pombeiros with their coffles of slaves on foot and caravans of human porters.

An important advantage for the Vili was that their European trade connections were with the Dutch, and later with the French and English merchants, rather than with the Portuguese. They were thus able to obtain more favourable terms of trade, and also access to the all-important trade in firearms.

To the south of the main Luanda trade route up the Kwanza valley to Kasanje and Lunda there rose the Bihe plateau, which was inhabited by the Ovimbundu and related peoples. At least as early as the seventeenth century the Ovimbundu had begun to form little kingdoms, similar in structure to the early Kongo kingdoms, but with some Lunda features, passed on to them no doubt by the Imbangala. By the middle of the eighteenth century these Ovimbundu kingdoms were deeply involved in the Atlantic slave trade. At first they sold their captives through Ndongo to Luanda, but later they took to trading directly with the southern port of Benguela. This had been founded early in the seventeenth century as a colony of settlement for Portuguese fishermen and farmers rather than for traders. Some of these farmers moved inland and settled in the Bihe highlands, marrying local women and becoming *sertanejos*, backwoodsmen, the pombeiros of the southern region. By the middle of the eighteenth century, Benguela had begun to overtake Luanda as the main Portuguese slaving port, and by the end of the century the Ovimbundu kingdoms had expanded to dominate a vast region stretching northwards nearly to the Kwanza and southwards to the Cunene. They thus became the most southerly exponents of the political and social influences of the Kongo and Lunda political traditions.

12   From the Lualaba to the Zambezi

On the East African plateau, as we have seen, the essential feature of the later Iron Age was the advent of northern influences from the basin of the upper Nile, associated in pottery manufacture with roulette-decorated wares, the wide distribution of which betokened a much more complete occupation of the land by food-producers than had occurred in early Iron Age times. Specifically, it had meant a diffusion both of specialised pastoralism and of mixed cattle and cereal farming among peoples who had until then been almost exclusively vegecultural. On the Central African plateau, in eastern Zambia and Malawi, a similarly abrupt transition took place around the eleventh century, when the early Iron Age ceramic forms, traditionally made by men, were replaced by radically different ones, typified by that called Luangwa pottery, traditionally made by women. This coincided with a corresponding change in settlement patterns away from the concentrated villages of the early Iron Age to a more dispersed pattern, suggesting a change towards a more cattle-oriented style of farming.

In Central Africa to the west of the Luangwa tributary of the middle Zambezi, however, the later Iron Age meant something very different. The key region here was the Shaba (Katanga) province of Congo (Zaïre), where the later Iron Age material culture seems to have resulted from a period of accelerated development within the region itself. Primarily, this was an improvement in metallurgical techniques which occurred in and around the northern Copperbelt, and which caused a general enrichment of the whole material culture. From Shaba it spread southwards into western Zambia, and westwards across the Kasai to Angola. The transitional phase between the early and later Iron Age culture probably began towards the end of the first millennium AD, but successive stages of its development continued to ripple outwards until about the seventeenth century. In social and political organisation, the crucial developments probably occurred fairly late on, making some use of systems and ideas which spread southwards from the later Iron Age kingdoms of the East African plateau, especially those situated in Rwanda, Burundi and Kivu. Not many parts of southern Central Africa were suited to specialised pastoralism, or to the kind of political and economic interaction between

180

pastoralists and cultivators characteristic of the later Iron Age cultures of the East African plateau. Nevertheless, in both north-eastern and south-western Zambia there were some societies in which pastoral aristocracies played an important role, and the same was certainly true of later Iron Age societies in Zimbabwe.

THE LUBA AND THE LUNDA

The central population of the Shaba region was the Luba. They lived between the Lualaba and the Bushimai, in a land drained by a hundred rivers and tributary streams flowing northwards in long, straight, parallel valleys towards the forested centre of the Congo basin. Though Lubaland is often described as savanna, in fact its valleys are mostly filled with forest galleries, and even the intervening ridges are quite heavily wooded. It is essentially a land of fishermen and riverside planters, who use the ridges mainly for hunting, and who are prevented by the prevalence of the tsetse-fly from keeping many cattle. Archaeologically, Lubaland is best known at its eastern extremity, where the Lualaba flows through a series of lakes filling the lower parts of the Lupemba depression. Here, at the end of the first millennium, lakeside fishermen, almost certainly Luba, were moving into a phase of later Iron Age culture known as Early Kisalian. This was succeeded from about the eleventh till about the thirteenth century by a phase called Classical Kisalian, which may have overlapped from about the twelfth century onwards with another, intrusive culture called the Kabambian. Kisalian pottery, though distinctive, is clearly reminiscent of early Iron Age wares, and the metal artifacts, both jewellery and weapons, are mostly of iron. Kabambian pottery, by contrast, is almost undecorated, though finished with a shiny red slip, and the characteristic metal goods are of copper, including very elaborate articles of jewellery and large quantities of small copper croisettes, which must have been used for currency and must indicate the existence of a considerable network of local trade.

All these developments in material culture appear to have preceded the political reorganisation of Lubaland, which forms the starting-point of Luba traditional history, and which refers to a period around the fourteenth and fifteenth centuries. The traditions describe a double process of infiltration and conquest which established ruling lineages known as *balopwe*, whose members came to hold all but the most local kind of chiefly offices in a series of four main kingdoms embracing most of northern and central Lubaland. The southern part of Lubaland was unaffected. As with the Kintu traditions of southern Uganda, the Luba traditions have personalised and telescoped a process which must have operated over a wide geographical area and through a considerable period of time. The first such personification is that called Kongolo, which is also the name of an ancient settlement area at the head of the Lualaba rapids to the north of eastern Lubaland. The second figure is that of Ilunga Mbili, who is associated with the region to the east of the Lualaba, then occupied by peoples called Kunde and Kalanga. As traditionally presented, Ilunga reached Lubaland during the lifetime of Kongolo, and married his daughter, whose son Kalala eventually overthrew, and thus succeeded, his maternal grandfather. But this is a common traditional formula for concealing and legitimising a change of dynasty. The reality was probably that one set of outside influences was followed, perhaps much later, by a second. At all events, from these episodes northern Lubaland acquired some political coherence, which was reinforced by many of the common rituals of centralised kingship systems in use all the way from Darfur to Zimbabwe. Like so many others, Luba kings ate and drank in secret and concealed other natural functions. They practised royal incest with their queen-sisters, shared ritual authority with their queen-mothers, and used spirit mediums to communicate with royal ancestors. Human sacrifices were a part of the elaborate rituals surrounding their death and burial. As their principal symbol of authority they used royal fire, kindled at their accession and kept burning until their death, from which the fires of all subordinate chiefs had annually to be rekindled.

The developments referred to in the traditions of Kongolo and Ilunga Mbili used to be described as the first and second Luba 'empires'. This was certainly to convey a wholly misleading conception of the nature of political change in this and other parts of Africa during our period. No more than in the Uganda of the Kintu traditions were large kingdoms created by invading armies at one fell swoop. The earliest Luba kingdoms were certainly very small and probably very numerous. The more successful among them grew slowly at the expense of the others. Defeated dynasties often migrated to try their luck elsewhere. Above all, military forces were minute. Often they consisted of little groups of hunters, who naturally tended to be more mobile and better armed than the settled communities of farmers and fishermen.

The same considerations apply when we turn from the early history of the Luba to that of their western neighbours the Lunda, who lived astride the Kasai and its tributaries. The key figure connecting the history of the two regions is that of Chibinda Ilunga, presented in oral tradition as a Luba hunter, who moved into eastern Lunda and married Lueji, the 'granddaughter' of a small-scale Lunda chief, Yala Mwaku, whom he eventually succeeded as ruler. Lueji's 'brothers', Kinguri and Chinyama, refusing to recognise Chibinda's authority, migrated westwards and southwards, and founded dynasties among the Imbangala of central Angola (above, pp. 175–6) and the Luyana (Lozi) of north-western Zambia. In this case, it is today accepted that the names in the story are those not of individuals but rather of hereditary titles. Similarly, the relationships attributed to them are those of 'perpetual kinship', indicating seniority or juniority in the foundation of the title by the use of kinship terms such as 'father', 'son' or 'brother', while conquests and amalgamations are referred to as 'marriages', with the senior or victorious partner described as the husband and the subordinate one as the wife. The Chibinda Ilunga of the tradition is likewise not to be understood as a personal name but as the leadership title of a Luba hunting expedition despatched westwards into Lunda country by the ruler of one of the Luba kingdoms to the east. Throughout the region described in this chapter, it was in fact the custom for large-scale military or hunting expeditions to be commissioned by the ruler, who conferred his own title upon the leader as his personal representative. The subordinate chiefs would contribute their own contingents to the expedition, the officers in charge of which would bear the titles of the chiefs whom they represented. In this way, an expedition was organised as a scale-model of the parent kingdom. All that was necessary to complete the act of political reproduction was for the expedition to settle permanently in its hunting grounds, imposing its authority over the people of the area concerned. A new kingdom would have come into being with a superstructure similar to that of its parent, whose acquiescence would be secured by the payment of tribute, at least for a time.

The essential message of the tradition of Chibinda and Lueji is, therefore, that a long process of centralising conquest and amalgamation of small Lunda chiefdoms was set in motion by a band of adventurers of Luba origin, causing some of the older Lunda authorities to submit to them, while others moved away in an attempt to maintain their independence by imposing themselves on other Lunda living further to the west and the south. It was a process, not an event. It consisted of a series of often repeated episodes, widely spread over time and space. In the words of Joseph Miller, who has contributed much to the modern understanding of the problem, 'Early Lunda history should be . . . visualised as a gradual movement through several stages of political development characterised by progressively more centralised state structures.'[1] What began as the conquest of a tiny corner of Lundaland by a handful of Luba adventurers developed into an indigenous movement among the Lunda themselves. Probably it took some two or three centuries to reach the stage at which most Lunda-speaking people had been included within a single overarching political system, ruled by a dynasty stable enough for its historical traditions to present a sequence of reigns, each associated with a set of outstanding events. This stage was reached only about the middle of the seventeenth century, when a ruler (*mwata*) called Yamvo Naweji achieved a position of such prestige that all his descendants took his name for their title, so that the main Lunda kingdom was known as that of the Mwata Yamvos.

Lunda kingship seems to have developed as a much more effective instrument of political centralisation than its Luba progenitor. Very largely, it resulted from the pre-existing Lunda system of small matrilineal chieftainships over village communities (*tubungu* or *mwantangand*), each completely independent of its neighbours, but yet arranged in groups observing ties of perpetual kinship. It was a system which could be quite easily integrated under a central superstructure providing defence and security in exchange for taxation and tribute. The classic pattern of accommodation between Lunda tubungu and Luba balopwe was first worked out among a group of fifteen village settlements occupying a section of the valley of the upper Bushimai river, where all the later capitals (*musumba*) of the growing kingdom were to be built. The tubungus were recognised as 'chiefs of the land', rulers of the traditional communities, and the priestly intermediaries with the unseen world of ancestral spirits. In token of this, the tubungus of the fifteen original settlements held positions of the highest honour at the royal court, and exercised a central role in the selection, initiation and investiture of successive kings. As the kingdom expanded beyond its original nucleus, fresh groups of related tubungus made their submission to the kingship and were confirmed in their traditional functions. The only royal official operating at the local level was the *chilolo*, who established a village of his own at some central point among a group of related village settlements. Unlike that of the tubungu, the authority of the chilolo was purely secular and mainly fiscal. He collected the tribute

[1] Joseph C. Miller, *Kings and Kinsmen* (Oxford, 1976), p. 115.

from his district and forwarded it to his permanent representative at the royal court. In districts close to the capital the tribute was paid mainly in beer and foodstuffs. More distant districts paid in salt or copper, or else in manufactured goods such as tools and weapons, palm and raphia textiles, pots and basketry. The peripheral districts in a constantly expanding circle were those in which organised expeditions were still operating, and these returned the products of warfare and hunting, especially ivory and slaves.

The initial direction in which the Lunda kingdom expanded was westwards, across the Kasai to the Kwilu. All this country was already Lunda-speaking. Moreover, even before the arrival of the Mwata Yamvo's expeditions, this had been the direction taken by the eastern Lunda refugees, the followers of the Kinguri and the Chinyama title-holders in their flight from the Chibinda Ilunga. These had prepared the way for the later empire-builders. Already during the reign of Mwata Yamvo Naweji, these western Lunda provinces were visited by long-distance caravans from the Portuguese colony in Angola, bringing guns and cloth, spirits and tobacco, which were exchanged for the slaves and ivory captured by the Mwata Yamvo's frontier forces. Henceforward, the tribute requirements of the kingdom were increasingly geared to the needs of the long-distance trade. Expeditions were undertaken among non-Lunda peoples to the north and south of Lundaland, and in time this led to conquest and permanent occupation. The first non-Lunda to be absorbed were the Kosa living to the south of eastern Lundaland, and the significance of this extension of the kingdom was that it opened the door to a whole new line of eastward expanson to the south of the Luba kingdoms, among the politically fragmented peoples of the Congo–Zambezi watershed, such as the Kaonde and the Sanga, the Lembwe and the Shila, the Lemba and the Aushi. Here, in the late seventeenth and early eighteenth centuries, a series of expeditionary leaders bearing the title of Kazembe established tributary kingdoms too distant to be effectively controlled by the parent state, but where the supposed Lunda ancestry of the ruling groups was sufficient to maintain loose bonds of community and mutual respect. In the later eighteenth century the easternmost of these Kazembes, operating from a capital in the fertile and densely populated Luapula valley south of Lake Mweru, built up an empire even larger than that of the Mwata Yamvos, which stretched from the sources of the Lualaba to the south-western shores of Lake Tanganyika. Meanwhile, at the opposite end of the Lunda dominions, similar colonies were being formed beyond the effective borders of the parent state, of which the

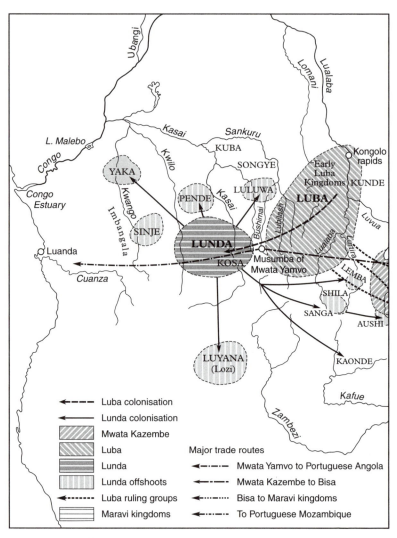

21 From the Lualaba to the Zambezi

largest was that founded among the Yaka people of the Kwango valley
by a Lunda conqueror who took the title of Mwene Mputa Kasongo.
Others were the kingdom of Kapenda Kamulemba among the
Shinje, that of Mwata Kumbana among the Pende and that of Mai
Munene among the Lulua.

Thus, by the later eighteenth century a wide swathe of Central
186   Africa from the Kwango to Lake Tanganyika was under the rule of

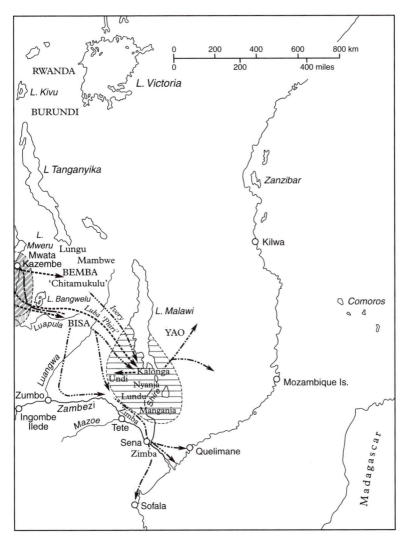

Lunda kingship, directly or indirectly tributary to the Mwata Yamvo residing in his capital town or musumba, which was rebuilt in every reign, but always in the narrow plain between the Bushimai and Lulua rivers. To the westward this great political complex traded with the Portuguese of Luanda through the Imbangala, who were themselves in a sense an offshoot of the Lunda expansion. To the eastward it traded through the Bisa and other intermediaries with   187 the Portuguese on the Zambezi, and it would soon do so directly with the Swahili merchants of the Zanzibar coast. In its geographical extent the Lunda empire of the eighteenth century was by far the largest political hegemony to emerge anywhere in Bantu Africa. In sheer size it rivalled the largest empires of the Sudanic belt. Yet this Lunda hegemony was in reality only the very lightest kind of super-structure. Except for tribute payments, every village community in the empire was self-governing, and, at least in the more distant dis-tricts, the amount of the tribute was mainly determined by the local willingness to pay. In these circumstances the longer-distance tribute payments became almost indistinguishable from trade, because substantial gifts were made in exchange for them. If it is true that tribute was the life-blood of the empire, it was not only, or even mainly, for fiscal reasons, but because tribute helped to stimulate the arteries of commerce. The military forces of the Mwata Yamvo were never large. Expeditions of 300 or 400 men, with only a handful of guns among them and mainly armed with swords and spears, were sent to capture slaves and to hunt elephants for their ivory in the Luba-ruled territories to the north and east of the capital. Otherwise little compulsion was used. But the flow of tribute ensured that all roads led to the musumba, which thus remained the principal centre of redistribution in Central Africa until, in the mid-nineteenth century, trading caravans from the outside became well enough armed to carve their own direct routes to the resources they wished to exploit.

THE SOUTH-EASTWARD SPREAD OF LUBA SYSTEMS: MARAVI, BISA AND BEMBA

During the same period that Luba systems of empire were spreading out westward into Lunda territory and beyond, a similar movement was in progress to the east of the Lualaba, in the region between Lake Mweru and the lower Zambezi, and in all probability reaching to the Zimbabwean plateau as well. But whereas the westward move-ment produced results which were still clearly visible during the nineteenth century, the traces of the south-easterly movement were nearly obliterated, on the one hand by the expansion of the Lunda Kazembes across the area of its origin, and on the other hand by the invasion and settlement of the Ngoni peoples of Zulu origin right up the highlands of the Malawi–Zambia frontier. These developments of the late eighteenth and early nineteenth centuries caused the sup-pression of much traditional evidence concerning earlier periods, and it has only been through the very careful scrutiny of what little survives, in the light of early Portuguese documentation of the region, that it has been possible to reconstruct the outlines of its earlier history.

It is clear that the most significant group involved in this whole process was that which called itself Maravi or Malawi (meaning 'flames') in order to distinguish the immigrant aristocracy of Luba origin from the Nyanja, Chewa and Manganja populations among whom they had settled. The leading element among the Maravi was the Phiri clan, which provided the royal dynasties for a number of loosely organised kingdoms existing in the region to the west and south of Lake Malawi at least from the fifteenth century and perhaps somewhat earlier. The senior Maravi kingdom, which apparently sired the others, had its capital towns among the Nyanja people around the southern shores of the lake. It was ruled by Phiri kings, who bore the title of *kalonga*, and whose queens, bearing the title of *mwali*, had to be drawn from the Banda clan. To the south of the Kalonga's kingdom, among the Manganja of the lower Shire valley, was another Phiri kingdom, that of the Lundu. A third Phiri kingdom, of which the ruler's title was *undi*, was founded during the sixteenth century among the Chewa living to the west of the Kalonga's kingdom, in the area where the modern frontier between Zambia and Malawi meets that of western Mozambique.

The Maravi kingdoms have sometimes been described as confederacies, in that they were all composed of smaller kingdoms ruled by hereditary dynasties, of which the rulers lived, like the paramount kings, in capital towns called *zimbabwe* and were addressed by the same honorific title of *mambo*. As in the Lunda kingdoms, a very wide autonomy existed even at the level of village communities, which were ruled by 'chiefs of the land' (*mwene mudzi*) each supposedly descended from the founding settler who first cleared the bush. In the Maravi polities kingship was essentially concerned with tribute, and tribute involved a two-way process of acceptance and redistribution which came very close to trade. Kings stored the grain collected as tribute and used it to relieve famine. They redistributed cattle and salt. Above all, they conducted long-distance trade with outside regions in iron goods and ivory. The Maravi were renowned as miners, smelters and smiths, and their tools and weapons were in demand all over the lowland country north and south of the lower Zambezi, where iron was very scarce. The Maravi were likewise deeply involved in the ivory trade. Their country abounded in elephants, which they trapped in pits, and it was the immemorial custom that the tusk which fell nearest to the ground was the tribute payable to the mambo. The inception of the ivory trade on the lower Zambezi can be dated from the rich trading site of Ingombe Iledi, just above the Luangwa confluence, to a period around the late fourteenth or early fifteenth century, and it is likely that the valley of the Shire tributary, running down to the Zambezi from Lake Malawi, would have begun to contribute to the trade at least by this date. If the Maravi conquerors were not already established in the lands of their settlement, it is likely that their advent soon afterwards would have given a new dimension to the trade by enlarging the political framework within which it could operate.

Certainly, in the sixteenth century, when the Portuguese replaced the Swahili traders on the lower Zambezi (below, pp. 207–8), and when their governors began to place monopolistic restrictions on the trade of the river, the reactions of the Maravi were swift and formidable. First the Lundu, and later the Kalonga sent fearsome military expeditions eastwards through the country of the Lomwe and Makua to open alternative trade routes with the Indian Ocean coast between Angoche Island and Kilwa. The forces of the Lundu, remembered variously as the Marundu and the Wazimba, practised terror tactics of the most extreme kind by killing and eating their war captives in a manner reminiscent of the conduct of the Imbangala (themselves an offshoot of the Luba military system) in the hinterland of the Portuguese colony of Angola (above, pp. 175–6). In 1588 or 1589 a Zimba war-band sacked Kilwa and Mombasa, and was only narrowly defeated outside Malindi. In 1592 other bands destroyed Portuguese forces sent against them from Tete and Sena. The situation was only restored in 1622, when the Kalonga with Portuguese help defeated the Lundu and extended his own trading network to the Indian Ocean coast. This hegemony continued until the end of the seventeenth century, when it was gradually replaced by that of the Yao, who ran their ivory caravans down the Lujenda and Rovuma river valleys to Ibo and Kilwa.

To the north of the Maravi kingdoms, and linking them geographically with those of the Luba and Lunda, were the multiple small kingdoms of the Bisa and the Bemba. Here, the population as a whole was culturally akin to that of eastern Lubaland, though it included some elements drawn from the patrilineal and partly cattle-keeping peoples, such as the Lungu, Mambwe and Ila, who lived in the high watershed country to the south of Lake Tanganyika. The ruling groups were certainly of Luba origin. The royals were known as balopwe and their capitals as musumba. Some time in the seventeenth century a fresh group of Luba royals of the Bena Ngandu or Crocodile clan established themselves in a part of Bembaland under a chief with the title of *chitimukulu*. During the eighteenth century the chitimukulus gradually built up a ritual pre-eminence among a circle of some twenty neighbouring Bemba kingdoms, which in the nineteenth century was misinterpreted by early European observers as a political paramountcy. In reality, however, the chitimukulus never exercised political or economic control over their client dynasties. In all secular matters these dynasties, like those of the Bisa, acted independently, their power deriving largely, as Andrew Roberts has expressed it, 'from their command of material wealth and their ability to circulate it among their subjects' through the interconnected systems of tribute and trade.[2]

All this was a region rich in ivory, but very deficient in iron ore. Tools and weapons had therefore to be imported, either from the Mambwe and Lungu to the north-east or from the Maravi to the south. In the eighteenth century, with the establishment of the Kazembe kingdom on the Luapula, the Bisa became the commercial intermediaries between the eastern Lunda on the one hand and the Maravi and the Portuguese on the other. Like the Nyamwezi of central Tanzania and the Yao of northern Mozambique, the Bisa became specialists in the organisation of long-distance caravans. A Portuguese officer who travelled through their country in 1831 described a society in which the villages were inhabited mainly by old men, women and children, because most of the adult men were away on caravan service. Above all, the Bisa carried the ivory and copper of the Mwata Yamvo's kingdom and all its southern offshoots and sold them, at first to the Portuguese at Tete and Zumbo, and later increasingly to the Yao on the south-eastern shores of Lake Malawi, whose own caravans carried them on to the Swahili coast, where prices for it were higher than on the Zambezi.

In 1806 the Portuguese governor of Angola sent two literate African trading agents (pombeiros) on a mission to explore the overland route from Luanda to Tete. So far as is known, this was the first caravan to cover the whole distance from one Portuguese colony to the other. The mission took five years to accomplish, but only because the Mwata Kazembe of the Luapula, jealous for his own monopoly over the central part of the route, delayed the travellers at his capital for four years. The actual travelling time for the double journey was less than one year, and at no stage was it necessary for

---

the caravan to diverge from well-beaten tracks with river ferries and recognised halting-places, or from a framework of authority sufficient for goods to be carried in reasonable security. At the time of the pombeiros' journey, these routes had all been in existence for nearly a century. The economic watershed between east and west, which was also the last link to be forged in the chain of communications, lay on the borders of the Mwata Yamvo's home territory and that of the Luapula Kazembe. This marked the divergence between an export trade in slaves which flowed mainly to the west and a trade in ivory which flowed mainly to the east. Copper moved in both these directions, but also in others, for it was much less exclusively an article of intercontinental commerce. Imports from the Atlantic coast consisted of European textiles, arms and ammunition, glass beads and other hardware, and of Brazilian rum and tobacco. An incidental introduction, perhaps more significant than any of these things, was the Brazilian root crop called manioc or cassava, which spread into the heart of the continent along the trade routes. It was capable of much more intensive cultivation and of much longer storage than the millet and bananas which it increasingly replaced. It was thus especially significant as a staple food for towns and trade routes, and all the greater chiefs developed plantations, worked by slaves, from which to exercise the hospitality expected of them. The main imports from the Indian Ocean coast were Indian textiles and other manufactured goods. 'King Cazembe', the pombeiros noted, 'has tea-pots, cups, silver spoons and forks . . . and gold money. He has a Christian courtesy: he doffs his hat and gives good day.'[3]

Throughout this region the connection between political organisation and long-distance trade is so obvious that it would be intellectually satisfying if the whole process of state formation could be linked with the development of trade routes. In such a scheme the ivory trade would assume the key position. Already attested in the region around the lower Zambezi by the tenth century, it would have spread its tentacles up the Zambezi tributaries – the Shire and the Luangwa – to the copper-rich watershed between the Zambezi and the Congo, and thence, using the hunting organisations of the Luba and Lunda, it would have extended itself westwards to the Kwango, before meeting the rival system spreading inland from the South Atlantic. There are, unfortunately, at least two flaws in this otherwise attractive theory. The first is the ubiquitous tradition that polit-

---

[3] R. F. Burton (trans.), *Lacerda's Journey to Cazembe in 1778, also the Journey of the Pombeiros* (London, 1873), p. 230.

ical systems spread mainly from north to south – from the Songye to the Luba and thence to the Lunda on the one hand and to the Maravi on the other. The second is the chronological evidence, which seems to indicate that only in the late seventeenth or the early eighteenth century did the Zambezi trading system make contact with that of the Congo basin. The momentum for change thus appears to have been political rather than economic, and its direction seems to have been down the centre of the subcontinent from north to south. In this region, no less than in the interlacustrine region to the north of it, political developments seem to have had precedence over economic ones – unless indeed the economic factors were of a much more local kind.

Here, Andrew Roberts has delineated more clearly than any other author the significance of a rich and populous stretch of river valley as the focus of political integration. This is true both in the case of the Kazembe's kingdom on the Luapula and in the Luyana (Lozi) kingdom on the upper Zambezi. In the Luapula valley the economic basis for a dense population consisted in the combinantion of fishing with flood plain agriculture, using manioc introduced by the Lunda conquerors as an easily storable and relatively trouble-free starchy root crop. On the upper Zambezi the Luyana pastured great herds of cattle on the wide flood plain of the river, and practised intensive agriculture on the edges of the valley. In both areas density of population and continuity of settlement favoured the imposition of a structured system of territorial chieftainship, and the development of military forces capable of conquering and laying under tribute the scattered and shifting societies of the less favoured countryside all round. Roberts has described the Kazembe's capital as 'a clearing-house where the products of the river were exchanged for those of the surrounding woodland', and the same was certainly true of the much more centralised system evolved by the powerful Luyana kings during the course of the late seventeenth and eighteenth centuries.[4] Here, as elsewhere in Africa, we have the salutary reminder that human societies evolve not only in accordance with their received inheritance but also in response to the promptings of diverse environments.

[4] Andrew Roberts, *A History of Zambia* (London, 1976), pp. 95–7.

13   The approaches to Zimbabwe

We saw in chapter 9 that until almost the end of our period the later
Iron Age societies which were emerging on the great plateau of East
Africa had practically no connection with the Indian Ocean coast.
From Mogadishu in the north to Vilanculos bay and the Bazaruto
archipelago in the south, the Zanzibar coast was a world of its own,
based on the coastal plain and the offshore islands, oriented towards
the sea, and exploiting only tenuously even the immediate hinterland as a source of ivory and slaves. The population of the coast from
the Tana river southwards had been since early Iron Age times
almost entirely Bantu-speaking, its many, still closely related, languages descending from the most recent and rapid phase of the
general Bantu dispersion. The Pokomo of the lower Tana valley, the
Giriama and the Digo north and south of Mombasa, the Bondei
around the mouth of the Pangani river, the Zaramo between Dar es
Salaam and the Rufiji, the Makonde and Makua between the
Rovuma and Mozambique Island, were all, basically, peoples who
lived by a combination of fishing, hunting and farming in the coastal
plain and in the wooded hillsides leading up towards the central
plateau, governing themselves in small clan and family units and
interacting little with the townspeople who lived so near them. Even
on the offshore islands, such as Pemba and Zanzibar, there were
wholly rural African communities which existed independently of
any system of rule by strangers. Yet in their midst there were growing
up other, far more dynamic urban communities which were participating actively in a much wider world.

From at least the beginning of the Christian era, the East African
coast had been the western shore of a far-flung oceanic commercial
system, bounded on the east by the Indonesian archipelago and the
lands surrounding the South China Sea, on the north by the coasts
of southern India and Sri Lanka, and on the north-west by the
Persian Gulf and southern Arabia. During the early Christian era,
the dominant maritime societies had been those of South-East Asia,
and it is likely that Indonesians had been among the earliest seafarers to reach and settle on the East African coast. They travelled in
fleets in their big sailing canoes, their freeboards built up with sewn
planks and equipped with outriggers to balance them in rough seas.

And they brought with them the living shoots of bananas and coco-nuts, taro and the large *colocasia* yams, which added so much to African woodland diets. On the mainland of the continent their identity and language soon disappeared through intermarriage, but on the great island of Madagascar, which was still uninhabited at the time of their arrival, their Malayo-Polynesian language established itself to the point at which it could absorb the later arrivals from Bantu Africa.

Although Indonesian trade and settlement persisted, at least with Madagascar, until the Portuguese arrival in the Indian Ocean, when it was being transported in large junks capable of carrying hundreds of passengers and many tons of cargo, its early predominance was gradually overtaken from the eighth century onwards by a rival trading system based in the Muslim lands around the Persian Gulf and southern Arabia. As recent archaeology has shown, the early Muslim settlers were humble people, whose trading activities may have been limited to exports of dried fish and the mangrove poles cut from the adjacent coastal forests which were used for house-building in the treeless lands around the Gulf. The earliest remains of mosques built at Shanga in the Lamu archipelago were simple con-structions of mud and wattle, accommodating no more than a dozen or so worshippers. Only over the course of two or three more centu-ries did their descendants grow rich enough to build mosques and tombs and some of the largest houses in coral rag collected from the raised beaches of earlier sea levels. Later still, in a few major seaport towns, the mosques and the palaces might be constructed of *porites* coral, mined from the submerged shoals of living coral, which could be cut with a saw into matching blocks before they hardened by exposure to the air.

The Arabs and Persians of the East African coast have often been presented as a ruling race, leading lives quite distinct from those of the surrounding African peoples. But in fact it is likely that of those who came to trade few settled permanently, and of these most took local wives and built up large households of children, dependants and slaves, so that the inhabitants of the emerging mercantile towns remained predominantly African. In all of them Bantu languages were spoken, and even the mercantile class used a Bantu lingua franca known as *Kiswahili*, 'the language of the coast', which was most closely related to the languages of eastern Kenya, though enriched over time with many words of Arabic origin. Very likely, it emerged as the language of the first African sailors to engage in the coastal trade, and was carried by them southwards along with the 195

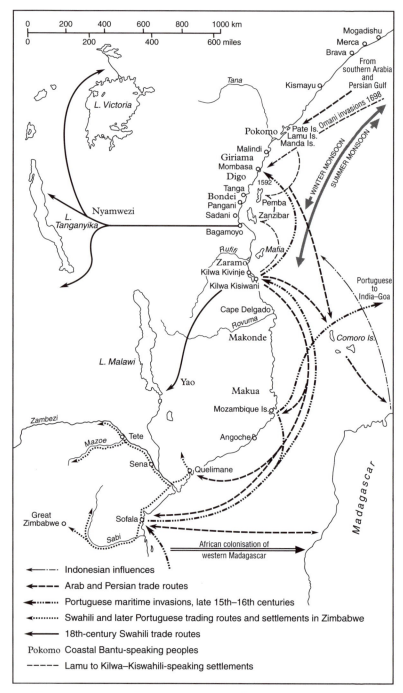

| 0 | 200 | 400 | 600 | 800 | 1000 km |
| 0 | 200 | | 400 | | 600 miles |

L. Victoria

Tana

From southern Arabia and Persian Gulf

Mogadishu
Merca
Brava
Kismayu

Pate Is.
Pokomo
Lamu Is.
Manda Is.

Malindi
Giriama
Mombasa
Digo
Tanga
Bondei
Pangani
Sadani
Bagamoyo

Nyamwezi
L. Tanganyika

1592

Pemba
Zanzibar

Rufiji
Zaramo
Kilwa Kivinje
Kilwa Kisiwani

Mafia

WINTER MONSOON
SUMMER MONSOON
Omani invasions 1698

Portuguese to India–Goa

Cape Delgado
Rovuma
Makonde

Comoro Is.

L. Malawi

Yao

Makua

Mozambique Is.

Zambezi
Mazoe
Tete
Sena

Angoche

Quelimane

Great Zimbabwe
Sofala
Sabi

Madagascar

African colonisation of western Madagascar

← – · – Indonesian influences
← – – – Arab and Persian trade routes
← · · · · · Portuguese maritime invasions, late 15th–16th centuries
◄ · · · · · · Swahili and later Portuguese trading routes and settlements in Zimbabwe
←——— 18th-century Swahili trade routes
Pokomo Coastal Bantu-speaking peoples
– – – – – Lamu to Kilwa–Kiswahili-speaking settlements

196   22 The approaches to Zimbabwe (see also Map 2, p. 6)

movement of the trading frontier. Language apart, these communities were linked by the fact that the ruling groups professed Islam, that their economic activities were bound up with maritime trade, and that their social and material culture was considerably influenced by their overseas contacts.

By the eighth century, the Muslim seafarers from the Persian Gulf had explored the East African coastline to at least as far south as the Zambezi and quite possibly as far as the Limpopo. The tenth-century Arab geographer al-Masudi claimed himself to have travelled the route in 922 AD, as far as 'a great kingdom of the blacks', where ivory of the best quality was to be had in profusion, and also some gold. This kingdom extended to 'Sofala' – a stretch of low-lying coast which probably included the site of the later port of that name, well to the south of the Zambezi delta. Thenceforward, Swahili settlements along the coasts of Somalia, Kenya, Tanzania and Mozambique had developed steadily. The earliest of the harbour towns were sited on the offshore islands – Pate and Manda in the Lamu archipelago, Pemba, Zanzibar, Mafia, Kilwa, the Comoro Islands – and the north-eastern coast of Madagascar, all probably by the tenth century, and it would appear that early Arab voyages to the Sofala coast used some of these places as staging posts. By the twelfth century, however, seaport towns were growing up all down the northern mainland coast – at Mogadishu, Merca, Brava, Malindi and Mombasa, while many smaller places dignified by mosques and tombs in coral rag were to be found at intervals of only a few miles.

Economically, the Swahili settlements were self-supporting in the essentials. Their inhabitants lived on fish and goatsmeat, bananas and coconuts, millet and rice. In the northern towns they wove their own camel-hair cloth. Further south, cotton was planted, spun and woven, so that Muslims might be clothed with the required attention to decency and dignity. Many of the settlements had their own masons and boat-builders, blacksmiths and leather-workers. The climate was humid, but otherwise pleasant. Life, at least for the well-to-do, was comfortable and easy-going. Trading dhows came southwards in their hundreds with every winter monsoon, filled with luxury textiles of silk and cotton, carpets, hardware, glazed pottery from Persia and porcelain eating-bowls from Canton. They sailed northwards again every summer, loaded with mangrove poles (*bariti*) for house-building, with rice from Madagascar, with the large, soft ivory used especially for women's bangles in all the Hindu countries, and with the copper and gold of Zimbabwe which helped to fertilise the trade of the whole system. Curiously enough, slaves are little mentioned as articles of export from the East African coast. Presumably they were more easily obtained in the countries of the Horn, where larger kingdoms with better organised armies were constantly warring with their neighbours (above, p. 130).

That it was gold which really sustained all the other branches of the East African coastal trade can be demonstrated both from the history of Kilwa and from that of Zimbabwe, which was the only sector of the vast interior which was deeply penetrated by long-distance trade with the coast. The strategic significance of Kilwa was that it marked approximately the limit of a single season's sailing for dhows based in southern Arabia and the Persian Gulf. South of Cape Delgado the monsoon winds diminished, and ships sailing beyond this point risked a whole year's delay in making their return. Kilwa was thus the ideal port of transhipment for the Sofala coast and also for Madagascar. With its magnificently sheltered roadstead between the island and the mainland, it was the natural headquarters for vessels plying over the southern sector of the route. Extensive archaeological investigation carried out over seven seasons by Neville Chittick established the importance of the settlement and the chronological stages of its development. Ruled since the eleventh century by a dynasty claiming to have originated in the Persian city of Shiraz, but which had probably settled for some time on the Somali coast before moving south, Kilwa grew steadily in importance during the twelfth and thirteenth centuries, and reached the peak of its prosperity in the fourteenth century under a new dynasty, that of the Mahdali, whose origins and main connections were with Aden and the Red Sea rather than with the Gulf. During this period much of the town was rebuilt in coral, the Great Mosque was enlarged and adorned with vaults and cupolas, and a splendid new palace, the Husuni Kubwa, was erected on a low cliff overlooking the roadstead at the northern tip of the island. This was equipped with a reception hall of great magnificence, with an elegant, octagonal bathing pool on the edge of the cliff, and with a large warehouse compound for the storage of trade goods. The numerous finds of Chinese porcelain associated with the buildings of this period show the growing wealth of the Mahdali sultans. For small transactions a minted copper coinage was in widespread use. Three-legged steatite (soapstone) eating and funeral vessels made in northern Madagascar indicate a regular trade with the great island, the bulk of which was probably in foodstuffs, especially rice. A contemporary site at Vohémar in north-eastern Madagascar shows the existence there of at least one Muslim settlement which was importing the same trade goods as Kilwa. However, the indigenous chronicles of Kilwa, compiled in the sixteenth century, leave no doubt that the main commercial interests of the town lay along the Sofala coast. By the fourteenth century, if not before, Sofala had come to denote a specific settlement in the neighbourhood of modern Beira, which was ruled by governors sent from Kilwa. The fourth of the Mahdali sultans, Daud, had held this post during his father's reign, and both he and his successor were said to have grown rich on the Sofala trade.

Though Kilwa seems to have suffered a brief period of decline at the end of the fourteenth century, the fifteenth century saw a marked revival, and when the Portuguese first landed at Sofala in 1497, they found it still ruled by a governor from Kilwa. It can be concluded that during these two centuries Kilwa controlled the lines of maritime communication leading southwards towards Madagascar and the Mozambique mainland. As we shall see, this period corresponds with the great period of political development of the Shona people in the lowlands of central Mozambique and on the Zimbabwe plateau behind them. It was also the period when western Madagascar was extensively colonised by African people from the Mozambique mainland. These migrants are likely to have been attracted by the seafarers' tales of waters rich in fish and pastureland as yet unoccupied by the Indonesian Malagasy, who were still concentrated around the eastern shores of the island. Presumably, both the pioneers and their animals would have made the 300 mile sea-crossing in the ships of the coastal traders.

THE KINGDOMS OF THE SHONA

In the earlier years of scholarly research, the historians of Zimbabwe painted a picture that was far too concentrated upon the highland plateau south of the middle Zambezi, to the virtual exclusion of the lowlands between the plateau and the coast. The impression was created of kingdoms emerging in the interior without any reference to events at the coast, and of a great gold-mining industry developing without any stimulus from a world market. Only with the emergence of the Mutapa empire in the fifteenth century was Shona rule in the coastal lowlands discussed in any detail. However, the discovery in the 1970s at Manekweni, only 30 miles from the coast at Vilanculos, of a stone-built capital site, with a series of radiocarbon dates running from about 1150 to about 1600, showed that, all through the period of stone building at the plateau site of Great 199

Zimbabwe, the same culture was present in the lowlands of central Mozambique.[1] It would appear that the earliest coastal trading stations in central Mozambique grew up in the coastal plain around Vilanculos bay and on the islands of the Bazaruto archipelago, with one site, at Chibuene, which yielded Persian pottery and Islamic glassware of the ninth century and similar to that found at the earliest period of occupation at Manda Island on the northern Kenya coast. This trading network spread far inland to the middle Limpopo, where by the twelfth century Mapungubwe hill had become the capital of a powerful kingdom rich in cattle and trade goods. In many respects the political and economic transformations visible at Mapungubwe, the rulers of which were doubtless in contact with their counterparts at Manekweni, would seem to have had a direct influence on the development of the culture centred at Great Zimbabwe. At Manekweni, as at Mapungubwe and at most of the comparable sites on the plateau, cattle ownership was the main preoccupation of the ruling class and prime beef the diet of those who inhabited the main stone-built enclosure.[2]

In the light of these archaeological findings at Manekweni and Chibuene, it is quite reasonable to suppose that al-Masudi's 'great kingdom of the blacks' was situated in the lowlands of the Sofala coast. 'The sailors of Oman', he wrote, 'and the merchants of Siraf go on the sea of the Zanj as far as Sofala, which is the extremity of the country of the Zanj and the low countries thereabout . . . which produce gold in abundance and other marvels. [The Zanj are] constantly employed in hunting elephants and gathering ivory. [Tusks] go generally to Oman and from there are sent on to China and India.'[3] Very likely, this tenth-century kingdom was the ancestor of that known to the sixteenth- and seventeenth-century Portuguese as Kiteve, then a recent and still reluctant tributary of the Mutapa empire centred on the northern plateau of modern Zimbabwe, but in earlier times an important broker kingdom linking the maritime enterprise of the Swahili and Arab traders with the sources of gold and ivory in the interior. While the political systems of Kiteve, and of other neighbouring Shona kingdoms, were undoubtedly of African origin, it is perfectly conceivable that the stimulus to large-scale gold-

---

[1] P. S. Garlake, 'An Investigation of Manekweni, Mozambique', *Azania* 11 (1976), pp. 25–48.

[2] P. S. Garlake, 'Pastoralism and Zimbabwe', *Journal of African History* 19 (1978), pp. 479–93.

[3] Al-Masudi, *Les Prairies d'or*, ed. and trans. C. Barbier de Maynard and P. de Courteille (Paris, 1861–77), vol. III, pp. 36–7.

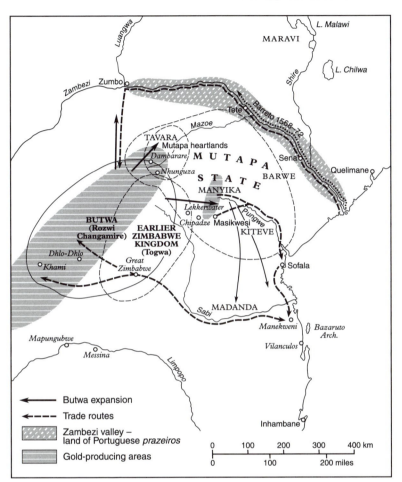

23 Between the Zambezi and the Limpopo

mining and ivory-hunting should have resulted from the contacts
with the maritime traders of the Indian Ocean coast. As in so many
other regions of Africa, it was easiest for the largest concentrations of
political and economic power to develop in the interior, away from
direct contact with outsiders who would tend to play off one coastal
kingdom against another. Nevertheless, the external trade could be a
powerful influence even in the politics of interior regions. The main-
stay of the economy in kingdoms like Mapungubwe and Great
Zimbabwe may have been the control and utilisation of cattle, but
the increase in the political power of their rulers was probably made   201

possible by the external trade in gold and ivory, which attracted the imported luxuries, probably mostly textiles, with which the rulers could reward their most important subjects.

There is no doubt that by the beginning of our period the dominant polity on the interior plateau was that centred since the end of the eleventh century at Great Zimbabwe. The capital was not itself in the gold-producing areas, which stretched around it in a wide arc from the west to the north-east. Rather, the place seems to have been chosen for its temperate climate and varied agricultural potential, midway between the dry grazing lands to the west and the misty mountains and damp valleys adjoining the eastern scarp. Here, in a landscape of little ridges topped with granite boulders and valleys dropping gently to the Sabi river, a royal township, supplied with beer and vegetable food by the local cultivators, and with milk and meat from the royal herds kept moving around the country in a regular pattern of transhumance, could be comfortably supported for more than four centuries. At its western extremity an unusually steep, granite-covered hill rising sheer from the valley floor was the ritual centre and, traditionally at least, the royal burial place of the kingdom. In the valley below its southern cliffs the royal enclosure had its main gateway facing towards the hilltop shrine. The town stretched away to the east along the valley floor.

For the first two centuries of its existence Great Zimbabwe was a fairly modest settlement. The royal enclosure was roughly walled with uneven slabs of granite. The holy hill had huts of pounded anthill standing upon roughly piled stone platforms. The local pottery was plain and undecorated. Only towards the end of the thirteenth century was there a sudden enrichment of the whole site, with improved styles of stone building, with burnished and richly decorated pottery, with jewellery of gold and ingots of copper, and with imported Chinese procelain and Persian glazed wares. Later on in this century, the whole of the royal enclosure was surrounded by a new girdle wall, more than 30 feet high, and built in courses so even and uniform as to give the appearance of cut stone. Again, during these centuries there appeared a few other stone-built sites constructed in the same style, though on a smaller scale, and yielding a selection of the same local artifacts and luxury imports. These sites – at Chipadze, Lekkerwater, Nhunguza and Ruanga – were spread around the north-eastern edges of the plateau. They were, once again, primarily pastoral sites, although they might also have commanded some of the areas of gold production nearest to the Zambezi valley. It looks very much as though they were the provincial outposts of a Great Zimbabwe kingdom that was expanding its territory north-wards during this period.

Essentially, the evidence for the political character of the kingdom based on Great Zimbabwe rests upon the archaeological evidence that a single, widespread 'court culture' co-existed with a number of local 'plebeian cultures'. As Peter Garlake has expressed it, 'While most of the later Iron Age ceramic traditions of Zimbabwe can be equated with particular Shona dialect clusters, this does not apply to the Great Zimbabwe tradition. This represents a social or political entity spread over the whole interior plateau and, as Manekweni demonstrates, far beyond. It existed at the same time and in the same areas as other traditions and presumably interacted with them.'[4] The implication of all this would seem to be that the rulers of Great Zimbabwe were a minority, not indeed of foreign origin, but at the very least a tightly organised, aristocratic group which established its authority over most of the area by conquest and succeeded for an unusually long time in maintaining a superstructure of political, economic and military power, heavily fortified by religious magic. Such was certainly the impression gained by the Portuguese when they began to penetrate the region in the early sixteenth century. By that time, however, the geographical centre of power had changed. Great Zimbabwe had been deserted, or at least had ceased to be a place of any importance. The paramount dynasty of the region now had its headquarters on the northern edge of the plateau above the Zambezi valley. The great question about how far it is legitimate to project backwards from the situation uncovered by the Portuguese turns upon how much continuity there was between the new system and its predecessor. On the whole, the evidence suggests that the element of continuity was large.

The abandonment of Great Zimbabwe as a major capital site is documented in archaeology by the fact that its luxury imports were all of the fifteenth century or earlier. The rise of a new paramountcy in the north is roughly datable from the tradition that its founder, Nyatsimba Mutota, preceded by four or five generations the *Mwenemutapa* with whom the Portuguese entered into direct relations in the 1560s. This would place the origins of the dynasty during the first half of the fifteenth century, when, following a widespread cliché of African traditions of dynastic change, Mutota was sent by his father, a king reigning in a stone-built capital far to the south, to explore for fresh sources of salt. These were eventually located in the

---

[4] Garlake, 'Investigation', p. 43.

land of the Tavara, a Shona subdivision, who occupied the northern edge of the great plateau and were prominent as hunters of elephant in the broad valley of the middle Zambezi which lay immediately below their homeland. The Tavara were conquered by Mutota, and his successor Matope went on to extend this kingdom into a great empire comprising most of the lands between Tavara and the Indian Ocean coast which had previously paid tribute to the Torwa dynasty of Great Zimbabwe. The story has some loose ends, notably about the precise relationship of the new paramount dynasty to the earlier one. What is sure from the archaeology of the northernmost sites built in the Great Zimbabwe tradition at Nhunguza and Ruanga is that, by the time of the emergence of the Mutapa kingdom, the influence of the southern capital was already well established over most of the northern plateau. The conquest of Tavara could therefore have originated in a relatively modest expansion, perhaps carried out by the frontier regiments, into the country west of the Mazoe valley. The Mutota who commanded the expedition was very likely a Torwa prince, who slowly asserted his independence, after the fashion of the many Kazembes who separated themselves from the Lunda kingdom of the Mwata Yamvos (above, pp. 185–6). The significance of the episode may have become apparent only when the second ruler, having become rich by exploiting the copper of Chidzurgwe and the ivory of the middle Zambezi, sent his armies eastwards to open a land route to the coast. The Torwa government at Great Zimbabwe may have continued to function normally throughout this phase of the northern secession. Only when Matope's armies overran Manyika, and the coastal kingdoms of Kiteve and Madanda, may the old capital have become untenable through the northward diversion of the main long-distance trade routes.

At all events, by the time the Portuguese reached the coast of Mozambique, the centre of Shona power had already shifted from south to north. João de Barros, the great historian of Portuguese enterprise in the Indian Ocean, writing about 1550, reported information collected at Sofala about a capital city of the ancient gold mines called Zimbabwe, which was 'built of stones of marvellous size, and there appears to be no mortar joining them'.[5] It was still guarded by a nobleman, and there were always some of the Mwenemutapa's wives quartered there. The sixteenth-century capital, however, was approached up the Zambezi, where the Swahili merchants of the coast

---

[5] G. M. Theal, *Records of South-Eastern Africa* (Cape Town, 1898–1903), vol. VI, pp. 267–8.

had already established trading settlements at Quelimane, Sena and Tete. From Tete it was a mere five days' march up the Mazoe valley to the fairs on the edge of the metropolitan district, where the foreign merchants were required to trade. The capital town itself, lying to the north of the region of granite outcrops, was built like most other African towns of clay, wood and thatch and was surrounded by a wooden stockade, which could be circumambulated in about one hour. It contained a public enclosure where the king did his business; another for his wives and their attendants, who were said to number 3000; and a third for the pages and bodyguards, who were young, unmarried men, recruited from all parts of the kingdom and destined for later service as soldiers and administrators. The annual distribution of brands from the royal fire was here, as in so many other African kingdoms, the main symbol for the conferment of authority. The royal shrines, and the cult of the royal ancestors, involving the ritual consultation of the spirits through living mediums, were served by priests called *mhondoros*, whose descendants continued to live around the site of the capital until recent times. It has been from them that the traditions of the dynasty have best been recorded.

THE PORTUGUESE IMPACT

The Portuguese who entered the Indian Ocean in 1497 in the three ships commanded by Vasco da Gama were already consciously bound for India. Their expedition was the culmination of ten years of research by explorers despatched through the Middle East, who had travelled the Red Sea and the Persian Gulf as far as Cananor in the pepper country of south-western India. The Portuguese knew that their prime objective was to begin the capture of the spice trade from the Arabs who had monopolised it for five centuries past. What they had still to learn by experience was that trade goods brought from Lisbon were of little interest to the Hindu merchants of Calicut, Goa and Cananor. What the Indians wanted was ivory and gold. What the Portuguese had to do, therefore, was to oust the Arabs from the trade of Sofala. This could be achieved only by force. The new plan was put into operation in 1505, when Francisco de Almeida was appointed the first governor of Portuguese India. On his way out, he subjected and built forts at Sofala and Kilwa and imposed a Portuguese monopoly on their external trade. Within eight years, the trade of Kilwa was so nearly defunct that the fort there was demolished and the garrison withdrawn. There could be no firmer proof of the dependence of Kilwa on the Sofala trade. 205

By about 1515 the Portuguese had established virtually complete naval superiority over Arab shipping in the Indian Ocean, operating from a chain of fortified bases on Mozambique Island, at Ormuz and Muscat in the Persian Gulf, at Diu, Goa and Cochin in western India, and at Malacca in the strait between the Malay peninsula and Sumatra. Henceforward, the luxury trade of the Sofala coast followed almost its ancient pattern, but with the elimination of the Arabian link. Indian silks, cottons, hardware and glass beads were brought to Mozambique in Portuguese ships, transhipped into coastal and river vessels, and used to buy ivory and gold from the various sub-kingdoms of the Mutapa empire at the fairs still visited by the Swahili merchants of Sofala and Inhambane, Quelimane, Sena and Tete. The gold and ivory reaching Mozambique from the interior was forwarded to Goa and there used to fertilise the trade in spices. But between south-eastern Africa and South Asia the Portuguese were now the carriers.

Once they had firmly established this position, the Portuguese did not greatly concern themselves with the rest of eastern Africa, or with the trade which continued in small vessels plying up and down the coast. They maintained friendly relations with Zanzibar and Malindi, but to the other Swahili townships north of Cape Delgado they behaved mainly as pirates, making brief naval expeditions to loot their accumulated wealth. Generally speaking, there were no garrisons north of Mozambique until, in 1592, the Portuguese decided to occupy Mombasa. Even this was a defensive measure, undertaken to block the southward penetration of the only Muslim fleet which they had not succeeded in destroying – that serving the Ottoman provinces in the Red Sea. Their installation at Fort Jesus in Mombasa was accompanied by a closer control of the offshore islands from Lamu to Kilwa, but it did not involve them in any relations with the peoples of the mainland. Like that of the Swahili before them, Portuguese interest in the African interior was limited to the lands immediately above and below the Zambezi. Even here, their objectives were few and simple. They needed to ensure that the production of gold and ivory continued and increased. And they needed to see that as much as possible of what was produced would pass out of Africa through their own hands and not leak away into the small-boat traffic of the Swahili maritime system. To achieve the first aim, they needed good relations with the Shona kings, who controlled the production of their subjects. To achieve the second, they needed to extend their own system of communications up the Zambezi and install themselves alongside the settlements of the Swahili merchants.

During the first sixty years of the sixteenth century, relations between the Portuguese and the Shona developed amicably enough. Besides the official garrisons, a number of private adventurers and deported criminals, many of them drawn from the Portuguese settlements in Asia, were landed at Sofala. They quickly made their way into the hinterland as backwoodsmen (*sertanejos*), living alongside the Swahili merchants at the inland fairs, and even taking service with the Shona kings as interpreters and political advisers. One of them, Antonio Fernandes, succeeded between 1512 and 1516 in travelling through virtually all the major Shona kingdoms, from Kiteve and Manyika in the east, through the Mwenemutapa's metropolitan district and on to the kingdom of Butwa, which comprised most of modern Matabeleland in the far south-west. With the help of such rough-and-ready ambassadors, the Captains of Sofala were able to work out a system of commercial relations with the Mwenemutapa and his tributary kings. The first serious breakdown occurred in 1561, when a Jesuit missionary, Gonçalo da Silveira, penetrated to the Mwenemutapa's court, where he persuaded his host to accept Christian baptism, only to be murdered a few days later at the instigation of the Muslim merchants at the capital. After lengthy preparations, the Portuguese in 1568 mounted an expedition of 1000 men under Francisco Barreto, conceived partly as an anti-Muslim crusade and partly in the hope of bringing the gold mines under Portuguese control. Though penetrating far up the Zambezi, the greater part of the force succumbed to the local diseases, and by 1572 the survivors had retreated to their base. Nevertheless, the expedition had some important results. The Swahili traders of the Zambezi were massacred with revolting cruelty and their places taken by Portuguese, whose descendants, taking African wives and assimilating progressively to African customs, gradually developed into the largely self-governing 'estate holders' (*prazeiros*) of the lower Zambezi valley. Sena and Tete retained tiny garrisons, supported henceforward by increasing numbers of African mercenaries and dependants, who became an important factor in the politics of the Shona kingdoms to the south of the river valley and of the Maravi kingdoms to the north.

The relationship of the Portuguese with the eastern Shona kingdoms has been aptly described by Richard Gray as one of 'subordinate symbiosis'.[6] Throughout the remainder of the sixteenth and the whole of the seventeenth century the Mutapa kingdom, like those of

---

[6] Richard Gray, in *CHA* IV, p. 586.

Manyika, Kiteve and Madanda, retained basic control of its territory and of the economic production of its subjects. In particular, fierce penalties were exacted from any individual or group attempting to mine gold without the ruler's licence. Equally, every Portuguese Captain on taking up his office at Mozambique paid a subsidy (*curva*) to the Shona rulers for permission to trade at the established fairs, where a duty of 50 per cent was levied on all trade goods imported. It was only during comparatively rare moments of internal disorder, during succession struggles, rebellions and inter-kingdom warfare, that Shona kings sometimes appealed to the Portuguese for military help. It was during such crises that successive Mwenemutapas ceded peripheral land in the Zambezi valley for Portuguese *prazos*, and occasionally, as in 1607 and 1629, signed treaties (which were never put into effect) giving the Portuguese possession of the gold mines or declaring themselves the vassals of the Portuguese Crown.

More realistically, what did happen during the seventeenth century was that the Mwenemutapas gradually lost their paramountcy over many previously tributary kingdoms. In particular, Kiteve, Madanda and Manyika ceased to pay tribute, while a new kingdom known as Barwe emerged on the southern side of the lower Zambezi valley. All this would probably have happened in any case, but it may have happened rather sooner as a result of Portuguese contact with these kingdoms. The most serious threat to the Mutapa kingdom, however, seems to have come from the south and the south-west, that is to say, from the central lands of the old Torwa kingdom of Great Zimbabwe. The course of events in this part of the region is more obscure than elsewhere, but already in the early sixteenth century there came reports of a ruler with the title of *changamire*, who invaded the Mutapa kingdom from a base in the southern part of the plateau. By the seventeenth century this title was definitely associated with the Rozwi dynasty of the rising kingdom of Butwa. The Rozwi were great pastoralists, and their capital towns were stone-built in the general style of Great Zimbabwe. They included such well-known sites as Naletale, Dhlodhlo, Matendere and Khami – all in the area between modern Bulawayo and Fort Victoria. Though lacking any pre-sixteenth-century deposits, all these sites are rich in material of the seventeenth and eighteenth centuries. They testify to the existence of a kingdom with sophisticated local industries and rich enough to import all the luxury goods of the Portuguese Indian Ocean trade. At first this trade probably passed through Kiteve and Madanda, but later the entrepôt market was at the Portuguese trading station at Zumbo, at the confluence of the Zambezi and the Luangwa.

By the late seventeenth century Butwa, under the leadership of a changamire called Dombo, was actively challenging the hegemony of the Mutapa kingdom in the region as a whole. In 1684 Dombo's forces encountered and decisively defeated those of the Mwenemutapa Mukombwe on the southern borders of the metropolitan district. In 1693 Mukombwe died, and there ensued a succession struggle in which the Portuguese backed one contestant and Dombo another. Dombo thereupon razed the fair-town of Dembarare, situated at the very approaches to the Mutapa capital, wiping out the Portuguese traders and their entire following. In 1695 Dombo overran the rich gold-producing kingdom of Manyika, and even descended to the lowlands on the eastern edge of the country to destroy the Portuguese fair-town at Masikwesi. Dombo now controlled the whole arc of gold-producing territory from Butwa in the south-west to Manyika in the north-east.

Unlike the Mwenemutapas, who had always permitted subordinate rulers to bring their own tribute to the capital at the time of the annual ceremonies, the changamires installed their own tax collectors to reside in the conquered provinces. The control of mining could thus be effectively enforced. Although the fair at Masikwesi was eventually reopened, it remained a firm principle of the Butwa hegemony that henceforward no Portuguese should set foot upon the plateau. Trade with Butwa itself was carried out at Zumbo, whence only the African agents (*mussambazes*) of the Portuguese traders were permitted to organise caravans to the main towns of the country. One consequence of Butwa's dominance over the plateau, which lasted throughout the eighteenth century, was that the Portuguese in the Zambezi valley shifted their interest increasingly from the south bank to the north. Here, Portuguese backwoodsmen and prospectors who had been expelled from the Shona kingdoms made numerous, mostly small, gold strikes in the lands of the Maravi, Chewa and Senga peoples, whose earlier political unity was fast crumbling at this period. In these circumstances most of the gold was mined under various arrangements with the local chiefs by the prazeiros and sertanejos, who set up temporary mining camps (*bares*), which were worked by their retainers and slaves. Meanwhile, the ivory trade of the Luangwa basin and of the Kazembe's kingdom on the Luapula was being carried through the Maravi country by the Bisa, and it was the hope of attracting this trade to the Zambezi settlements rather than to the Zanzibar coast that inspired the exploration of the coast-to-coast route described above (pp. 191–2).

THE RETURN OF THE ARABS

On the East African coast to the north of Cape Delgado the zenith of Portuguese power was reached during the forty years from 1592 till 1631. Under the watchful eyes of the Fort Jesus garrison, the former ruling house of Malindi, transplanted now to Mombasa, reigned over Malindi, Mombasa and Pemba. North of Malindi, the island settlements of the Lamu archipelago were all careful to pay tribute. There were Portuguese sertanejos settled on Zanzibar, Pemba and Pate, and Augustinian missionaries at Mombasa, Zanzibar and Faza. The situation, however, was not completely peaceful. In 1595 or 1596 the Swahili governor of Pemba was poisoned on becoming a Christian. Even the friendly Sultan Ahmad was always complaining of the insulting treatment he received from the Portuguese Captains of Fort Jesus. His son and successor, Hassan, quarrelled openly with the Portuguese and in 1614 ran away to the mainland. He was replaced first by a brother, who was deposed four years later, and then by a nephew, Yusuf Chingulia, who was taken away to Goa and educated for twelve years in an Augustinian priory before being allowed to assume office. How little the Portuguese were really tolerated is best shown by the sequel. In the year after his return to Mombasa Yusuf abjured Christianity for his native Islam and incited a revolt of the townspeople in which the entire Portuguese garrison was murdered. The neighbouring towns joined in the rebellion, and the first punitive expedition of 800 Portuguese sent from Goa in 1632 was beaten off. Yusuf thereupon demolished the fort and decamped to Arabia, whence he continued the struggle in a series of naval raids.

Though the Portuguese reoccupied Mombasa and rebuilt Fort Jesus in 1635, they never recovered full control of the northern coast. It was a period when the Portuguese empire all round the world was suffering disasters at the hands of the Dutch, who between 1631 and 1641 conquered Pernambuco, Elmina, Luanda, Ceylon and Malacca. The Portuguese had already in 1622 been ejected by the Persians from Ormuz, and in 1650 the Omanis drove them from Muscat on the opposite shore of the Persian Gulf. There were Omani merchants settled in all the towns along the East African coast, whose trade was taxed and hampered by the Portuguese, and it was inevitable that the Omanis of the Gulf should follow up their own liberation by fomenting trouble in East Africa. Already in 1652 their fleets raided Pate and Zanzibar, wiping out the Portuguese settlers. In 1660 they attacked the town of Mombasa under the noses of the Portuguese in the fort. In 1669 they raided as far south as

Mozambique Island. The Mombasa garrison, increasingly isolated, at last succumbed in 1698 to an Omani siege lasting two and a half years. The place was briefly recaptured by the Portuguese in 1728–30, but in general it was Arab sea-power that dominated East African waters north of Cape Delgado throughout the eighteenth century. Once more, the big sailing dhows of the Gulf replaced the small coasting vessels of the Portuguese period. The Swahili communities of the coast, now increasingly supplied with firearms, began to develop the trade in slaves and ivory of the far interior. Symbolic of the new commercial interest was the emergence of a new Kilwa, situated on the mainland 12 miles to the north of the medieval island site. Unlike its predecessor, the new Kilwa faced inland. It was the coastal base of new caravan routes leading far to the west. In the early 1770s Kilwa was visited by a French trader, Morice, who was interested in building up a regular supply of slaves for the sugar plantations of Mauritius and Réunion. He was told of the existence of a great inland sea, which must have been Lake Malawi, and beyond it of an immense country, which had been traversed in two months by native caravans to another ocean visited by European shipping.

The case of Kilwa was not, however, unique. On the Kenya coast, the old towns of Mombasa and Malindi, Pate and Lamu did not perhaps change their character very greatly. They had survived the Portuguese period, and they were to survive into modern times, mainly as the centres of slave-worked plantation agriculture, more or less self-contained within the coastal belt. But other towns grew up in the later eighteenth century, especially along the Tanzanian coast, at Tanga and Pangani, Saadani and Bagamoyo, which like Kilwa Kivinje were oriented inland, and were to develop as the coastal termini of trade routes leading westwards to Lake Tanganyika and the Congo basin, to Uganda, to Kilimanjaro and north into Kikuyu and Kavirondo. As we saw above (pp. 149–50), it was around the third quarter of the eighteenth century that the kingdoms of the interlacustrine region began to receive luxury imports from the outside world, while by the end of the century even bulky goods like cotton textiles were appearing there in some quantity. Here, as on the more southerly routes to Lake Malawi and beyond, it was at this stage the peoples of the interior who did most of the actual travelling. It was not until the nineteenth century that the coastmen themselves started to venture inland in any numbers. But already in the eighteenth century the trade of the interior was becoming one of their main preoccupations.

14   The peoples of the South

After the Sahara desert, the great spaces of southern Africa include more land that is too dry for cultivation than any other region of the continent. In most of southern Angola, in virtually all of Namibia and Botswana and in much of the old Cape Province of South Africa, rainfall is less than 20 inches a year. River valleys apart, all this is at best ranching country for sheep or cattle. It is only the eastern third of the region, from the present Botswana–Transvaal border southwards across the highveld to the Indian Ocean in the vicinity of Port Elizabeth, that offers the possibility of dense agricultural settlement. Such is the geoclimatic logic underlying the distribution of South Africa's language-families, which were, to the west, the old Khoisan languages of the surviving hunting and gathering peoples and the nomadic pastoralists of sheep and cattle; and, to the east, the Bantu languages of the Iron Age farmers.

HUNTERS AND HERDERS

Of the two families Bantu was the intruder, in a process that had begun to occur early in the first millennium AD. Well into the second millennium, however, late Stone Age hunters and herders were still occupying most of the fertile east as well as the drier west, with the newcomers settling among and interacting with the older inhabitants. It was not until about the time of the earliest Portuguese voyages around southern Africa in the late fifteenth century that the cultivators could be said to have gained a decisive ascendancy over the hunters and herders living in the Bantu-speaking lands. Indeed, as recently as the eighteenth century identifiable communities of San hunter-gatherers were still inhabiting the mountainous country of the Drakensberg, Lesotho and the eastern Cape Province, much of the plateau of the Orange Free State and the valleys of the Orange and the Vaal. Each of the small hunting and gathering bands spoke its own tongue, which might be understood by its immediate neighbours but certainly not by more distant groups. The extraordinary diversity of the San languages suggests that their speakers had been present in southern Africa for a very long time.

The herders, on the other hand, though very widely dispersed, spoke a single language, with only minor variations of dialect. Unlike the San, most of the Khoi were pastoralists rather than hunter-gatherers, moving around in communities of 500 to 1000 persons and tending large herds of longhorn cattle and flocks of fat-tailed sheep. They occupied, although sparsely, a vast area of the subcontinent, stretching from northern Namibia down both sides of the Kalahari desert to the Cape of Good Hope, and thence eastwards perhaps as far as Natal, making their tongue one of the most widely spread in Africa. Their remarkable linguistic homogeneity would seem to indicate a comparatively recent dispersal extending over not much more than two millennia. Their practice of shepherding may have begun in Stone Age times, for sheep bones have been found in association with pottery and stone tools in cave sites near the Cape of Good Hope, which have been dated to around the beginning of the Christian era. Cattle-herding must have come significantly later, and must have reached the northern Khoi through Bantu intermediaries in Angola or Zambia during Iron Age times, for there is as yet no archaeological evidence of Stone Age cattle-keeping anywhere to the south of the Kenya highlands.

All this is highly relevant to the occupation of eastern South Africa by the South-Eastern Bantu, whose languages not only assimilated the clicking sounds of San and Khoi, but also adopted Khoi terms for 'cattle', 'sheep' and 'milk'. The implication would seem to be that pastoralism was not widely or intensively practised by the South-Eastern Bantu at the time of their penetration of the eastern lands, and that they came to value it more highly by interacting with the Khoi on their western and southern borders. Certainly, at the beginning of our period the Khoi were the supreme cattle-keepers of southern Africa. Their staple diet was the milk of cows and ewes. Their clothing was of leather and sheepskin. They gelded their bulls and used them for riding and baggage. Though not skilled as smiths, they knew the use of metals, wearing a profusion of copper ornaments and wielding some iron weapons in addition to wooden bows and staves. The scale of Khoi cattle-keeping societies was at its most impressive in the northern Cape region, with the stone-walled herder sites of the so-called 'Type R' culture in the triangle of grassland above the confluence of the Orange and the Vaal, which have been dated to around 1350–1600 AD, and the somewhat similar sites around Dithakong of about a century later. Whatever the actual relationships between hunters, herders and Iron Age farmers, the historical importance of the Khoisan peoples, and especially of the Khoi   213 pastoralists, cannot now be doubted. The Khoi and San interacted continuously with the Bantu farmers settled in their midst, and were by no means a race of downtrodden clients. Intermarriage with them conferred prestige even upon the ruling houses of the Bantu, who doubtless appreciated the access to storable and rapidly growing wealth in cattle which might come from such alliances.

THE SOUTH-EASTERN BANTU

The earliest occupation of southern Africa by Iron Age peoples, almost certainly speaking Bantu languages, dates to the third and fourth centuries AD. Anthropologists and linguists are agreed that the South-Eastern Bantu complex comprises three main subdivisions – the Tsonga, the Sotho-Tswana and the Nguni – together with a number of smaller languages, such as Venda, which would seem to be more closely related to Shona than to the rest. The Tsonga are the people of the lowlands of southern Mozambique, who at one time also occupied most of Swaziland and northern Natal. They were cultivators and fishermen of the coastal plain, keeping few cattle and paying even marriage dowries in hoes and other metal goods. They were the earliest of the Bantu-speaking inhabitants of southern Africa, with their roots in the early Iron Age and their main affiliations with the coastal Bantu of central and northern Mozambique and the eastern parts of Tanzania and Kenya. Next there were the Sotho-Tswana, basically the Iron Age population of the Transvaal highveld, who later spread across the Orange Free State towards Lesotho and southern Botswana. The Sotho practised a mixed economy of agriculture and stock-raising, with a preference for living in large, almost urban settlements, which were often protected by stone walling. The northern Sotho had a particularly well-developed interest in mining and metallurgy, in copper and gold as well as iron, which they shared with their northern neighbours the Venda, with dates for mining sites going back into the first millennium. Finally, there were the Nguni, who may in origin have been indistinguishable from the Sotho, for the linguistic divergence between the two sets of languages is very slight. The Nguni, during the past six or seven centuries, came to occupy the lowlands between the Indian Ocean and the escarpment of the great interior plateau, all the way from Swaziland to the Transkei, and, perhaps owing to closer contact with the Khoi, became more strongly pastoral than the Sotho, living in beehive huts around their cattle kraals, dispersed more or less evenly across the landscape.

At the beginning of our period, the most developed part of southern Africa, both politically and economically, was the north-east. The Tsonga cultivators and fisherfolk of the coastal plain of southern Mozambique had been among the earliest of the Iron Age inhabitants of the subcontinent. Their iron-working has been dated to the fourth century AD. They had been in touch with the maritime trade of the Indian Ocean for almost as long as the Shona of the Kiteve and Madanda kingdoms in the Pungwe and Sabi river valleys (above, pp. 199–200). The Zimbabwe-like structure at Manekweni, sited just inland from the trading centre at Vilanculos, the earliest date for which is about 1150, stood in what was almost certainly Tsonga territory, and perhaps represented the extension of a Shona-like political system over a northern Tsonga population. Further south, they were organised in their own small kingdoms, which together controlled the approaches to the Limpopo valley, with its riches in copper and ivory, and its tributary river, the Olifants, with its deposits of gold, copper, tin and iron.

On the highveld plateau of the central and western Transvaal the earliest Iron Age settlement sites have been dated to the fifth century AD, and these are presumed to be the work of the earliest speakers of a Sotho-like language. Unlike the early Iron Age sites of the coastal belt, the plateau sites do bear evidence that some cattle and sheep were being kept from the first, although not in large numbers. In this respect as in others, they resembled most closely the sites of the Gokomere people of the Zimbabwean plateau and the early Iron Age peoples of central Zambia. They belonged, that is to say, to a more westerly stream of early Iron Age cultural diffusion than that of the Tsonga. In somewhat more recent times the northern Sotho – the Pedi – had a particularly well-developed interest in mining and metallurgy, in copper and gold as well as iron, with dates for mining sites dating from as early as the eighth and ninth centuries AD at Phalaborwa and other sites on the north-eastern side of the plateau. Indeed, the whole of the Transvaal plateau from the Zoutpansberg in the north to the Witwatersrand in the south is pitted with ancient workings and with the remains of countless smelting furnaces. Much of this evidence comes from terrain that must have been quite unsuited to cattle-keeping, either because of tsetse-fly or because it was covered with dense thorn forest which had to be slowly and painfully cleared before the land could be used either for agriculture or for grazing. That mining and pastoralism do not normally go hand in hand was recognised by the Sotho themselves in the popular saying that 'where the sound of the hammer is heard, the lowing of   215

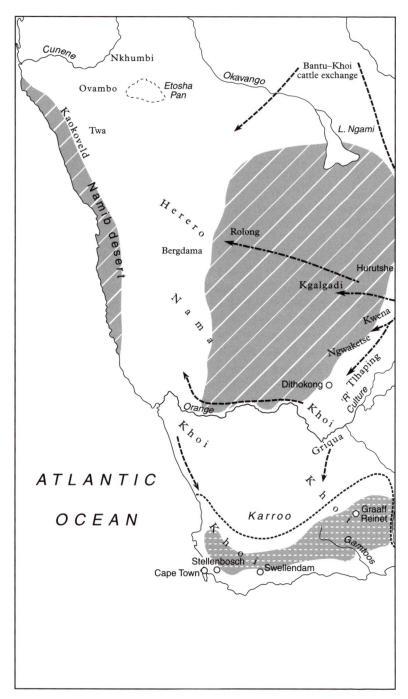

Cunene

Nkhumbi

Okavango

Bantu–Khoi
cattle exchange

Ovambo

Etosha
Pan

Twa

L. Ngami

Kaokoveld

Namib desert

H e r e r o

Rolong

Bergdama

Hurutshe

Kgalgadi

Kwena

N a m a

Ngwaketse

'R' Tlhaping
Culture

Dithokong

Orange

Khoi

Griqua

Khoi

K h o i

ATLANTIC

OCEAN

Karroo

Graaff
Reinet

Gamtoos

K h o i

Stellenbosch

Cape Town

Swellendam

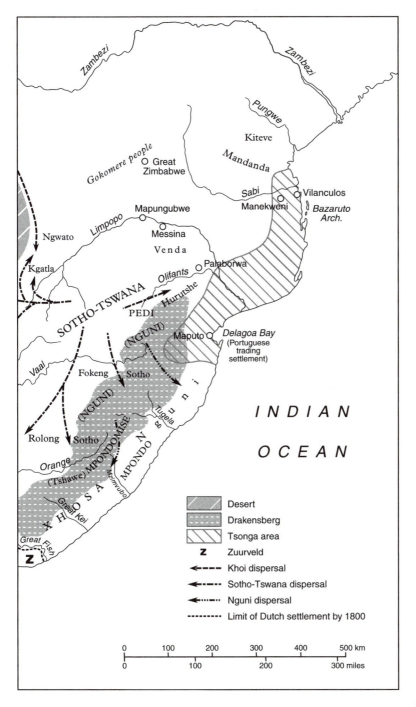

Zambezi

Zambezi

Pungwe

Kiteve

Mandanda

Gokomere people ○ Great
Zimbabwe

Sabi ○ Vilanculos
Manekweni *Bazaruto Arch.*

Mapungubwe

Ngwato

Limpopo

○ Messina

V e n d a

Kgatla

SOTHO-TSWANA

Olifants ○ Palaborwa

Hurutshe

PEDI

(NGUNI)

Maputo ○ *Delagoa Bay*
(Portuguese trading settlement)

Vaal

Fokeng

Sotho

(NGUNI)

Rolong

Sotho

Orange

(Tshawe) MPONDOMISE

MPONDO

Great Kei

X H O S A

Great Fish

Z

Tugela

Mzimvubu

N g u n i

INDIAN

OCEAN

	Desert
	Drakensberg
	Tsonga area
z	Zuurveld
◄----	Khoi dispersal
◄-·-·-	Sotho-Tswana dispersal
◄-··-··-	Nguni dispersal
········	Limit of Dutch settlement by 1800

0   100   200   300   400   500 km

0   100   200   300 miles

cattle is not there'.[1] It is not only that pastoralists make a significantly smaller use of metal tools than cultivators. It is also that mining, especially for copper and gold, was essentially a communal activity, undertaken with agricultural tools and at seasons of the year when large numbers of people were free from work in their fields and able to camp out around the mining pits.

It seems likely that it was not until the early centuries of the second millennium AD that the ancestors of the Sotho-Tswana and Nguni peoples expanded into southern South Africa, with the Nguni to the south and east of the Sotho, in the south-eastern Transvaal and Lesotho. In the course of time small bands of Nguni drifted over the escarpment into the lowlands of Natal and the eastern Cape. In the more open country to the west and south of the highveld plateau, however, the spread of more intensive cattle-keeping alongside cereal agriculture was bringing about a rapid increase of population. This enabled the patrilineal and polygynous lineages of Sotho-Tswana clans to expand at the expense of both Khoi and San. The density of later Iron Age settlement throughout a wide arc of territory from Zeerust in the south-western Transvaal to Lydenburg in the south-east is shown by the thousands of stone ruins across this area. Villages were built around cattle byres, in which senior male elders were buried. Elders and clan-heads based their social dominance on wealth in cattle, which enabled them to buy brides for their young men and to secure the allegiance of clients through gifts of cattle. The growth in the size and scale of political societies on the highveld and mountains north of the Vaal can be traced back at least to the sixteenth century, but it may well have begun much earlier. In the course of the seventeenth century the process seems to have accelerated, particularly in the wake of a civil war among the senior Tswana lineage, the Hurutshe, when Kwena and Kgatla chiefdoms scattered in all directions from the Sotho-Tswana heartlands. Some Kwena moved westwards into south-eastern Botswana, while Kgatla migrated eastwards into the country of the Pedi. Rolong, who were already in southern Botswana, expanded their influence over the chiefs of the Khoi herders to the north of the Orange river. Other Rolong migrated across the Kalahari into the Herero country of central Namibia. Parties of Rolong, Kgatla and Kwena moved into the southern Sotho heartlands in the northern Orange Free State, and this set off the dispersal of Fokeng and other Sotho lineages into the lowlands of the upper Caledon valley.

[1] Cited by David Birmingham and Shula Marks, in *CHA* III, p. 604.

It is during this period of explosive increase in the human and bovine population of the highveld that traditional history gives us our first glimpses of Nguni-speaking 'Ndebele' people dispersing from the vicinity of modern Pretoria across the central Transvaal into central Botswana. These were either Nguni who had never crossed the Drakensberg into the lowlands of Natal or else groups who had moved in the opposite direction as mercenaries or brigands, as the Sotho word *matabele* implied. Either way, they are unlikely to have been the earliest Nguni to penetrate the lowlands, where most of the early part of the second millennium must have been devoted to the slow clearance of the forests, and the opening up of the land to a system of farming in which, although millet and vegetables were planted, pride of place was given to cattle-keeping. 'After about 1500', writes the archaeologist Tim Maggs, 'the evidence clearly indicates that the Iron Age people [of the south-eastern coastal region] were directly ancestral, culturally, linguistically and physically, to today's black population. There is nothing to suggest that the cultural traits that distinguish Nguni-speaking groups from others within the Late Iron Age originated or developed outside the historic Nguni-speaking regions.'[2]

Owing to the great upheavals which affected the northern half of Nguniland with the rise of the Zulu nation just after the end of our period, it happens that historical traditions concerning the period from the fifteenth till the eighteenth century have survived better in the southern half of Nguniland than in the north. From these it would appear that the royal clans of the Xhosa, Mpondo and Mpondomise peoples all descended from the same Tshawe lineage, which had its earliest remembered centre around the sources of the Mzimvubo river, in the mountainous borderlands of southern Lesotho. During the seventeenth century the dynasty moved by stages down the Mzimvubo to the coast, and there divided, as its followers spread out across southern Natal and the Transkei. By the mid-seventeenth century the Xhosa royal kraal was established on the Kei. In 1702 there occurred the first skirmish between the Xhosa frontiersmen and the Dutch cattle-traders from Cape Town in the valley of the Fish river.

For northern Nguniland the genealogical evidence is much more fragmentary, but the scattered references in Portuguese maritime literature of the sixteenth and seventeenth centuries establish with

---

[2] 'The Iron Age Farming Communities', in Andrew Duminy and Bill Guest (eds.), *Natal and Zululand from Earliest Times to 1910* (Pietermaritzburg, 1989), pp. 267–8. 219

certainty that, at least by the middle of the sixteenth century, all the country from the Transkei to northern Natal was thickly settled by people whose main wealth lay in their herds of sleek, well-fed cattle. They also show that throughout this region chiefs were known by the Nguni word *nkosi*, which differentiated these southern Africans from the Khoi to the west of the Kei and from the Tsonga living to the north of Santa Lucia Bay in the far north of Natal. In particular, a journal kept by one of the survivors from a Portuguese ship wrecked on the Transkei coast in 1593 describes the overland march of four months from the Bashie river to Delagoa Bay, passing through the whole length of the Nguni country.

These Kaffirs [wrote the anonymous author] are herdsmen and husband-men. Their husbandry is millet, ground between two stones or in wooden mortars. They make flour, and of this they make cakes, which they bake under the embers. Of the same grain they make wine, mixing it with a lot of water, which after being fermented in a clay jar, cooled off and turned sour, they drink with great gusto. Their cattle are numerous, fat, tender, tasty and large, the pastures being very fertile. Most of them are polled cows, in whose number and abundance their wealth consists. They also subsist on their milk and on the butter which they make from it. They live together in small villages, in huts made of reed mats, which do not keep out the rain. The dress of these Kaffirs is a mantle of calf-skins, with the hair on the outside, which they rub with grease to make it soft. They are shod with two or three soles of raw hide fastened together in a round shape, secured to the foot with thongs and with this they run with great speed. They carry in their hand a thin stick to which is fastened the tail of an ape or of a fox, with which they clean themselves [i.e. whisk away flies] and shade their eyes when observing.[3]

There can be no doubt that 'these Kaffirs' were Nguni, or that they had already attained a density which presupposed that forest clearance was already far advanced.

Meanwhile, far to the west, on the Atlantic side of the subcontinent, a not dissimilar pattern of settlement was evolving, with Bantu-speaking people in the north and Khoi in the south. There can be little doubt that at the beginning of our period most of the inhabitants of this vast region were hunter-gatherers, although some bands had already turned to the raising of sheep. The majority of these hunters and herders were ethnically similar to the San of South Africa, but some, such as the Twa of the Kaokoveld and

---

[3] C. R. Boxer (ed.), *The Tragic History of the Sea 1589–1622* (Cambridge, 1950), pp. 121–2.

the Bergdama around the site of modern Windhoek, were Khoi-speaking Negro people. During the first half of our period, the ancestors of the Ovambo, Herero and Nama peoples moved into Namibia from every landward direction and settled among the Stone Age peoples. Those who came to inhabit the thorn savanna and dry woodlands on either side of the Cunene valley and north of the Etosha Pan were related, both in language and culture, to the Ovimbundu (above, p. 179). Most sections of these South-Western Bantu were cattle keepers, their stock coming originally from the Bantu-speaking groups of the middle Zambezi, following a narrow corridor of grassland on either side of the Okavango river. Meanwhile, the Ovambo and Nkhumbi were building up dense agricultural populations in the fertile flood plains of the Cunene and Cuvelai rivers, while to the west of them the Nyaneka people settled the productive Huila highlands. By the end of the eighteenth century, the Nyaneka, Nkhumbi and Ovambo had become involved in the slave-raiding and ivory-trading activities of the Ovimbundu and the Portuguese sertanejos from Benguela. Their response was to coalesce into larger groups and chiefdoms, but these were never as powerful as the Ovimbundu kingdoms further north.

South of Ovamboland was the high dry country settled by the Herero, the most southerly of the South-Western Bantu, who moved into Namibia from the Okovango basin of northern Botswana. While still in the Okovango, the Herero seem to have obtained their sheep and cattle, and indeed a whole cattle culture, from neighbouring Khoi people. At all events, they abandoned agriculture and became fully pastoral. They were the only Bantu-speaking group to make the full transition. The whole of the southern and much of the central Namibian plateau was settled by Khoi nomads called Nama. According to tradition, the Nama first entered Namibia from the lower valley of the Orange river, probably sometime in the seventeenth century. In the first stages of their settlement, the Ovambo and the Herero interacted closely and peaceably with the aboriginal peoples. By the end of our period, however, the dominant population groups were all encroaching on each other's territory – the Nama herders on the land of the Herero, the Herero on that of the southernmost Ovambo chiefdoms. These last disputes concerned not only grazing grounds but control of the copper deposits of Tsemeb. Thus the stage was set for the more widespread violence of the nineteenth century, when, supplied with firearms by traders from the Cape as well as from Benguela and Mossamedes, Ovambo chiefdoms and Herero and Nama clans became enmeshed in ever more destructive conflicts.

It seems clear from the historical traditions of both Sotho and Nguni that, in the Transvaal and Natal, the eighteenth century was a period of increasing violence owing to the jostling between small kingdoms for the control of land. As always in the history of eastern and south-eastern Africa, one has to suspect that the main cause of overcrowding was due to the increase of cattle rather than people, but it does seem that one important factor may have been the spread of maize as a staple food, following its introduction by the Portuguese and then the Dutch traders at Delagoa Bay. In good years maize could yield three times as much cereal food as either millet or sorghum. Although the earliest of the Tswana towns on the highveld and in eastern Botswana may have predated the eighteenth century, it seems that they really emerged as large conurbations only during the second half of that century, and that their defensive walling was a symptom of increasing competition for productive land.

Another feature of the mid-eighteenth century was the nature of the mercantile contact between the interior regions of the subcontinent and its coastal outlets. Previously, most of the initiative in trading ivory and other products of the chase had come from the peoples of the interior, who had carried their goods in small parties, travelling long distances to obtain very small returns. Now, the initiative passed to the Tsonga kingdom that dominated Delagoa Bay and to the Dutch traders at the Cape, who began to send larger, and better armed caravans into the interior, which offered tempting quantities of textiles and hardware in exchange for ivory and skins, as before, but also now for slaves. At the northern end of Nguniland, the new trading network radiated from the trading station established at Delagoa Bay, by the Dutch in the early 1700s. In response to it, the Tsonga chieftaincy of Maputo soon moved in to organise regular supplies of ivory and slaves. These were brought down to the coast either in canoes or on foot. The warlike activities of the Tsonga set up chain reactions deep into northern Natal, into the country which, a few decades later, was to become Zululand. There, chiefs were attempting to monopolise external trade, so as to increase their patronage and attract followers. As these rose, so did the numbers of their cattle. This led to ever greater tension over the ownership of grazing land, and to ever more aggressive warfare between ruling clans. The trade of Delagoa Bay reached its peak in the 1780s, after which supplies began to diminish, and the Maputo chieftainship turned to the production of foodstuffs for European whaling ships.

THE TAVERN OF THE SEAS

To the Portuguese the Cape of Good Hope was, despite its name, a cape of storms, which was best given a wide berth by their ships sailing to and from the East. With the discovery by the Dutch in the early seventeenth century of sailing routes to the Far East based upon the trade winds of the Atlantic and southern Indian Ocean, whereby voyages were made in wide sweeps across the two oceans, the Cape assumed a new significance as a half-way landfall between Holland and Java, and so as a vital source of fresh provisions for scurvy-ridden sailors. Though French and English had likewise used it as a watering place, where it was also possible to obtain cattle by barter from Khoi herders, it was the Dutch who in 1652 actually occupied the Cape peninsula – largely as a pre-emptive move to exclude the English with whom they were then at war. The Dutch East India Company's plans contained no hint of wider African colonisation, as the instructions to the first commander, Jan van Riebeeck, made plain. They merely said that it was essential that its fleets might find there 'the means of procuring vegetables, meat, water and other needful refreshments and by this means restore the health of their sick'.[4] There was to be a fort, surrounded by a market garden and a stock farm. Significantly, van Riebeeck himself was by profession a surgeon.

The first few years were precarious. The settlement could not even feed itself, but had to rely on rice brought from Madagascar and the Dutch East Indies. In an effort to cut costs and provide more efficient supplies, nine Company servants were released in 1657 as 'free burghers' and settled on tracts of 135 acres each a few miles from the fort, in a valley sheltered from the summer gales. These were laid out on land traditionally grazed by the Khoi, an action which provoked the first armed skirmish between the Europeans and the Khoi. The Company next obtained two shiploads of slaves, one from Dahomey and one from Angola, to perform the manual work on the new farms. In an act resonant with symbolism for the future, van Riebeeck planted a thorn hedge of bitter almonds in a vain attempt to enclose the Dutch settlement. By the 1680s some of the more enterprising free burghers were being settled on farms in the interior beyond the sandy Cape Flats, and in 1688 the first significant numbers of genuine colonists arrived, in the persons of Protestant Huguenots fleeing from persecution in France. By this

---

[4] Cited in Robert Ross, *Beyond the Pale* (Hanover, NH, 1993), p. 13.

time, further African slaves were being imported, mainly from Madagascar but also from the Mozambique mainland, to labour on the farms and in Cape Town, while skilled artisans and domestic slaves were shipped in from South India and the Dutch East Indies for sale to the wealthier farmers and officials. These were often convicts and political exiles, and many were Muslims. By the early nineteenth century the Muslim community, known locally as the Cape Malays, numbered over 2000.

By the end of the seventeenth century there were more than 1500 free burghers in the settlement, and about a similar number of slaves. Not all of the Dutch officials welcomed the heady mixture of free land and slave labour. 'Having imported slaves', wrote one, 'every common or ordinary European becomes a gentleman and prefers to be served rather than to serve. We have in addition the fact that the majority of the farmers in this country are not farmers in the real sense of the word, but owners of plantations, and that many of them consider it a shame to work with their own hands.'[5] Those colonists who lacked the money, expertise or inclination to become settled farmers became 'frontiersmen' or *trekboers*, who moved right out of the narrow belt of Mediterranean climate of the southwestern Cape and on to the dry plateau of the interior, where extensive pastoralism combined with hunting was the only possible basis for existence. Unfortunately, it could be done only at the expense of the Khoisan hunters and herders who had lived there by the same means for centuries before.

In 1702 the Company officials bowed to the reality of extensive land settlement, and instituted a system of farm loans, after which 6000 acres became the average size of a ranching farm. Between 1702 and 1743 farmers obtained legal possession of more than 100,000 acres by this means. By the 1770s more than 1 million sheep and 250,000 head of cattle were being reared in the colony. By the middle of the century a few hundred rich and powerful wine and wheat farmers, living in grand château-like farmsteads, designed and built by skilled slaves, formed the gentry class of the Dutch settlement in the country districts near the Cape. A traveller around 1780 wrote that he had seen on these farms 'a magnificence which I am certain can be found in no other colony, nor even in the richest cities of any country in the world'.[6] The gentry class, moreover, soon spread beyond the fertile area of the south-western Cape. By 1800

---

[5] Cited in Robert Shell, *Children of Bondage* (Hanover, NH, 1994), p. 7.

[6] Ross, *Beyond the Pale*, p. 28.

many of the upcountry stock farmers had become similarly commercialised, producing cattle for the shipping that called at Cape Town. The Cape gentry were to be one of the most potent forces in nineteenth-century South Africa.

The impact of the first half-century of European settlement at the Cape upon the local Khoi population was immense and, generally, calamitous. By the early 1700s, within a radius of 100 miles or more from Cape Town, the Khoi had lost the pastures necessary for the transhumance of their cattle and sheep. They had lost many of their herds through coercive trading or theft. They had lost, also, much of their social cohesion. In these circumstances, the arrival of smallpox in their midst was the last straw. It was introduced in 1713 in ships' laundry washed by slaves, and this and subsequent outbreaks through the rest of the century decimated the Khoi bands. The survivors of these man-made and natural disasters who remained in the colony had to work as farm labourers, or as guides and herders for the white hunter-farmers and cattle-traders beyond the limits of the Company's jurisdiction. The only Khoi who fared well in the new circumstances were those who acted as middlemen with the cattle-traders from the colony. These took charge of the white man's trade goods, his horses and his arms and ammunition, and moved ever further inland towards the frontier between the Khoi and the Bantu, where they obtained the cattle and ivory and skins and ostrich feathers which made up the long-distance trade of the Cape. By the early nineteenth century some Khoi were doing what many other good men did when dispossessed by European settlement. They joined the colonial army.

Considerable numbers of Khoi, however, moved out of the immediate orbit of the colony to join with the bands of dispossessed San hunters, runaway slaves and socially rejected offspring of the many temporary liaisons inevitable in an international port of transit. These mixed groups of refugees and outlaws soon acquired horses and firearms, with the help of which they raided the European colonists living on the frontier, and resisted and sometimes retarded their northward and eastward encroachments. By the end of the eighteenth century they were forming a number of distinctive political societies spread along the valley of the middle Orange river, which became closely engaged with the larger urbanised kingdoms of the Tswana living to the north of them. These frontier societies of so-called Griqua had some similarity with the little republics set up by the Dutch Voortrekkers on the highfeld during the nineteenth century.

The Colony itself grew slowly but steadily, the number of free burghers rising from 2000 at the beginning of the eighteenth century to 20,000 by its end. By then, the labour force of the Cape consisted of 26,000 slaves and 27,000 'Cape Hottentots', which term included all the same ethnic components as the Griqua, but denoted those who had preferred to remain in the Colony rather than face the risks and discomforts of flight. Among the white colonists, males at first predominated. There was some intermarriage, much concubinage, and, especially among the female slaves, much casual sex with the crews of passing ships. Thus there emerged that part of the population later to be called Cape Coloured. Cape Town itself remained first and foremost a bustling port, but it was also the market and the administrative centre for the prosperous wine and wheat and cattle farmers of the settled colony. It has been estimated that in 1800 the population of independent Xhosa, living beyond the colonial frontier in what is now the eastern Cape, numbered approximately 100,000.

In the interior, trekboers and Xhosa were expanding simultaneously and in convergent directions, and by the 1770s their advance guards had started to mingle in the area between the Kei and the Gamtoos rivers, which had previously been occupied only by Khoi pastoralists. Up until this time, Bantu farmers had only been marginally affected by European settler expansion. Indeed, when they first came in contact with them, the Xhosa described the white pastoralists as 'pale Hottentots'. Although the authorities of the Dutch Company tried to control the situation by designating geographical boundaries, in practice there was an open frontier over the Zuurveld, which was the most sought after strip of land, so named because of the quality of its grazing. All three groups contended for the area and for possession of its cattle. However, in 1793 a severe drought brought on the inevitable crisis, and in the resulting war many Dutch colonists were forced to flee from the Zuurveld. The frontier conflict remained unresolved through the first British administration of the Cape (1795–9) and the brief period of restored Dutch rule as the government of the Batavian Republic (1803–6). At last, in 1811 the British decided not just to pacify the frontier zone, but to drive the Xhosa out of the Zuurveld once and for all. To the colonists, the Xhosa might be armed rivals but they were also labourers, trading partners, and at times even allies. To the British military commander, Lieutenant-Colonel John Graham, the Xhosa were simply the enemy, 'horrid savages' as he called them. He ordered his troops, which included Khoi members of the Cape Regiment, to beat the Xhosa warriors back to their kraals, where 'every man Kaffir' who could be found, including if possible the chief, should be destroyed.[7] In the ensuing campaign, the Zuurveld up to the Fish river was largely cleared of Xhosa. In the 1830s, with the full strength of a British colonial garrison in support, the frontier was finally pushed back to the Kei. And there it remained. The southernmost Nguni were not yet conquered, but they were threateningly encircled and their potential for further expansion blocked.

[7] Cited in Richard Elphick and Hermann Giliomee (eds.), *The Shaping of South African Society 1652–1840* (Cape Town and London, 1989), p. 315.

Epilogue

At the end of the eighteenth century Africa as a whole was still very far from losing its pre-colonial independence. Indeed, the only large area of theoretically dependent territory was that comprised within the Ottoman empire – Egypt, Tripoli, Tunis and Algiers – and even here the central authority had declined so far that the system could almost be described as rule by locally based military élites of foreign origin. The pashas of Timbuktu had a similarly theoretical relationship to Morocco, as did the Mazruis of Mombasa and various other East African coastal dynasties to the Albusaid Imams of Oman. European dependencies in Africa were in comparison very small. There was Mozambique Island, with its cluster of trading outposts and its nearly Africanised prazo-holders in the lower Zambezi valley. There was Angola, with its two slightly garrisoned trade routes running inland from Luanda and Benguela. There were the fortified warehouses and slave-pens of Dutch, Danes and British on the Gold Coast and the Gambia, and of the French on the Senegal. And, in a class by itself, the Dutch colony at the Cape, soon to be taken over by the British, where the trekboers had expanded by the end of the century about half way to the Orange River. Such dependent areas were neither the most important nor the most dynamic of African polities. Except for the Cape, none of them was expanding, and some were obviously wearing away.

Looked at from another point of view, the eighteenth century was of course the peak period of the African slave trade, when it has been calculated that some 6,500,000 persons were transported across the Atlantic to the New World. This figure takes no account of those exported across the Sahara or the Indian Ocean. In the view of some writers this in itself is enough to situate the eighteenth century (and indeed the seventeenth and sixteenth also) within the colonial period of African history. This, however, is to miss a vital distinction between the colonial period in the New World and the colonial period in Africa. It was because the European nations were engaged in opening up colonies in the Americas that they looked to Africa for slaves to meet the labour needs of their plantations in Brazil, Central America and the Caribbean. But to colonise is to occupy and rule another country by main force, and of this Africa knew very little

228

until the late nineteenth century. The African kingdoms and corporations which engaged in the slave trade, whether westwards across the Atlantic or northwards across the Sahara, did so for the most part as free and willing agents. This is not to say that commercial profit was their only motive, although sometimes it was so. Often enough, however, the slave trade was an almost incidental element in African political aggrandisement. A ruler extended his kingdom's frontiers, and sold some of his war captives in exchange for horses or firearms with which to extend the frontiers still further. Alternatively, a ruler sold captives for imported textiles and other luxuries in order to reward his military captains for the last campaign and to whet their appetite for the next one. Eventually, the ruler of a successful kingdom might reach a stage where his frontiers were so distant from his capital that the game was no longer worth the candle. Or the expanded frontiers might reach those of another rising power which had been pursuing the same course. Then the supply of slaves from that particular region would dry up, and the foreign merchants would be forced to seek another source. Neither did the trade in slaves – nor any other goods – make those Africans who engaged in it dependent upon European (or Islamic) mercantile capitalist interests. It is true that the Europeans supplied firearms and other commodities which African rulers found useful or desirable. But these rulers were not in any quantifiable sense dependent on the European suppliers of firearms. However useful these might be as an improvement of technology, they were not essential to the functioning of African kingdoms and chiefdoms. Rather, the European mercantile capitalists were dependent on Africa for the supply of slaves, which were crucial for their colonies in the New World.

Thus, although the slave trade was an important and almost ubiquitous element in the relations between Africa and the outside world, and particularly so during the final century of our period, it was not the main motive force of social and political change in Africa itself. This is rather to be sought in the necessity felt in nearly every part of Africa during this period to seek the enlargement of political groupings. This necessity was probably in the main a function of the growth of population experienced in all the more favourable environments of the continent following the spread of later Iron Age technology. It was at least as marked in interior regions, such as Rwanda and Lunda and Asante and Oyo, as it was in the coastal areas or those of the desert fringes. It seems likely that, even if there had been no external contacts and no external slave trade, the enlargement of political scale would still have been the dominant theme of our period, and that slavery and deportation would have been among its by-products. The medieval states of the Sahel – Ghana, Mali, Songhay, Kano, Katsina, Bornu, 'Alwa and Ethiopia – had all practised the removal of war captives from neighbouring communities to the metropolitan districts of their own kingdoms. Asante, Oyo and Benin had all followed this example. The Lunda kingdoms all employed slaves in agriculture, especially in the neighbourhood of their capital towns. It is certain that there was a large slave class in Kongo before the Portuguese contact. It is to be presumed that the stone-built capitals of Great Zimbabwe and its successor states were built by some kind of impressed labour. All in all, it seems likely that, even at the height of the Atlantic slave trade, there were many more African slaves serving within Africa than outside it. At this rate, there would be no reason to assign a dominant role in African history to the supply of the external trade. By and large, it would seem that European traders proposed, but that it was African rulers who disposed. This situation would remain broadly unchanged until the era of the rifle and the machine-gun, and meantime the enlargement of political scale among the indigenous kingdoms of independent Africa would continue.

It is important to remember, however, that the enlargement of political societies did not affect all of the peoples of Africa during our period. Even at the end of the eighteenth century there remained countless smaller political entities which still managed to flourish in the spaces between and beyond the big players, and many more which somehow survived the inroads of conquest and slave-raiding. Whether we consider the large and growing kingdoms, or these more humble chiefdoms and village neighbourhoods, the evidence suggests an impressive vitality of political innovation and imagination. The varieties of African inventiveness in the art of ruling societies big and small, and ensuring their survival through time, is almost breathtaking, and this includes the patterns developing in the Muslim lands of Mediterranean Africa no less than those of Africa south of the Sahara. Successful expansion required exceptional skill in assimilating the conquered. Likewise, the successful avoidance of conquest required skill in adapting to changes of organisation and sometimes of environment also. Always in Africa political change involved corresponding adaptations in religion and ritual. Here again, the evidence suggests that African spirituality, Islamic as well as traditional, was still vibrant on the eve of the fateful nineteenth century. In these political and religious areas of experience most African communities were still independent of outside influences and certainly free from changes enforced by foreigners from other continents.

There is another sense in which the Africa of the eighteenth century was still largely independent, and it concerns the whole field of design and technology, art and imagination. In the eighteenth century, as in the thirteenth, nearly all of the material goods in use in Africa were made in Africa. Metal goods in particular – the axes, hoes, cutlasses, knives, spears and jewellery of all kinds, especially of copper – were still made by local smiths from locally mined and smelted ores. Only in the late nineteenth century would they begin to be displaced by the products of Western blast furnaces, to the ruin of the local industries. In the fields of wood-carving and leatherwork African imaginations could still range freely around indigenous themes in all the rich diversity which in the twentieth century would so largely disappear into the banality of 'airport art'. Traditional music, song and dance, heroic recitation, and representational art, though inhibited by the progress of Islam in some parts of the continent, did not yet have to face the competition of mass-produced sound and verbiage that would come from the printing presses, the record players, the film industries and the radio stations of the outside world. One does not need to think that the Africans of our period were unduly resistant to change. They accepted new food crops and learnt how to grow and prepare them. Those who were in contact with the intercontinental trade routes were quick to note the superiority of cotton textiles over bark, leather and platted grasses and to begin the growing and weaving of cotton, which became a major industry all along the Sudanic belt of Africa. Until the coming of the rifle, the skilled blacksmiths of African kings could often repair the simpler firearms introduced from Europe and the Middle East. They learnt to make gunpowder and to fashion workable ammunition. They dealt with foreign traders and other visitors confidently, as equals. They had no doubts about who was in charge.

If the end of the eighteenth century marks the end of an era, therefore, it is not because of any dramatic development in the unfolding of the historical process, but rather because of a change in the nature of historical evidence. The nineteenth century saw the widespread exploration of independent Africa by literate observers from the outside world. It saw the first recording of much oral tradition, of which the latest parts were the most reliable and the least disguised under hidden esoteric meanings. From this time forward it is possible to reconstruct the history of nearly all of Africa in some detail and with a considerable degree of confidence. This we have tried to do in our book called *Africa since 1800*, of which the fourth revised edition was published in 1994.

Further reading

GENERAL

Curtin, Philip, Steven Feierman, Leonard Thompson and Jan Vansina, *African History from Earliest Times to Independence* (revised edn, New York, 1995)

Fage, J. D., *An Atlas of African History* (revised edn, London, 1978)

Gray, Richard (ed.), *The Cambridge History of Africa*, vol. IV, *c.1600–c.1870* (Cambridge, 1975); cited below as *CHA* IV

Iliffe, John, *Africans* (Cambridge, 1996)

Isichei, E., *A History of African Societies to 1870* (Cambridge, 1999)

Niane, D. T. (ed.), *General History of Africa*, vol. IV, *Africa from the Twelfth to the Sixteenth Century* (London, 1984); cited below as *General History* IV

Ogot, B. A. (ed.), *General History of Africa*, vol. IV, *Africa from the Sixteenth to the Eighteenth Century* (London, 1992); cited below as *General History* V

Oliver, Roland, *The African Experience* (revised edn, London, 1999)

Oliver, Roland (ed.), *The Cambridge History of Africa*, vol. III, *c.1050–c.1600* (Cambridge, 1977); cited below as *CHA* III

Phillipson, David W., *African Archaeology* (Cambridge, 1985)

BY CHAPTER

Chapter 2 Egypt

Ayalon, David, *Studies on the Mamluks of Egypt* (London, 1977)

Daly, M. W. (ed.), *The Cambridge History of Egypt*, vol. I, *Islamic Egypt 640–1517*; vol. II, *Modern Egypt from 1517 to the Twentieth Century* (Cambridge, 1999)

Dols, M. W., *The Black Death in the Middle East* (Princeton, 1977)

Garcin, J. C., 'Egypt and the Muslim World', in *General History* IV, pp. 371–97

Holt, P. M., 'Egypt, the Funj and Darfur', in *CHA* IV, pp. 14–57

Hrbek, I., 'Egypt, Nubia and the Eastern Deserts', in *CHA* III, pp. 10–97

Lewis, Bernard, *The Middle East, 2000 Years* (London, 1995)

Marsot, A. L. al-Sayyid, 'Egypt under the Mamluks', in *Egypt in the Reign of Muhammad 'Ali* (Cambridge, 1984)

Raymond, André, *Le Caire* (Paris, 1993)

Vesely, R., 'The Ottoman Conquest of Egypt', in *General History* V, pp. 137–69

Further reading

Chapters 3 and 4 The Maghrib

Abun-Nasr, J. M., *A History of the Maghrib in the Islamic Period* (Cambridge, 1987)

Bourqia, R. and S. G. Miller (eds.), *In the Shadow of the Sultan: Culture, Power and Politics in Morocco* (Cambridge, MA, 1999)

Brett, Michael, *Ibn Khaldun and the Medieval Maghrib* (London, 1999)

Brett, Michael, and Elizabeth Fentress, *The Berbers* (Oxford, 1996)

Cherif, M. H., 'Algeria, Tunisia and Libya: The Ottomans and Their Heirs', in *General History* V, pp. 233–61

El Mansur, M., *Morocco in the Reign of Mawlay Sulayman* (Wisbech, 1990)

Fisher, George, *Barbary Legend: War, Trade and Piracy in North Africa 1415–1830* (Oxford, 1957)

Hess, Andrew, *The Forgotten Frontier: A History of the Sixteenth Century Ibero-African Frontier* (Chicago, 1978)

Hrbek, I., 'The Disintegration of Political Unity in the Maghrib', in *General History* IV, pp. 78–101

Laroui, Abdallah, *A History of the Maghrib* (Princeton, 1978)

Chapters 5 and 6 West Africa

Abitbol, M., 'The End of the Songhay Empire', in *General History* V, pp. 300–26

Ajayi, J. F. A., and Michael Crowder (eds.), *A History of West Africa*, vol. I (3rd edn, London, 1985)

Alagoa, E. J., 'Fon and Yoruba, the Niger Delta and the Cameroon', in *General History* V, pp. 434–52

Curtin, Philip D., *Economic Change in Precolonial Africa: Senegambia in the Era of the Slave Trade* (Madison, 1975)

   The Atlantic Slave Trade: A Census (Madison, 1969)

Daaku, K. Y., *Trade and Politics on the Gold Coast 1600–1720* (Oxford, 1970)

Feinberg, M., *Africans and Europeans in West Africa: Elminas and Dutchmen on the Gold Coast during the 18th Century* (Philadelphia, 1989)

Hodgkin, Thomas, *Nigerian Perspectives* (2nd edn, London, 1975)

Hopkins, A. G., *An Economic History of West Africa* (London, 1973)

Hopkins, J. F. P. and N. Levtzion, *Corpus of Early Arabic Sources for West African History* (Cambridge, 1981)

Inikori, J. E., 'Africa in World History: The Export Slave-Trade from Africa and the Emergence of the Atlantic Economic Order', in *General History* V, pp. 74–112

Law, Robin, *The Horse in West African History* (Oxford, 1980)

   The Oyo Empire c.1600–1836 (London, 1978)

   The Slave Coast of West Africa 1550–1750 (Oxford, 1991)

Levtzion, N., 'The Western Maghrib and Sudan', in *CHA* III, pp. 331–462; and 'North-West Africa from the Maghrib to the Fringes of the Forest', in *CHA* IV, pp. 142–222

McIntosh, R. J., *The Peoples of the Middle Niger* (Oxford, 1988)
Rodney, Walter, *A History of the Upper Guinea Coast 1545–1800* (Oxford, 1970)
Ryder, A. F. C., *Benin and the Europeans 1445–1897* (London, 1969)
Saad, Elias, *The Social History of Timbuktu: The Role of Muslim Scholars and Notables 1400–1900* (Cambridge, 1983)
Wilks, Ivor, *Asante in the Nineteenth Century: The Structure and Organisation of a Political Order* (2nd edn, Cambridge, 1989)

Chapter 7 Nubia, Darfur and Wadai
Fisher, H. J., 'The Central Sahara and Sudan', in *CHA* IV, pp. 58–141
Hasan, Y. F., *The Arabs and the Sudan* (Khartoum, 1973)
Hasan, Y. F., and B. A. Ogot, 'The Sudan 1500–1800', in *General History* V, pp. 170–99
Kropáček, L., 'Nubia from the Late 12th Century to the Funj Conquest', in *General History* IV, pp. 398–422
Lange, D., 'The Kingdoms and Peoples of Chad', in *General History* V, pp. 238–65
O'Fahey, R. S. and J. L. Spaulding, *Kingdoms of the Sudan* (London, 1974)
Spaulding, J. L., *The Heroic Age in Sinnar* (East Lansing, 1985)

Chapter 8 The north-eastern triangle
Haberland, E., 'The Horn of Africa', in *General History* V, pp. 703–49
Hassen, Mohammed, *The Oromo of Ethiopia, a history 1570–1860* (Cambridge, 1990)
Tamrat, Taddesse, *Church and State in Ethiopia 1270–1527* (Oxford, 1972)
'The Horn of Africa: The Solomonids in Ethiopia and the States of the Horn of Africa', in *General History* IV, pp. 423–54

Chapter 9 The upper Nile basin and the East African plateau
Cohen, D. W., *The Historical Tradition of Busoga: Mukama and Kintu* (Oxford, 1972)
Karugire, S. K., *A History of the Kingdom of Nkore in Western Uganda to 1896* (Oxford, 1971)
Ogot, B. A., *History of the Southern Luo*, vol. I (Nairobi, 1962)
'The Great Lakes Region', in *General History* IV, pp. 498–524
Sutton, J. E. G., 'The Antecedants of the Interlacustrine Kingdoms', *Journal of African History* 34 (1993), pp. 33–64
Vansina, Jan, *L'Evolution du royaume Rwanda des origines à 1900* (Brussels, 1962)
Webster, J. B., B. A. Ogot and J.-P. Chrétien, 'The Great Lakes Region 1500–1800', in *General History* V, pp. 776–827
Wrigley, Christopher, *Kingship and State: The Buganda Dynasty* (Cambridge, 1996)

Further reading

Chapter 10 The heart of Africa
de Dampierre, Eric, *Un Ancien Royaume Bandia du Haut-Oubangui* (Paris, 1967)
Harms, Robert, *River of Wealth, River of Sorrow* (New Haven, 1981)
Martin, P. M., *The External Trade of the Loango Coast 1576–1870* (Oxford, 1972)
M'Bokolo, E., 'From the Cameroons Grasslands to the Upper Nile', in *General History* V, pp. 515–45
Vansina, Jan, 'Equatorial Africa and Angola: Migrations and the Emergence of the First States', in *General History* IV, pp. 551–77
   Paths in the Rainforests (Madison, 1990)
   The Children of Woot: A History of the Kuba Peoples (Madison, 1978)
   The Tio Kingdom of the Middle Congo (Oxford, 1973), especially pp. 439–69

Chapter 11 The land of the blacksmith kings
Balandier, Georges, *Daily Life in the Kingdom of the Kongo* (London, 1968)
Birmingham, David, *Trade and Conflict in Angola* (Oxford, 1966)
Miller, Joseph C., *Kings and Kinsmen: Early Mbundu States in Angola* (Oxford, 1976)
Thornton, John, *The Kingdom of Kongo: Civil War and Transition 1641–1718* (Madison, 1983)
Vansina, Jan, *Kingdoms of the Savanna* (Madison, 1964)
Vansina, Jan, and T. Obenga, 'The Kongo Kingdom and Its Neighbours', in *General History* V, pp. 546–87

Chapter 12 From the Lualaba to the Zambezi
Alpers, Edward A., *Ivory and Slaves in East Central Africa* (London, 1975)
Nziem, Ndaywel è, 'The Political System of the Luba and Lunda', in *General History* V, pp. 588–607
Phiri, K. M., O. J. M. Kalinga and H. K. Bhila, 'The Northern Zambezia – Lake Malawi Region', in *General History* V, pp. 608–39
Reefe, Thomas Q., *The Rainbow and the Kings: A History of the Luba Empire* (Berkeley, 1981)
Roberts, Andrew, *A History of Zambia* (London, 1976)
   History of the Bemba (London, 1974)

Chapter 13 The approaches to Zimbabwe
Beach, David, *The Shona and Zimbabwe 900–1850* (London, 1980)
Chittick, H. Neville, 'The East Coast, Madagascar and the Indian Ocean', in *CHA* III, pp. 183–221
Freeman-Grenville, G. S. P. (ed.), *The East African Coast: Select Documents from the First to the Earlier Nineteenth Century* (Oxford, 1962)
Garlake, P. S., *Great Zimbabwe* (London, 1973)

Kent, R. K., 'Madagascar and the Islands of the Indian Ocean', in *General History* V, pp. 849–94

Matviev, V. V., 'The Development of Swahili Civilisation', in *General History* IV, pp. 454–80

Mudenge, S. I. G., *A Political History of Munhumutapa c.1400–1902* (Harare, 1988)

Newitt, Malyn, *A History of Mocambique* (Bloomington, 1995)

Nurse, Derek and Thomas Spear, *The Swahili: Reconstructing the History and Language of an African Society 800–1500* (Philadelphia, 1985)

Sutton, J. E. G., 'Kilwa', *Azania* 33 (1998), pp. 113–69

Chapter 14 The peoples of the South

Birmingham, David and Shula Marks, 'Southern Africa', in *CHA* III, pp. 567–620

Duminy, Andrew and Bill Guest (eds.), *Natal and Zululand from Earliest Times to 1910* (Pietermaritzburg, 1989)

Elphick, Richard, *Kraal and Castle: Khoikhoi and the Founding of White South Africa* (New Haven, 1985)

Elphick, Richard and Hermann Giliomee (eds.), *The Shaping of South African Society 1652–1840* (Cape Town and London, 1989)

Hall, Martin, *The Changing Past: Farmers, Kings and Traders in Southern Africa 200–1860* (Cape Town, 1987)

Hamilton, Carolyn (ed.), *The Mfecane Aftermath* (Johannesburg, 1995). Earlier chapters on pre-Mfecane situation

Marks, Shula and Richard Gray, 'Southern Africa and Madagascar', in *CHA* IV, pp. 384–468

Ross, Robert, *Beyond the Pale: Essays in the History of Colonial South Africa* (Hanover, NH, 1993)

Shell, Robert, *Children of Bondage: A Social History of Slave Society at the Cape of Good Hope* (Hanover, NH, 1994)

Index

Index

Index

Connent